Everyday Violence in the Irish Civil War

Everyday Violence in the Irish Civil War presents an innovative study of violence perpetrated by and against non-combatants during the Irish Civil War, 1922–3. Drawing from victim accounts of wartime injury as recorded in compensation claims, Dr Gemma Clark sheds new light on hundreds of previously neglected episodes of violence and intimidation – ranging from arson, boycott and animal maiming to assault, murder and sexual violence – that transpired amongst soldiers, civilians and revolutionaries throughout the period of conflict. The author shows us how these micro-level acts – particularly in the counties of Limerick, Tipperary and Waterford – served as an attempt to persecute and purge religious and political minorities and to force redistribution of land. Clark also assesses the international significance of the war, comparing the cruel yet arguably restrained violence that occurred in Ireland with the brutality unleashed in other European conflict zones.

Gemma Clark is a Postdoctoral Research Fellow at the Global Irish Studies Centre, University of New South Wales.

Everyday Violence in the Irish Civil War

Gemma Clark

Global Irish Studies Centre,
University of New South Wales

CAMBRIDGE
UNIVERSITY PRESS

University Printing House, Cambridge CB2 8BS, United Kingdom

Cambridge University Press is part of the University of Cambridge.

It furthers the University's mission by disseminating knowledge in the pursuit of education, learning and research at the highest international levels of excellence.

www.cambridge.org
Information on this title: www.cambridge.org/9781316635278

First published 2014
First paperback edition 2016

A catalogue record for this publication is available from the British Library

Library of Congress Cataloguing in Publication data
Clark, Gemma M. (Gemma Mary), 1984–
Everyday violence in the Irish Civil War / Gemma Clark, Global Irish Studies Centre, University of New South Wales, UNSW Sydney.
pages cm
Includes bibliographical references and index.
ISBN 978-1-107-03689-5 (hardback)
1. Ireland – History – Civil War, 1922–1923. 2. Violence – Ireland – History – 20th century. 3. Political violence – Ireland – History – 20th century. I. Title.
DA963.C43 2014
941.5082′2 – dc23 2013040530

ISBN 978-1-107-03689-5 Hardback
ISBN 978-1-316-63527-8 Paperback

In memory of my grandparents, Walter and Maureen Cassin, and Maureen and Tony Clark

Contents

Figures

Maps

Tables

Acknowledgements

This book developed out of postgraduate research funded by the Arts and Humanities Research Council. My studies at the Queen's College, Oxford, would not have been possible without the support of the AHRC; I am very grateful for the help I received through the Research Preparation Master's and Doctoral Award schemes. I also thank the British Association of Irish Studies for a bursary that funded research in Dublin. The students and staff at Queen's made it a wonderful college to be a part of as an undergraduate and graduate; I thank Dr John Davis for his wise words over the years and the Governing Body for travel grants.

Prof. Roy Foster's fascinating Further Subject on Irish nationalism at Oxford stimulated my interest in the Irish Revolution. I thank him for this and for his guidance as my Master's and D.Phil. supervisor; his comments on my thesis drafts helped to shape and direct my research and writing. His great understanding of the field was invaluable, and I thank Roy for connecting me with academics and archivists who helped with my research. He has continued to offer support since I left Oxford and has advised me during the writing of this book. His insights on 'Urban experiences' were particularly helpful in the preparation of Chapter 4. I also thank Roy's secretary, Jules Iddon.

I also owe a great deal to Dr Matt Kelly. Not only was he an inspiring undergraduate tutor, but also his discovery of a 1924 pamphlet on house burnings gave me a fascinating topic for an undergraduate dissertation that eventually developed into this book on civil-war violence. He encouraged me to pursue postgraduate study and has continued to offer support. I thank Matt and Prof. Ian McBride for inviting me to present my research at a vital stage during my D.Phil. – at the 2010 Conference of Irish Historians in Britain.

Dr Tim Wilson has been instrumental to the development of my academic interest in violence and has shaped this book from its beginnings. As my doctoral co-supervisor he motivated and directed me, and helped me – more than did anyone else – to think conceptually and comparatively about violence in Ireland. Since I finished my doctorate, his advice on job seeking and publishing has been invaluable. His great support continues from afar. I wrote key sections of Chapter 3 during the first months of my postdoctoral position at the University of New South Wales and, during that time, I consulted Tim on the comparative role of arson in conflict in Northern Ireland. He gave generously of his time and expertise, even checking, on my behalf, references for material I was unable to retrieve in Australia. I am very grateful for his input on this book and for his help in setting me on my career path.

Matt, Tim, Dr Aurelia S. Annat, Dr Lauren Arrington, Dr Frances Flanagan, Dr Ultán Gillen, Dr Mike McCabe, Dr Marc Mulholland, Dr Ciarán O'Neill and others, are/were members of the supportive Irish Studies network that formed around Roy Foster's Seminar in Irish History. I thank them all for their advice. Indeed, I thank all who discussed my doctoral research with me in Oxford and beyond, including my assessors for Transfer and Confirmation of D.Phil. status; conveners and attendees of seminars in Irish and Modern British History at Hertford and St John's Colleges, and conferences and local community events outside Oxford; my friend and sounding board, Dr Eve Colpus; and Dr David Thackeray, for information on pre-1920s relief campaigns for British Loyalists.

I thank my D.Phil. examiners, Marc Mulholland and Prof. Richard English, and the anonymous readers of my manuscript, for comments that helped to improve my work and sharpen my conclusions. I also thank Richard for his help and advice since my viva exam; his support was central to the development of my D.Phil. research into this book.

During the final months of Sydney-based book writing, I had two very helpful and generous email correspondents. I thank Dr Andy Bielenberg for sharing his new work on the Protestant 'exodus' from the Irish Free State, and for his advice on 'Urban experiences' and Irish demographic change more generally. Dr Pat McCarthy has shared, over a number of years, his extensive local knowledge of Co. Waterford. I thank him for his time and his cheerful words, and particularly for his insights on 'Urban experiences' and Munster's military situation.

Researching the book was facilitated by knowledgeable staff in the History Faculty and Bodleian libraries in Oxford, the National Archives (TNA, Kew, London), the Public Record Office of Northern Ireland (Belfast), the National Library and National Archives of Ireland (NAI, Dublin), the Irish Military Archives (Cathal Brugha Barracks, Dublin), the Representative Church Body Library (Churchtown, Dublin), the Archdiocesan Archives (Drumcondra, Dublin), the libraries of UNSW and the University of Sydney, and the State Library of New South Wales. I am particularly grateful to Catriona Crowe (NAI), for generously granting me access to the un-catalogued compensation material in the first place. I also thank the county historians and archivists from Limerick, Tipperary and Waterford, who responded to enquiries and recommended sources.

I thank Celine Steinfeld who drew Map 1 using UNSW-owned facilities and software (ASTER GDEM is a product of METI and NASA). I also thank Donal and Nancy Murphy (Relay Books, Co. Tipperary) for allowing me to publish the images in Figure 4. Permission to reproduce the images in Figures 1, 3 and 5 was granted by Hugh Alexander (TNA); I also thank Hugh for providing digital copies of the photographs.

Parts of Chapter 3 appeared, in an earlier form, in 'The fiery campaign: New agendas and ancient enmities in the Irish Civil War: A study of arson in three Munster counties', in Brian Griffin and Ellen McWilliams (eds.), *Irish Studies in Britain: New Perspectives on History and Literature* (Cambridge: Cambridge Scholars Publishing, 2010). All six chapters draw on the research I carried out for my B.A., Master's and Doctoral dissertations; my D.Phil. thesis is available, from August 2014, via the Oxford University Research Archive.

I thank all of my new colleagues for making me feel so welcome in my first academic position, Sarah Sharkey Postdoctoral Research Fellow at the Global Irish Studies Centre, UNSW. I thank especially the Centre's director, Prof. Rónán McDonald, and administrator, Angela McLoughlin, for their support and for giving me time to finish my book.

I thank Michael Watson at Cambridge University Press for considering my initial proposal and for all his help in turning it into this book. I also thank Amanda George, Jeanie Lee, Shashank Shankar, Andrea Wright and all who were involved in its editing, production and marketing, and professional indexers Robert and Cynthia Swanson (Fairfield, IA).

I am forever thankful for the kindness and encouragement of my parents, Mary and Greg; my brothers, Patrick and Dominic; and the wider Clark, Cassin and Goodwin families. My granddad, Walter, was a true Irish history scholar; he, and my grandma, Maureen, always encouraged and inspired me. This book is dedicated to the memory of all my grandparents. Heartfelt thanks go also to my Manchester girls, my other dear friends, and my boyfriend, Ed Blakey. His love and support kept me going through job hunting, book writing and a move to Sydney; this project, and many others, have benefitted greatly from his advice and technical help.

Abbreviations

DI	Detective Inspector
GSWRC	Great Southern and Western Railway Company
ICCA	Irish Claims Compensation Association
IGC	Irish Grants Committee
IMA	Irish Military Archives, Cathal Brugha Barracks, Dublin
IPP	Irish Parliamentary Party
IRA	Irish Republican Army*
JBS	*Journal of British Studies*
NAI	National Archives of Ireland, Dublin
NLI	National Library of Ireland, Dublin
O/C	Officer-in-Command
P&P	*Past and Present*
PRONI	Public Record Office of Northern Ireland, Belfast
RIC	Royal Irish Constabulary
RM	Resident Magistrate
SILRA	Southern Irish Loyalist Relief Association
TD	Teachta Dála: member of the lower house (Dáil Éireann) of the Irish parliament (Oireachtas)
TNA	The National Archives, Kew
UIL	United Irish League

*The ratification of the Anglo-Irish Treaty on 7 January 1922 split the IRA. Michael Collins's (pro-Treaty) followers within the organization made up what would become the Free State Army (or National Troops). The anti-Treaty IRA, known as Irregulars, protested against the Treaty's maintenance of Ireland's link with Britain and held out for a republic. This book is chiefly concerned with the actions of the anti-Treaty IRA and uses the contemporary label 'Irregulars' interchangeably with 'republicans'.

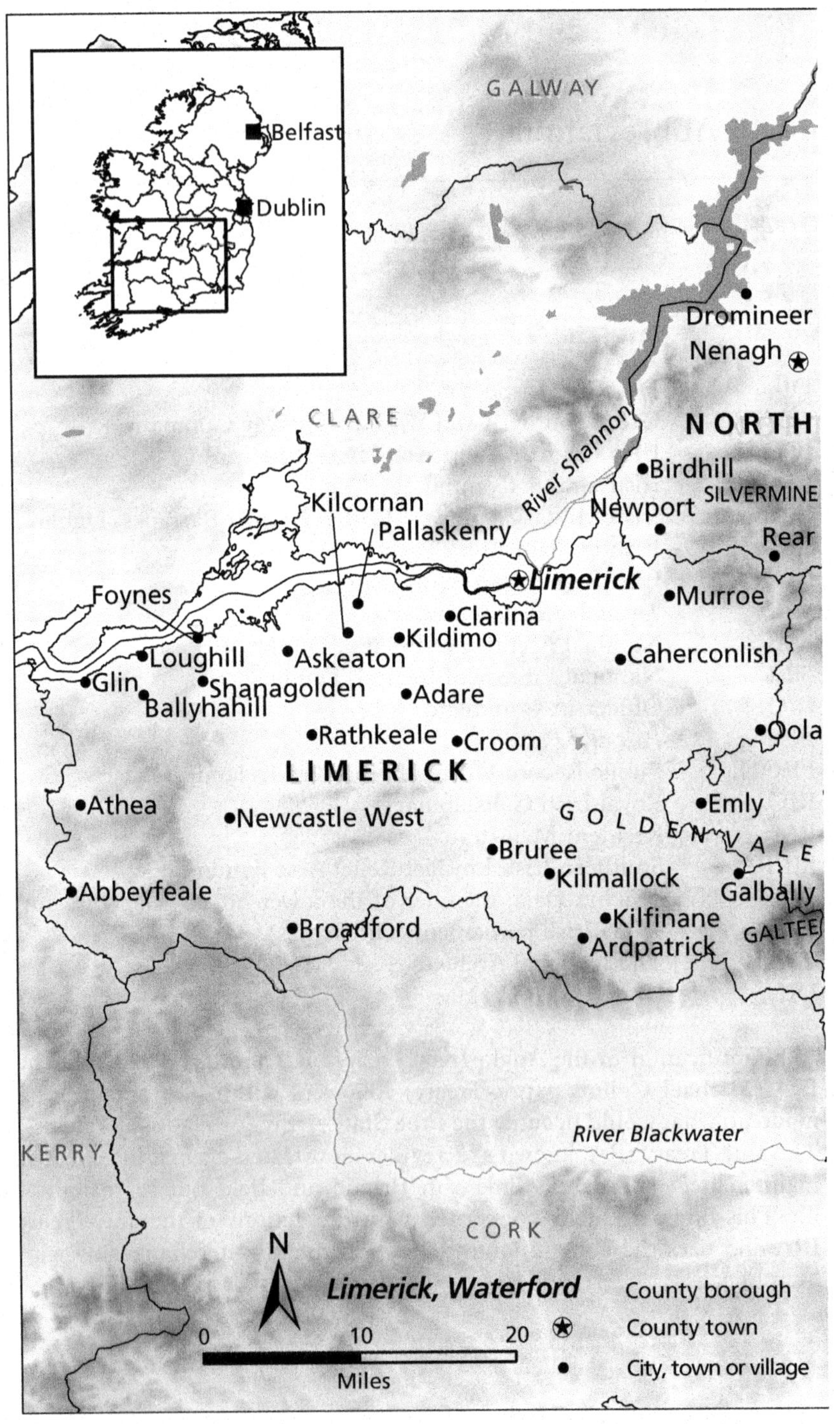

Map 1. Counties Limerick, Tipperary and Waterford, showing cities, towns, villages and other geographical features mentioned in the text.

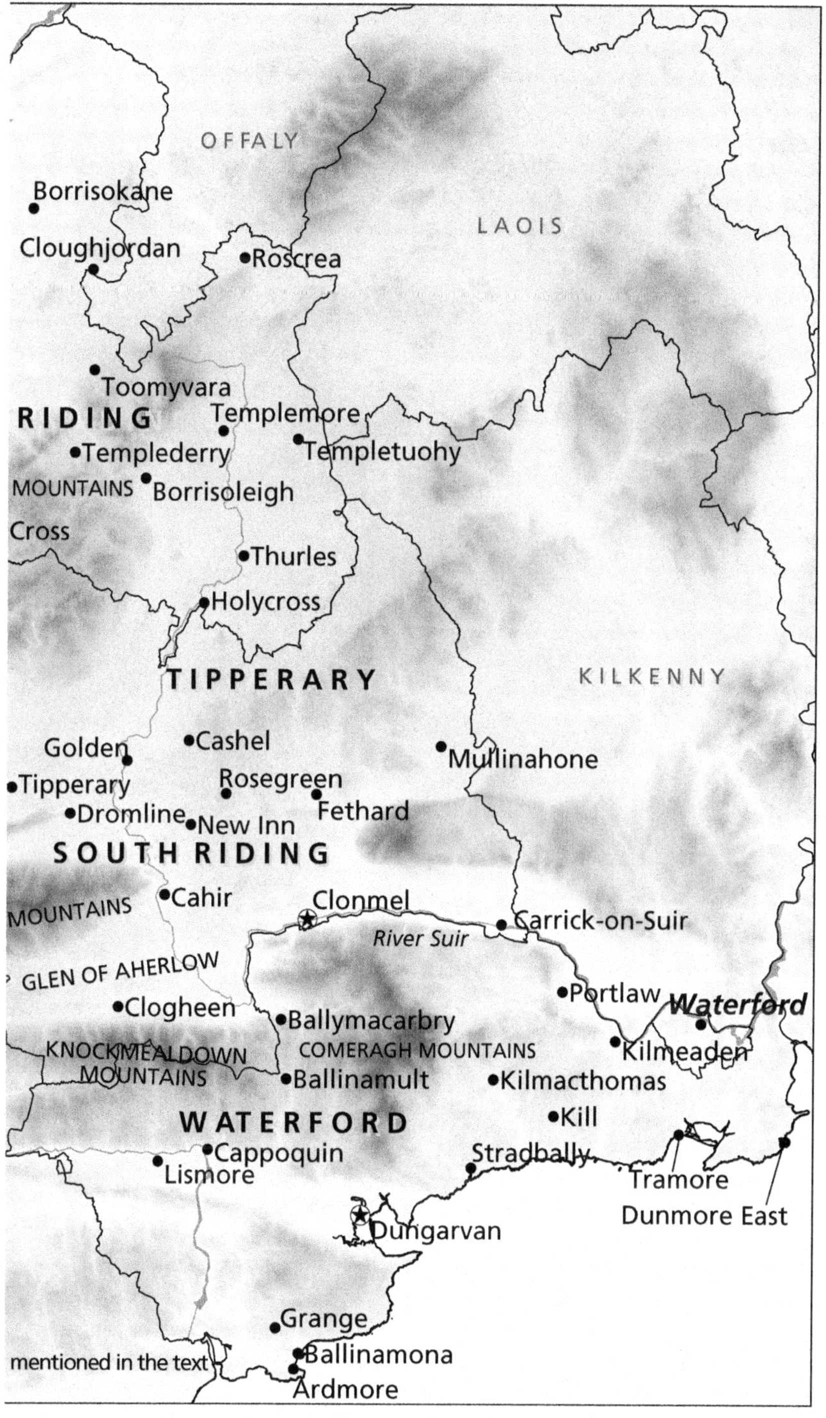
OFFALY
LAOIS
Borrisokane
Cloughjordan
Roscrea
Toomyvara
RIDING
Templemore
Templetuohy
Templederry
MOUNTAINS
Borrisoleigh
Cross
Thurles
Holycross
TIPPERARY
KILKENNY
Golden
Cashel
Mullinahone
Tipperary
Rosegreen
Fethard
Dromline
New Inn
SOUTH RIDING
Cahir
Clonmel
MOUNTAINS
Carrick-on-Suir
River Suir
GLEN OF AHERLOW
Portlaw
Waterford
Clogheen
Ballymacarbry
KNOCKMEALDOWN MOUNTAINS
COMERAGH MOUNTAINS
Kilmeaden
Ballinamult
Kilmacthomas
WATERFORD
Kill
Cappoquin
Stradbally
Lismore
Tramore
Dunmore East
Dungarvan
Grange
mentioned in the text
Ballinamona
Ardmore

1 Introduction

Civilized society describes violence using words (barbaric, indiscriminate, gratuitous) not in their true sense, but 'in order to express revulsion'.[1] Twenty-first-century governments and the media talk about 'mindless' acts of terrorism against innocent civilians, for example; this form of violence, which has 'engrossed so much of our attention' since 11 September 2001, 'seems to go straight off the chart of "common sense" – to be not only unjustifiable, but atrocious, mad'.[2] We disengage from the causes of violence to deliberately deceive ourselves about 'the subject of human nature',[3] because the truth is that violence is a rational, social phenomenon. Unpleasant acts (murder, intimidation, rape) are not side effects of conflict and war; violence is a feature of everyday life. There is, indeed, no such thing as 'mindless violence' because violence is, by definition,[4] the *deliberate* infliction of injury to persons or property. Violence is behaviour with *intent*, and it is the task of the historian and social scientist to work out the intention of, or reason for, violence, 'however obscure this might be'.[5]

Hannah Arendt pioneered the interrogation of violence as an academic subject. In 1970 she argued that violence could be examined, independently of war studies and military history, as a 'phenomenon in its own right'.[6] Scholars of violence have increasingly followed her lead, analyzing the range of harmful acts that occur in times of war and of relative

1 A.T.Q. Stewart, *The narrow ground: The roots of conflict in Ulster*, new ed. (London: Faber and Faber, 1989), 141.

2 C. Townshend, *Terrorism: A very short introduction* (Oxford: Oxford University Press, 2002), 1–2.

3 Stewart, *The narrow ground*, 142.

4 The *Oxford English dictionary* defines violence as 'behaviour involving physical force intended to hurt, damage, or kill'.

5 D. Muro-Ruiz, 'State of the art: The logic of violence', *Politics* 22, no. 2 (2002), 109–17 at 109.

6 H. Arendt, *On violence* (London: Allen Lane, 1970), 35.

peace.[7] Accompanying the recent global shift, from inter- to intra-state war, is the emergence of a particularly thriving field – civil-war studies. Civil war has been central to the formation of nations in the twentieth and twenty-first centuries,[8] and, as Stathis Kalyvas explains in his landmark 2006 study, internal strife unleashes brutal and intimate violence, much of which 'lacks conventional military utility and does not take place on a battlefield'.[9] The Greek conflicts of 1943–9 are his primary illustration of the 'logic' of violence in civil war: the deliberate infliction of harm on civilians (defined by him as anyone who is not a full-time soldier) cannot be reduced to 'madness'. Political actors instead use selective violence to coerce and control, that is, to maintain or establish rule over the populace within a contested territory.[10]

1. The Irish Civil War

This book tackles hostilities of a very different scale and intensity, the Civil War in Ireland, over the acceptance of the Anglo-Irish Treaty, during 1922–3. The Treaty, ratified in the Irish parliament, Dáil Éireann, on 7 January 1922, established the Irish Free State as a self-governing dominion within the British Commonwealth. Independence on these terms was anathema to republicans committed to the Proclamation of 1916; the Treaty split the Irish Republican Army (IRA). Michael Collins's (pro-Treaty) followers within the organization made up what would become the Free State Army (or National Troops).[11] The anti-Treaty IRA, known as 'Irregulars', protested against the maintenance of Ireland's link with Britain (symbolized by the oath of allegiance to the crown) and continued to fight for a republic.[12] In the first months of 1922, the anti-Treaty

7 R. Collins, *Violence: A micro-sociological theory* (Princeton: Princeton University Press, 2008); C. Tilly, *The politics of collective violence* (Cambridge: Cambridge University Press, 2003); A. Blok, *Honour and violence* (Cambridge: Polity Press, 2001).

8 Violence continues, in 2013, to claim lives and force displacement in South Sudan, for example; this independent state was formed in July 2011, after decades of civil war and at least 1.5 million deaths.

9 S.N. Kalyvas, *The logic of violence in civil war* (Cambridge: Cambridge University Press, 2006), 16.

10 Kalyvas, *Logic of violence in civil war*, 20, 27–9, 209.

11 M. Hopkinson, *Green against green: The Irish Civil War* (Dublin: Gill and Macmillan, 1988), 58–69. Michael Collins (1890–1922): IRB member; fought in 1916; director of IRA organization and intelligence during the War of Independence; delegate in the Anglo-Irish Treaty negotiations; Chairman and Minister for Finance of the Provisional Government; became Commander-in-Chief of the Free State Army and was killed in an ambush during the Civil War (22 August 1922).

12 Each TD (i.e., member of the lower house, Dáil Éireann) and Senator (member of the upper house, Seanad Éireann) was required to swear an oath of allegiance to the British crown on taking his seat in the Irish parliament (Oireachtas).

members of the IRA had the advantage – 'in terms of numbers and experience' – over pro-Treaty troops.[13] Active in Munster, the province at the heart of this study, during the Civil War, notorious IRA leader and War of Independence guerrilla Tom Barry believed that, with a more efficient deployment of their 30,000 men, the anti-Treaty republicans could have seized the initiative early on and ended the war in 'three days'.[14] The republicans instead chose a fatal, defensive policy and, during a short, geographically contained war, were never able seriously to compete with the superior firepower of the Free State.

This was, indeed, a limited war: military activity was confined to the first few months, July–September 1922, and large areas of the country remained relatively unaffected.[15] Exact casualty figures are elusive.[16] Michael Hopkinson, the author of the definitive military history of the war, finds it difficult even to approximate the numbers of civil-war dead and wounded.[17] He is sure, however, that more lives were lost during the Civil War than during the War of Independence. Total casualties during 1919–21 amounted to close to 1,400 (624 British forces and 752 IRA and civilians).[18] Nonetheless, the Irish Civil War certainly was not as bloody as was once proclaimed. Figures for combined pro-Treaty and anti-Treaty losses of 4,000 recently have been replaced with more conservative estimates:[19] by June 1923, total army fatalities numbered 927 (including 77 executed by the government).[20] Numbers of dead were also low by contemporary European standards; Alvin Jackson compares total wartime casualties in the Irish Free State of 'probably little more than 1,500' with 'the 30,000 or more who died in Finland's civil war – a country with population numbers similar to Ireland'.[21]

13 Hopkinson, *Green against green*, 58.

14 M. Ryan, *Tom Barry: IRA freedom fighter* (Cork: Mercier Press, 2003), 195–6.

15 There were no major battles, and the counties of Galway, Longford, Westmeath, Offaly, Kildare, Kilkenny, Monaghan, Wicklow, Meath, Cavan, Leitrim, Roscommon, Clare and Donegal saw hardly any fighting; see P. Hart, *IRA at war, 1916–1923* (Oxford: Oxford University Press, 2003), 41.

16 Daithí Ó Corráin and Eunan O'Halpin's research will soon remove much of the uncertainty surrounding Irish revolutionary deaths before the Treaty; *The dead of the Irish Revolution, 1916–1921*, forthcoming with Yale University Press, does not, however, cover the Civil War period.

17 Hopkinson, *Green against green*, 272–3.

18 Hopkinson, *The Irish War of Independence* (Dublin: Gill and Macmillan, 2002), 201.

19 F.S.L. Lyons, *Ireland since the Famine*, 2nd rev. ed. (London: Fontana, 1973), 467–8; J. Regan, *The Irish counter-revolution 1921–1936: Treatyite politics and settlement in independent Ireland* (Dublin: Gill and Macmillan, 1999), 374.

20 J. Augusteijn, 'Irish Civil War', in S.J. Connolly (ed.), *The Oxford companion to Irish history*, Oxford Paperpack Reference (Oxford: Oxford University Press, 2011), 277.

21 A. Jackson, 'The Two Irelands', in R. Gerwarth (ed.), *Twisted paths: Europe 1914–1945* (Oxford: Oxford University Press, 2007), 68.

The fighting began with the confrontation between National Troops and Irregulars in occupation of the Four Courts, Dublin, 28–30 June 1922. The Civil War did spread into counties, such as Sligo, that had been 'quiescent' during 1919–21.[22] However, the conflict was most intense in the War of Independence hot spots of the south-west, including the three counties (Limerick, Tipperary and Waterford) studied in detail in this book.[23] The Free State and anti-Treaty IRA clashed in the streets of the three counties' major towns and in ambushes in rural areas, and vied for control of local barracks. The 'exciting' scenes witnessed in the besieged Waterford city – freed after 'four days strenuous battle' – may not have been typical.[24] Colonel-Commandant Prout's National Army easily recaptured even Clonmel, the republicans' 'greatest strongholds in South Tipperary'.[25] Nevertheless, it was only after a number of what the Munster press termed 'lively' encounters in the summer of 1922 – and significant loss of life – that the Free State declared victory in the localities. 'Heavy street fighting' in Limerick, during 11–21 July 1922, took 'many casualties'. Republicans initially held the four main military barracks in the town, but National Troops met the 'Diehard' offensive with 'a fortnight's aggressive firing practice'.[26] Tipperary town witnessed 'fierce fighting', and Golden was won back from the anti-Treaty IRA after an 'all night battle'.[27] Free State Army Command Reports recall other 'sharp encounters', such as a clash at Ballymacarbry, Co. Waterford, between Irregulars and National Troops led by Captain Hayes.[28]

The military phase of the war was thus intense in some areas, but short-lived. By September, once the Free State had reasserted its authority in Cos. Limerick, Tipperary and Waterford, IRA opposition to the Treaty comprised small, isolated columns of Irregulars, limited to guerrilla activity and harassment of the public. Yet the war did not end until May 1923; this study offers a new perspective on the Irish conflict of 1922–3 by focusing on violence against (and often amongst) civilians,

22 R.F. Foster, *Modern Ireland 1600–1972* (London: Allen Lane, The Penguin Press, 1988), 512; M. Farry, *The aftermath of revolution: Sligo, 1921–23* (Dublin: University College Dublin Press, 2000), xii.

23 See Map 1. Cos. Limerick, Tipperary and Waterford were selected for study for a number of historical and practical reasons; see discussion later.

24 *Munster Express*, 29 July 1922.

25 *Clonmel Chronicle*, 12 August 1922. See Chapter 2 on John T. Prout.

26 P.J. Ryan, 'Armed conflict in Limerick', in D. Lee (ed.), *Remembering Limerick: Historical essays celebrating the 800th anniversary of Limerick's first charter granted in 1197* (Limerick: Limerick Civic Trust, 1997), 274–6 at 274.

27 *Clonmel Chronicle*, 2 August 1922.

28 Irish Military Archives (IMA), Operation/Intelligence Reports by Command, CW/OPS/1/A.

that is, the aggressive actions largely neglected by conventional military histories of the Civil War.[29] The war is losing its status as the great taboo of Irish history, but, outside the local case study, this readiness to challenge old interpretations still comes largely from a military and political perspective. John Regan tackles issues of state building and democracy,[30] for example, whilst Bill Kissane situates the Civil War in the general process of twentieth-century decolonization, explaining why divisions over the Treaty proved influential in the development of the Irish state.[31] These perspectives are useful, but insufficient; the 'martial paradigm', in Peter Hart's words, is clearly inadequate in describing the events of 1922–3.[32] Hart's research on Co. Cork has been crucial in peeling back the layers of polemic surrounding the history of the early IRA and charting local-community experiences of the 'Revolution' (1916–23) in Ireland's governance.[33] Pioneered by David Fitzpatrick,[34] the county study is, indeed, a useful model in researching these formative years. *Everyday Violence in the Irish Civil War* accordingly adds to important histories, of Cos. Clare, Cork, Longford, Derry, Dublin, Mayo, Wexford, Sligo and Monaghan,[35] by tracking violence in the under-researched, but strategic, counties of Limerick, Tipperary and Waterford, in the province of Munster, during the Irish Civil War.

2. A Three-County Study

Hart did challenge the theory that differences in actual physical geography explain the relative concentration of violence during the Irish

29 J.M. Curran, *The birth of the Irish Free State* (Tuscaloosa, AL.: University of Alabama Press, 1980); Hopkinson, *Green against green*; S. Mac Suain, *County Wexford's civil war* (Wexford: Séamus Mac Suain, 1995); E. Neeson, *The Civil War in Ireland* (Dublin: Poolbeg, 1989); C. Younger, *Ireland's civil war* (London: Frederick Muller, 1970).

30 Regan, *The Irish counter-revolution.*

31 B. Kissane, *The politics of the Irish Civil War* (Oxford: Oxford University Press, 2005).

32 Hart, *IRA at war*, 82.

33 Hart, *IRA at war* and *The IRA and its enemies: Violence and community in Cork, 1916–1923* (Oxford: Clarendon Press, 1998). The political transformation of 1916–23 (the transfer from Britain to Ireland of state power) has become known as the Irish Revolution, although Hart recognizes the wider debate in the historiography over how far these years actually should be characterized as a 'revolution'; see Hart, *IRA at war*, chapter 1.

34 D. Fitzpatrick, *Politics and Irish life, 1913–1921: Provincial experience of war and revolution* (Dublin: Gill and Macmillan, 1977).

35 M. Coleman, *County Longford and the Irish Revolution, 1910–1923* (Dublin: Irish Academic Press, 2006); Augusteijn, *From public defiance to guerrilla warfare: The experience of ordinary volunteers in the Irish War of Independence, 1916–1921* (Dublin: Irish Academic Press, 1996); Farry, *Aftermath of revolution*; T.A.M. Dooley, *The plight of the Monaghan Protestants, 1912–1926*, Maynooth Studies in Irish Local History (Dublin: Irish Academic Press, 2000).

Revolution.[36] 'Single-cause explanations about the geographical distribution' of revolutionary activity remain unconvincing.[37] It is nonetheless true that, during the Civil War, the republicans were at times able to use their surroundings (the mountainous districts in North Tipperary, in particular) to their advantage in resisting and undermining Free State authority.[38] In addition, administrative borders are useful demarcations for the purpose of historical analysis; certain provinces, such as Munster, and counties, such as Tipperary, are known for their propensity for radical nationalism, agrarian unrest and violence in general. Maps of violence compiled by Hart (and Fitzpatrick and Erhard Rumpf before him) suggest that the strength of opposition to the Treaty and intensity of Civil War violence, in the three counties under discussion, generally correlated with levels of aggression during the Land War and War of Independence.[39]

Tipperary's penchant for violence certainly stands out in the contemporary pamphlet that inspired my research on the Civil War.[40] In an undergraduate dissertation on civil-war arson, I address the 'bad preeminence' attained by Co. Tipperary in the Irish Claims Compensation Association's (ICCA) map of house burnings during 1922–3; see Map 2.[41] Master's and doctoral dissertations (on arson and other forms of civil-war violence) draw on the wartime experiences not only of Tipperary, but also the concomitant counties of Limerick and Waterford.[42] My unpublished research thus underlines the value of the local study in understanding a war in which violence was not the sole preserve of

36 Hart, 'The geography of revolution in Ireland 1917–1923', *Past and Present*, no. 155 (May 1997), 142–76 at 158–9.

37 Hopkinson, *Irish War of Independence*, 201.

38 Levels of republican strength and civilian support varied by area; see Chapter 5. Land War heroes such as the 'hillside committee' and 'Rory of the Hill' even reappeared as authors of threatening letters in circulation during the Civil War; see Chapter 4.

39 Hart, 'Geography of revolution', *P&P*, 148–53; Fitzpatrick, 'The geography of Irish nationalism 1910–1921', *P&P*, no. 78 (February 1978), 113–44 at 142; E. Rumpf and A.C. Hepburn, *Nationalism and socialism in twentieth century Ireland* (Liverpool: Liverpool University Press, 1977), 39–40, 52.

40 Irish Claims Compensation Association, *The campaign of fire; Facts for the pubic: A record of some mansions and houses destroyed, 1922–23* (Westminster, 1924), 2–3.

41 G. Clark, 'The Free State in flames: New politics or old prejudices? A study of arson during the Irish Civil War', Unpublished undergraduate thesis (B.A., University of Oxford, 2005).

42 Clark, 'Fire, boycott, threat and harm: Social and political violence within the local community. A study of three Munster counties during the Irish Civil War, 1922–3', Unpublished dissertation (D. Phil., University of Oxford, 2010); Clark, 'The fiery campaign: New agendas and ancient enmities in the Irish Civil War. A study of arson in three Munster counties', Unpublished dissertation (M.St., University of Oxford, 2007).

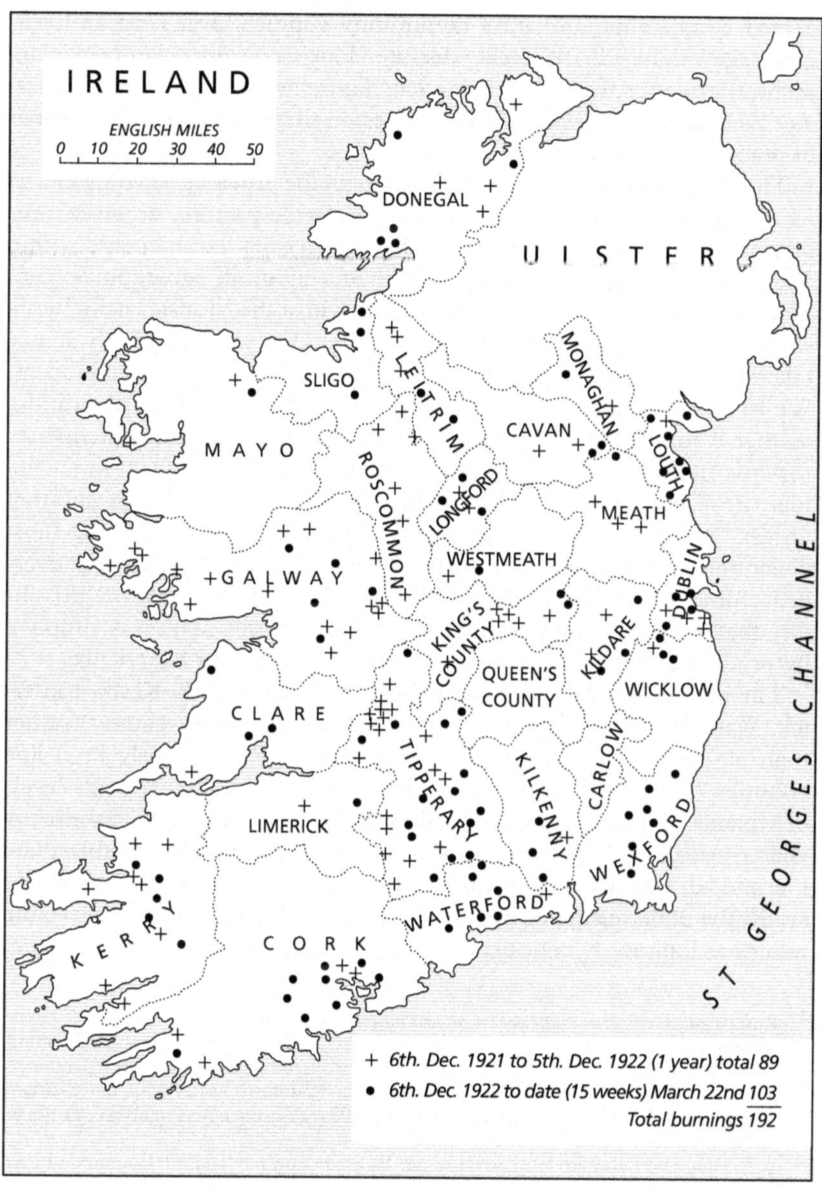

Map 2: Map showing mansions and houses burned, 6 December 1921–22 March 1923, as reported in the press

armed combatants, and intra-community conflicts over land and religion raged alongside the Treaty dispute. This study also relies heavily on archival evidence from Cos. Limerick, Tipperary and Waterford; *Everyday Violence in the Irish Civil War* focuses on these counties for a number of practical reasons.

The three counties cover a large portion of the province of Munster and its diverse topography (coast, mountains, fertile pasture, urban centres and pockets of industry). Worthwhile comparisons can be made within and between counties with varied, but not atypical, geographies, economies and wartime experiences. Indeed, whilst the Munster neighbours share some social and political features, including the anti-Treaty stance taken by their IRA divisions in 1922,[43] there are also crucial differences. Whilst west and north-west Waterford have a strong republican tradition, neither Waterford nor Limerick matches Tipperary's historical tendency towards radical politics and associated violence.[44] Waterford, in particular, does not share Limerick's and Tipperary's tradition of agrarian unrest.[45] I have not, in other words, hand-picked for study the most violent areas in the province; instead, I include in my analysis relatively peaceful areas (in Limerick and Waterford) in order to test the possibility that the 'everyday violence' at the heart of this book was simply a by-product of Tipperary's particularly intense civil-war experience.

The province of Munster comprises Cos. Clare, Cork, Kerry, Limerick, Waterford and Tipperary. This book offers a three-county (rather than all-province) study to, first of all, avoid the famously hard-line counties (Cork and Kerry) that experienced anomalously high levels of violence during the Irish Revolution. Hart, at any rate, has already charted successfully violence in the epicentre of the 1920s troubles, Co. Cork. And, whilst Co. Kerry has not yet been the focus of an academic study, the 2008 release of Irish Department of Justice files relating to the infamous Ballyseedy mine explosions will hopefully encourage scrutiny of

[43] Rumpf and Hepburn, *Nationalism and socialism*, 45–7, 58.

[44] Although one local historian argues that the county's quiet reputation may be misleading; 'militant nationalism' was not strong in Co. Waterford, during the War of Independence, but 'socialist activism' thrived. See P. McCarthy, 'Waterford hasn't done much either? Waterford in the War of Independence, 1919–1921: A comparative analysis', *Decies* 58 (2002), 89–106 at 106.

[45] W.E. Vaughan, *Landlords and tenants in mid-Victorian England* (Oxford: Clarendon Press, 1994), 283–6: when the thirty-two counties are ranked according to official nineteenth-century records of the 'number of agrarian outrages per 1000 agricultural holdings', Tipperary in particular shows consistently high rates of violence. Waterford, by contrast, was not 'convulsed' in nineteenth-century rural violence; M.B. Kiely and W. Nolan, 'Politics, land and rural conflict, c.1830–1845', in W. Nolan and T.P. Power (eds.), *Waterford: History and society: Interdisciplinary essays on the history of an Irish county* (Dublin: Geography Publications, 1992), 459–94 at 468–9.

revolutionary violence in this county.[46] In addition, key archival sources (compensation claims made to the British and Free State Governments for injuries sustained during the Civil War) are not available for all Munster counties.[47] Civil-war compensation files from Clare, amongst other Irish counties, are missing from the National Archives of Ireland. Indeed, whilst compensation claims made to the UK Government are organized and accessible via the National Archives' (TNA) CO 762 collection,[48] the National Archives of Ireland (NAI) has not catalogued its collection of compensation material from the Civil War.[49] This book brings to light many previously unseen testimonies on civil-war violence, by focusing on a manageable number of counties for which archival evidence is available.

The chronological parameters of this study also reflect practical considerations and archival exigencies. I examine acts of violence perpetrated in Cos. Limerick, Tipperary and Waterford between the ratification of the Treaty, on 7 January 1922, and the ending of the war, by the republicans' dumping of arms, on 24 May 1923. Compensation records are available for much of this period; in fact, British and Irish compensation committees invited claims for injuries suffered between the Truce (11 July 1921) and the passing of the Damage to Property Act (12 May 1923) that governed the compensation process in the Free State. That is not to say, of course, that violence ceased completely on 12 May, before the real end of the war. However, allowances were made, especially by the British Government body, the Irish Grants Committee (IGC), for late applicants. In addition, this study of violence does not rely solely on the compensation material, but draws on other sources such as the local press, government papers and military reports.

3. Categories of Violence

My research has been shaped and directed, in other words, by a vast body of administrative records of civil-war violence (and Chapter 2 explores in more detail the quirks of the compensation process). The most striking feature of the violence recorded in these sources is that it was targeted at

[46] National Archives of Ireland (NAI), Records of the Department of Justice, 2008/152/27.

[47] See Chapter 2 for a full exposition of the compensation process. After Partition, claimants from Northern Ireland could not seek compensation from the Irish Government and so there are no compensation claims from the six Northern counties. Compensation files from other Free State counties are also missing or at least inaccessible for researchers.

[48] Records of the Colonial Office, Records of the Irish Office, Irish Grants Committee: Files and Minutes.

[49] Catriona Crowe (NAI) generously granted access to unsorted boxes of compensation files from Cos. Limerick, Tipperary and Waterford.

certain social groups, namely the religious and political minority in southern Ireland. Protestants, Unionists, landlords and other representatives of British rule in Ireland were punished for their loyalty to the old regime, even after the creation of the Irish Free State; in *Campaign of Fire* (see earlier discussion, and Map 2) the London-based pressure group, ICCA, lamented the destruction of 'mansions and country houses', which had 'greatly... increased since the evacuation by British forces took place and the Free State Government assumed office'.[50]

The 'injustices suffered by Irish Loyalists' are not, however, the full story.[51] Catholics, small farmers and 'Free Staters' were not exempt from violence during this bitter, localized conflict. This book brings to light the wartime experiences of victims and perpetrators of violence from across Munster, examining the broad spectrum of harmful acts that occurred in local communities during 1922–3.[52] I categorize these diverse actions, including house burning, boycott, animal maiming, assault and murder, as 'everyday violence' because these acts of violence, far from being mundane, did nonetheless become commonplace in some areas. And the violence I describe in this book is violence that affected not only IRA and Free State soldiers, but also unarmed civilians, that is, men and women of all ages, classes and religions. Murder and rape did not happen every day; Ireland's Civil War was fairly restrained, at least by contemporaneous European standards. However, whilst grotesque violence and state brutality did not become the norm, Irish people and animals nonetheless experienced great cruelties during the Civil War.

My study, of '*everyday* violence' in the Irish Civil War, encompasses actions that are classified elsewhere in the historiography as '*political* violence' and/or '*social* violence'. Clarity of terms is important, because the history of Irish violence has been beset by particular difficulties and political and sectarian agendas. With the progress made since the Good Friday Agreement (1998) towards peace in Northern Ireland, historians today are better placed than those in more politically charged times to scrutinize Irish violence. Nevertheless, the role of violence in the overthrow of the British state in the 1920s remains a highly charged historical problem as evidenced, for example, in the Aubane Historical Society's reaction to the publication (1998) of *The IRA and Its Enemies*, and the

50 ICCA, *Campaign of fire*, 2.
51 Title of ICCA report to the House of Lords; see Chapter 2, Section 2.
52 This book identifies the three main categories of violence during the Irish Civil War – arson, intimidation and harm (assault and murder) – which are explored thematically, in Chapters 3 through 5.

bitter public wrangling over the 2004 anniversary of the controversial War of Independence ambush at Kilmichael, Co. Cork.[53]

The tradition of violence within Irish politics, and the centrality of 'organized armed force' to republican strategy until the 1990s,[54] have been well documented. Open insurrections in Ireland famously fell flat, but the 'courage' of the Young Irelanders who took up arms in 1848 'was remembered and their incompetence forgotten'.[55] Fenianism certainly taught its followers the function of violence as armed propaganda; for Irish nationalists, violence was a symbolic display of political demands and self-governing ambition that could (and did) extract 'concessions' from the British Government.[56] Whilst the old interpretation of the late-eighteenth-century to early-twentieth-century movement for Irish autonomy was one of tension between its constitutional parliamentarian and revolutionary separatist wings, more recently historians have suggested moral and physical force are not binary opposites, and that it is more useful to consider the spectrum of strategies employed by nationalists. Michael Wheatley, for example, analyzes the blurring of boundaries between constitutional and radical nationalism at a provincial level: in Cos. Leitrim, Longford, Roscommon, Sligo and Westmeath, advanced politics were contained within the Irish Parliamentary Party (IPP), even before the crisis of the third Home Rule Bill and World War I.[57]

Indeed, the idea that the Easter Rising and the violence that followed represented a sudden, almost mystical denouement of centuries of struggle has been revised in both academic and public history. Marie Coleman, for example, challenges 'creationism' in Irish history writing by beginning her study of Co. Longford's revolutionary experience in 1910.[58] And the relatively new permanent exhibition at the National Museum of Ireland, 'Soldiers and Chiefs: The Irish at War at Home and Abroad from 1550', incorporates the Easter Rising in the history of World War I, reminding visitors that extraneous circumstances did at times determine the course of events in Ireland. Opened at Collins Barracks in 2006, after the dismantling of 'The Road to Freedom' exhibit at

[53] See Chapter 5.
[54] M.L.R. Smith, *Fighting for Ireland? The military strategy of the Irish republican movement* (London: Routledge, 1995), 2.
[55] L. O'Broin, *Revolutionary underground: The story of the Irish Republican Brotherhood, 1858–1924* (Dublin: Gill and Macmillan, 1976), 2.
[56] Townshend, *Political violence in Ireland: Government and resistance since 1848* (Oxford: Clarendon Press, 1983), 360.
[57] M. Wheatley, *Nationalism and the Irish Party: Provincial Ireland 1910–1916* (Oxford: Oxford University Press, 2005).
[58] Coleman, *County Longford and the Irish Revolution.*

the National Museum, Kildare Street, 'Soldiers and Chiefs' proves that rebellion against Britain is no longer exempt from scrutiny as a discrete, sacred history. The exhibit's final display is a list of the 1,200 Irish men and women killed between 24 April and 12 May 1916 as a result of war at home *and* abroad. No cause is painted as more heroic, no death less tragic than another.

Charles Townshend's seminal *Political Violence in Ireland* still provides the most definitive analysis of the term; he explains why, in Ireland in particular, 'violent acts or threats continued for so long to be an acceptable supplement to, if not an actual substitute for, political dialogue'.[59] At the heart of 'political violence', for him, is the particular relationship between Ireland and the British state. Britain found it necessary to govern Ireland by force rather than consent; Irish groups, from the Irish Republican Brotherhood (IRB) to the IRA, resisted and rebelled; Britain responded with further coercion, in an ongoing and reciprocal process. This book examines political violence in the context of the Civil War; I look not to violent resistance of the British state, but the destructive acts involved in rebellion against the new, native government of the Irish Free State. Indeed, whilst the term 'political violence' was not used at the time, the key primary sources on which my research is based are records of political violence in the first instance. In the thousands of compensation claims made to the Free State's Ministry of Finance for injuries sustained during the Civil War, victims had to prove that the loss, destruction or damage described was committed by persons 'engaged in armed resistance' to the Provisional or Free State Government, or indeed by members of 'any unlawful or seditious association'. The British government compensation body, the IGC, similarly offered assistance to those civilians – loyal to the government of the United Kingdom prior to Irish independence – who were attacked during the conflict over the Treaty.[60]

Because of the original material on which it relies, my examination of everyday violence in the Irish Civil War has an inherent bias towards the political; this book looks primarily at subversive or rebellious acts against the Provisional Government, and the government of the Irish Free State,[61] carried out, in the main, by the anti-Treaty divisions of the IRA.[62] In terms of military encounters, this was a limited war. After

59 Townshend, *Political violence in Ireland*, viii.

60 See Chapter 2 for the Terms of Reference of compensation law.

61 The constitution of the Irish Free State was passed and the Provisional Government ceased to function on 5 December 1922.

62 The available evidence, as recorded in the compensation files, determines my focus on the so-called anti-state actions of 'Irregulars' and 'republicans'; I do not mean to pass judgement on the legitimacy (or otherwise) of political violence during the Civil War.

September 1922, once the Free State Army had recaptured the main republican-held towns in the three counties under discussion, IRA opposition to the Treaty comprised small, isolated columns, with little military organization. By April 1923, republican resistance had become 'a matter of small, scattered bands struggling to avoid arrest in remote areas'.[63] However, whilst I do not dispute Michael Hopkinson's assessment of the military situation, this book considers the broad range of subversive actions carried out by republicans. Attacks on civilians, intimidation, land seizures, the destruction of private property and the huge disruption to daily life in Munster did grant the republican army some success in undermining the authority of the Free State and the ability of the fledging government to protect its citizens.[64]

These were uncertain times; the Irish Free State of 1922–3 was far from a solid, established entity. Opposition to the Treaty settlement likewise came from a number of quarters. This book proves that political violence was not the sole preserve of the anti-Treaty IRA. 'Organised labour', for example, has been largely written out of the history of 1916–23.[65] However, in the communities I studied, disputes with employers were settled with violence.[66] Indeed, one of the main advantages of the compensation files is that they capture the violent episodes not usually mentioned in military histories or even in contemporary press reports. Thus this book examines not only political violence, broadly defined, but also 'social violence', that is, actions – including crop burning, cattle maiming, boycott and the serving of threatening notices – that are not always prosecutable or consistently recorded, but that nonetheless create a damaging atmosphere in the (often rural) communities in which they occur. Traditionally dubbed 'agrarianism', this 'peculiarly Irish' category of crime was increasingly used by the British authorities, from 1845, in recognition of Ireland's perceived tendency to certain modes of violence.[67] Since the Whiteboy outbreaks of the 1760s, rural discontent allegedly had become 'patterned into a particular tradition of action'.[68] In difficult times, before and after the Famine, particular counties, such as Tipperary, became known for their recourse to murders, robberies, house

[63] Hopkinson, *Green against green*, 245.

[64] See for example: Chapter 5 on the republican 'War of Destruction' and Chapter 4 on attacks on farmland.

[65] Foster, *Modern Ireland*, 514–15.

[66] See for example: Chapter 3 on the burning of saw mills, etc. on worker-occupied estates; Chapter 5 on the shooting of a Farmers' Party candidate, Godfrey Greene.

[67] K.T. Hoppen, *Elections, politics, and society in Ireland 1832–1885* (Oxford: Clarendon Press, 1984), 341.

[68] Hoppen, *Elections, politics, and society*, 341.

burning and houghing of cattle. This Munster county had a 'record of heroic consistency' as the 'worst' in Ireland for rural violence.[69]

In the past, the English countryside 'consumed only a fraction of the political attention . . . commanded by rural Ireland',[70] but it has by now become something of a historical truism that Ireland, more than Great Britain, had a particular propensity for outbursts of jacquerie or 'peasant unrest' – potentially organized, but generally spontaneous, reactions to 'momentary and local circumstances', such as high rent or food prices.[71] E.P. Thompson famously challenged the 'spasmodic' view of popular history, arguing that in eighteenth-century England, at least, collective rural violence did not represent 'compulsive responses to economic stimuli'. Communities acted instead in defence of 'traditional rights or customs', including commonly held views on, for example, fair prices or legitimate practices in food production and distribution. However, even though many historians have rejected the notion of the senseless and unorganized rural riot, and instead adopted and adapted Thompson's pioneering 'moral economy of the poor' thesis,[72] the 'complexities of motive, behaviour and function' often are still ignored by those writing on violence in a rural setting.[73] On the Irish Civil War specifically, some historians continue to draw the distinction between rural violence and the real conflict, over the Treaty.[74] For Terence Dooley, the Civil War simply created the 'anarchical conditions for agrarian radicals to operate freely', and tenants' associations in the counties had no central control or clear aims.[75] Hopkinson finds it 'difficult . . . to relate social protest and grievances in the regions to political developments at the centre'.[76]

Yet even if armed republicans and perpetrators of crop and outhouse burning, cattle driving and land seizures were not the same people, '[i]t is probably a mistake to distinguish too sharply between traditional violence and that motivated by contemporary politics. The distinction lies in the use of more deadly weapons; the bomb and machine-gun have

69 Vaughan, *Landlords and tenants in mid-Victorian England*, 157.
70 J.P.D. Dunbabin, *Rural discontent in nineteenth-century Britain* (London: Faber and Faber, 1974), 12.
71 P.G. Lane, 'Agricultural labourers and rural violence, 1850–1914', *Studia Hibernica*, no. 27 (1993), 77–87 at 77.
72 E.P. Thompson, 'The moral economy of the English crowd in the eighteenth century', *P&P*, no. 50 (February 1971), 76–136 at 79.
73 Thompson, 'Moral economy of the English crowd', *P&P*, 78.
74 N. Ó Gadhra, *Civil War in Connacht, 1922–23* (Cork: Mercier Press, 1999), 35.
75 Dooley, "*The land for the people": The land question in independent Ireland* (Dublin: University College Dublin Press, 2004), 40–2.
76 Hopkinson, *Green against green*, 90–1.

been added to the pistol and the pike'.[77] Thus whilst 'social violence' includes less sophisticated, non-lethal tactics (cattle driving, the posting of threatening notices and so on), it was not an irrelevant sideshow to the 'political violence' of the anti-Treaty IRA; both historical categories of violence are apt for inclusion in the analysis in this book.

Land issues recur throughout the book as the source of conflict in many communities. Violence gave added urgency to land reform; the new government responded to local conflicts, and imposed order on warring communities, by passing Land Acts in favour of land redistribution. In its original context, certainly, violence designated as 'agrarian' (surfacing in 'disturbances' or 'outrages') was more suggestive of serious resistance and protest than of simple rural anarchy. In 1836, British politician George Cornewall Lewis was the first to define 'rural violence' as a category distinct from normal acquisitive or malicious crime. Accompanying a British Government report on 'the Irish poor', Lewis sought the 'true origin and object' of the disturbances 'so prevalent in that country' for the past seventy years. Did the rural class in Ireland have an 'innate and indelible tendency' to crime and violence? Or was there another explanation for the murders, burnings and insurrections?[78] In answer, Lewis did not avoid the old cultural stereotypes entirely; he believed that the 'Whiteboy spirit' did account, in part, for the violence in rural Ireland. However, he also suggested that violent action was caused by more concrete, social and economic reasons (the 'wretched condition' of the mass of the peasantry, unemployment and dependence on land) and sought to classify crimes 'with reference to the motive, or effect they are intended to produce'.[79]

There had been fires and riots over the administration of the Poor Law in England, but, Lewis found, in this and 'most every . . . country', violence was motivated by 'malice or avarice, or . . . present want'. There is 'no stronger contrast' to these 'personal' crimes for instant gratification (homicide committed out of vengeance, for example, or a house broken into to obtain property) than violent acts in Ireland, which were intended 'to prevent or compel performance of some future act', and were 'committed by the offenders as administrators of a law of opinion, generally prevalent amongst the class to which they belong'. Threatening notices and malicious injury to property warned persons not to eject a particular tenant or servant, for example, or give evidence at a trial; beatings,

77 Stewart, *The narrow ground*, 153.
78 G.C. Lewis, *On local disturbances in Ireland, and on the Irish Church question* (London: B. Fellowes, Ludgate Street, 1836), iii, 1, 2.
79 Lewis, *On local disturbances*, 94, 98.

murder, cattle maiming, and house and hayrick burning punished those who did not comply.[80] Lewis overstates Ireland's special status; historians have shown that Thompson's 'moral economy', upheld by violence, functioned in other parts of pre-industrial Britain and Europe. Natalie Zemon Davis, for example, writes that the violent behaviour of crowds in sixteenth-century France was legitimated by religious belief and structured by ritual.[81] Nonetheless, Lewis's focus on the collective dimension of late-eighteenth and early-nineteenth-century agitation in rural Ireland, and categorization of violent acts according to their intention and implication, is helpful in conceptualizing agrarianism as a useful, historical label, and a key aspect of the everyday violence that occurred in Munster during 1922–3.

Whilst the military campaign fought by the anti-Treaty IRA did not achieve the permanent undoing of the Treaty and the Free State, collective violent struggle was more successfully directed towards local and legislative change. Agents of everyday violence – civilian and armed – won concessions from the government on, for example, land redistribution. Thanks to a series of Land Acts and improvements in the lot of the strong farmer, the nature of the land question had clearly changed since the Land War. However, the Ranch War, 1904–08,[82] and continued rural conflict during the Civil War prove that land still had the power to inspire resentments and incite hostilities; the general lack of interest in rural violence in the historiography, from the period from Parnell's death (1891) to independence, certainly is not justified.[83] Fergus Campbell's *Land and Revolution* is a recent and welcome exception. Campbell shows, like popular historians Thompson and Eric Hobsbawm have shown before him, how ordinary people enact change through violent action. Thompson's eighteenth-century rioters forced the authorities to take notice of the poor; crowd pressure, as well as market forces, determined food prices.[84] Hobsbawm's seminal history of the 'Swing' riots reveals that even apparently spontaneous violence 'quickly developed the nucleus of local organization', in England in the 1830s.[85] The 'multiform activities' (arson, threatening letters, wages meetings and assaults on overseers) carried out in Captain Swing's name had consistent aims: to attain a minimum living

80 Lewis, *On local disturbances*, 94–7.

81 N.Z. Davis, 'The rites of violence', in *Society and culture in early modern France: Eight essays* (Stanford, CA: Stanford University Press, 1975), 152–87.

82 See Glossary and Chapter 4, Section 3: 'Cattle Driving'.

83 See Chapter 4, Section 5. Charles Stewart Parnell (1846–91): Nationalist leader (of the 'home rule' IPP); president of the Land League.

84 Thompson, *P&P*, 'Moral economy of the English crowd', 125.

85 E.J. Hobsbawm and G. Rudé, *Captain Swing* (London: Lawrence and Wishart, 1969), 205.

wage and end rural unemployment.[86] In early-twentieth-century Connacht, Campbell argues, it was agitation on the ground, not high political concerns, that forced land reform on to the legislative agenda, resulting in the Wyndham Act (1903) and later laws. Public rallies called for the redistribution of grazing land and for landlords to sell their estates to tenants on fair terms; cattle driving, boycotting and intimidation enforced these demands in the local community. Campbell explains how the law of the British crown was replaced by the 'law of the League'; he offers the first full account of the role played by United Irish League (UIL) land courts in enforcing an agrarian agenda, and reveals what happened to those who transgressed agreed social and moral norms by refusing to surrender their land to 'the people'.[87]

Campbell's history of the West of Ireland is another successful application of the local study as a model for researching the revolutionary years in Ireland. My exploration of everyday violence in Cos. Limerick, Tipperary and Waterford will similarly contribute to scholarship on the still contentious and resonant Irish Civil War. A close examination of violence is facilitated by the book's structure. Four chapters examine the subject matter by topic, rather than chronologically, or by county. Chapter 2 offers an important introduction to the compensation process, the records of which provide the archival basis on which much of the research for the book was based. Chapter 2 also sets out the key questions of allegiance and identity, to be explored throughout the book. What was the status of the Protestant and Loyalist minority in the three counties? Were victims targeted because of their religion and politics? What was violence used for, if not to purge the old enemy from the community? In answer, Chapters 3 through 5 deal separately with arson (the burning of homes, crops and property), intimidation (being driven from one's home or livelihood by boycott, the destruction or seizure of property, cattle driving and other threatening actions) and harming civilians (killing, wounding and sexual violence). Using the largely unexplored compensation material, supplemented by other government records, local press and military reports, each chapter drives towards an understanding of the form, function and symbolism of the violent act.

[86] Hobsbawm and Rudé, *Captain Swing*, 195.

[87] F. Campbell, *Land and revolution: Nationalist politics in the west of Ireland 1891–1921* (Oxford: Oxford University Press, 2005), 153–6: one occupant of an evicted farm was subjected to boycott, physical threats and arson.

2 The Price of Loyalty: Violence, Compensation and the British in the Irish Free State

Thousands of previously unexplored episodes of violence are recorded in the compensation claims, files brought to light for the first time by this book. These sources also capture the complex administrative picture of 1922–3: during the transition from Westminster rule to Irish independence, both the Free State and British Governments faced liability for damage and injury perpetrated during the Civil War. The payment of compensation to claimants on both sides of the Irish Sea was a logistical and financial challenge; the process also revealed broader changes in attitudes. In responding to violence and providing relief for its victims, governments were forced to reconsider their duty towards certain social groups. What was the status of landlords, Unionists, Protestants and ex-British Servicemen, for example, in an independent Ireland? The 'suffering Loyalist' became an increasingly familiar figure in politics and the press; organizations such as the Southern Irish Loyalist Relief Association (SILRA) and Irish Claims Compensation Association emerged to supplement government schemes and draw attention to the 'injustices' endured by representatives of the old regime even after the new state came into being.

This chapter examines the 'Loyalist' motif and analyzes the process by which Loyalists and other groups sought compensation for violence suffered during the Civil War. In doing so, this chapter not only serves as a vital introduction to the primary sources on which Chapters 3 through 5 (on arson, intimidation and harming civilians) are largely based, but also addresses directly the questions of identity, nationality and loyalty at the heart of this book. I ask how far a person's national allegiance, religion, class and so on can be linked directly to the attacks against them. And who defined labels such as 'Loyalist' and 'Free Stater' in the first place – the victims, their attackers, or the administrators charged with picking up the pieces of war?

1. Compensation: Policy and Procedure

Dáil Éireann addressed the compensation issue before the Civil War had ended. A resolution of 1 November 1922 declared that, whilst the Free State Government would proceed with compensation legislation in due course, claims could be made in the interim; the Ministry of Finance (Aireacht Airgid) accepted claims for damage to or destruction of property, save that owing to accident, inflicted since 11 July 1921. In a procedure that continued under the Damage to Property (Compensation) Act, passed by the Dáil on 12 May 1923, applications for compensation were made by a standard form to the county and Dublin authorities. The judge at the local sessions assessed the claim and made a 'decree', which was then considered by the State Solicitor. The State Solicitor reported to the Ministry of Finance, which paid the decreed award, with adjustments or conditions. The emphasis in Free State legislation was on the perpetrator. Under the 1923 Act, applications were invited for compensation for 'loss, destruction, or damage',

> [c]ommitted by persons acting or purporting to act on behalf of any organization engaged in armed resistance to the Provisional or Free State Government or by persons belonging to or acting or purporting to act on behalf of any unlawful or seditious association.[1]

Usually claimants could prove the anti-Treaty Irish Republican Army (IRA) inflicted the injury in question, but the so-called Irregulars were not the sole definition of a 'seditious' group; often it was sufficient simply to show malice or premeditation on the part of the attacker. In the testimonies of victims of house burning, for example, descriptions of arsonists as 'masked and armed', or comprising gangs of up to fifty men, recur as evidence that the damage was deliberate.[2] Michael Carroll, whose long wait for compensation from the Ministry of Finance was the subject of a question in the Dáil,[3] was in bed when he 'began to feel suffocated'. He rushed out of home to find his 'whole property in flames'; the 'inflammable canvas burning all round the place' proved to this 'businessman' from Murroe, Co. Limerick, that this was indeed a planned attack, not an accidental fire.[4] Of course, we have to take Carroll's word for it. Fire

[1] 'Irish Free State. Compensation for injury to persons and property. Memorandum', p. 7, 1923, Cmd 1844, XVIII.115 (House of Commons Parliamentary Papers database).

[2] See for example, the following compensation claims made to the Free State: NAI, 392/122, 251, 401/646, 402/103 (Records of the Ministry of Finance, Un-catalogued compensation files: Series 392 [Limerick], 401 [Tipperary], 402 [Waterford]).

[3] Exchange between Padraig MacFhlannchadha TD and Minister for Finance, Ernest Blythe: *Dáil Éireann Debates* (http://historical-debates.oireachtas.ie), xii, 9 June 1925.

[4] NAI, 392/470: Carroll, Limerick.

is a crime of darkness. Incendiaries are notoriously difficult to trace and – historically – conviction rates for arson are low. Given these specific methodological problems, John Archer, who carried out a survey on arson in nineteenth-century rural Britain, advises taking 'on trust the accuracy of the evidence' from surviving official records, such as compensation claims, or court or insurance company reports. Government inspectors, Archer argues, generally were able to tell malicious fire from insurance scam: 'tell-tale signs of incendiary origin' included fresh footprints in the vicinity, occurrence during winter weekend nights, and simultaneous fires breaking out in different places.[5]

Irish Free State officials also took steps to verify claims. Whilst the Compensation Act (1923) technically covered injuries for which 'compensation could have been given under the Criminal Injuries Acts' of 1919 and 1920,[6] the Ministry of Finance did not entertain any and every claim for 'malicious' or 'criminal' loss or damage that took place within the Act's timeframe, from the Truce of 11 July 1921 to 12 May 1923.[7] The new government could not afford anything but the greatest stringency in its administration of compensation payments. To decide whether or not the claim was legally sound and the candidate genuine, the State Solicitor collected 'supporting evidence' from witnesses and associates of the victim, and inspectors from the Office of Public Works made site visits. Edmond Higgins's claim for the burning of twenty-five tons of hay, for example, seemed exaggerated. An inspection of his diminutive farm, and its poor quality land, proved that the amount Higgins claimed was indeed inflated.[8]

There were additional, specific constraints on Free State compensation. Looting and acts of vandalism often are explained by the breakdown in law and order that naturally accompanies war; consequently, the terms of the 1923 Act regarding theft were very strict for this reason. During the Civil War, armed men used violence and intimidation to levy goods (such as boots, tobacco and food) and services (lodgings

[5] John E. Archer, *By a flash and a scare: Incendiarism, animal maiming, and poaching in East Anglia, 1815–1870* (Oxford: Clarendon Press, 1990), 68–9. In Munster, during the Civil War, certain districts (such as Kilmallock, Co. Limerick) did see a number of fires break out over a few days; see Chapter 3.

[6] That is, had the appropriate avenue for redress (the local circuit courts) been open in wartime. See NAI, Records of the Ministry of Finance, FIN 1/3103: 'Official Notice'; FIN 1/1602: 'Circular to Councils: discharge of malicious injury decrees'.

[7] The Truce was a convenient cut-off date for government compensation bodies; separate committees dealt with injuries sustained before and after 11 July 1921. This book deals with the Civil War; its chronological parameters are 7 January 1922–24 May 1923; see Chapter 1.

[8] NAI, 392/125: Higgins, Limerick.

and transport) from the local community. Commandeering was common across all three counties, and thousands of compensation claims were submitted for lost and damaged vehicles, animals and other property. The seizure of motorcars, for example, was particularly prevalent in Co. Waterford and, in parts of Co. Limerick, 'Irregular communication' consisted entirely of 'bicycles and cars commandeered from country people'.[9] Soldiers often indulge in opportunistic acquisition during wartime. An Irish Fusilier in the Boer War wrote of the 'joy' and 'excitement' of looting.[10] And, after World War I, ex-soldiers and landless labourers were lured into violent counter-revolutionary movements in Central Europe by opportunities for 'theft, plunder and extortion'.[11] In Civil-War Munster, both sides exploited the local populace. In October 1922, 'Staters' were known to perform 'pretended raids of houses, where no real searches are made but meals for the raiders, numbering from 15 to 25, are always commandeered'.[12]

Full remuneration of victims of looting would have been extremely costly; the right to compensation did not, therefore, cover coins, banknotes or articles of 'personal ornament'.[13] Senator John Bagwell's wife and daughter, for example, were not entitled to any compensation from the Free State for jewellery destroyed, along with valuable books, furniture and paintings, in the fire at Marlfield mansion in Co. Tipperary.[14] Neither was compensation paid for 'consequential damages',[15] such as travel and accommodation costs associated with fleeing Ireland, and loss of income from an occupied farm or boycotted business. Edward O'Connell, a farmer from just outside Limerick city, received compensation for the destruction of a shed and 100 tonnes of hay in an arson attack on 26 December 1922.[16] However, he was not entitled to any money for the twenty-seven milch cows he had to sell as a consequence of the lost fodder. James Harty and Mary Tobin were similarly recompensed for the crops and farming implements burned in attacks on their farms in Co. Waterford, but the Ministry of Finance dismissed claims for

9 IMA, CW/OPS/2/M.

10 H. Slim, *Killing civilians: Method, madness, and morality in war* (London: Hurst, 2007), 238.

11 Gerwarth, 'The Central European counter-revolution: Paramilitary violence in Germany, Austria and Hungary after the Great War', *P&P*, no. 200 (August 2008), 175–209 at 189.

12 IMA, Captured Documents, Lot 4, A/0992/1.

13 Dooley, *The decline of the big house in Ireland* (Dublin: Wolfhound Press, 2001), 202.

14 See Chapter 3.

15 Dooley, *Decline of the big house*, 202.

16 NAI, 392/343: O'Connell, Limerick.

the extra feeding stuff that had to be purchased after the hay and straw were burnt.[17]

In its investigation of Free State compensation legislation, this book draws chiefly on claims made under the Damage to Property Act. The bias reflects archival exigencies: the Damage to Property files still exist, albeit in un-catalogued boxes, in the NAI, Dublin. By contrast, the files of another Free State body, the Compensation (Personal Injuries) Committee, unfortunately are missing from the archives.[18] The Personal Injuries Committee was appointed in April 1923 to 'receive, investigate and consider applications for compensation presented by any person who has suffered loss by reason of having been injured in his person or by dependents of any person who has died in consequence of having been so injured' since 21 January 1921.[19] The Committee considered injuries sustained by a 'non-combatant in the course of belligerent action between the British forces and the Irish National Forces', or those harmed in clashes between the Free State and anti-Treaty armies. Injured parties for whom 'the British Government have undertaken full liability' (crown forces eligible for army pensions, for example) were not entitled to make a claim.[20]

The Personal Injuries Committee was given 'wide publicity' and, by December 1924, had received 6,616 claims from the public.[21] Awards were made in almost 70 per cent of cases; more than £269,000 was paid in lump sums to the injured and dependents of the deceased, and compensation was also granted in the form of monthly allowances, or money held in trust, for victims' children. The Committee made 'searching enquiries' into applicants' statements, and sought advice from medical professionals on the authenticity of injuries claimed. His Honour Judge Johnson, Henry Kennedy DSc and Dr Thomas Hennessey FRCSI conducted most of their business in closed meetings, but the Committee also sat for 153 public hearings.[22]

17 NAI, 402/98: Harty, Waterford; 402/99: Tobin, Waterford.

18 Conversation with Gregory O'Connor, Duty Archivist, NAI, 24 April 2009: some records relating to the Committee remain (e.g., Terms of Reference, correspondence and final report), but the actual compensation claims from personal injury victims did not survive. It is very possible these files have been destroyed; certainly archivists do not know their location.

19 NAI, FIN 1/3103: 'Compensation (Personal Injuries) Committee'. Thus the Compensation (Personal Injuries) Committee covered the type of violence (maiming and murder) analyzed in Chapter 5.

20 NAI, FIN 1/1605.

21 NAI, FIN 1/3103.

22 NAI, FIN 1/3103.

Fairly comprehensive mechanisms for the settlement of wartime injuries had, in other words, been put in place by Free State legislation and departmental directives. The British Government nevertheless remained closely involved in the compensation process and, whether it liked it or not, continued to honour its financial responsibilities to former citizens of the Union. Officials had indeed already begun apportioning blame for Irish violence and wrangling over associated costs. Claims relating to the War of Independence (for injuries that had taken place between 1 January 1919 and 11 July 1921) were heard by Lord Shaw's Compensation (Ireland) Commission, which closed in March 1926 after dealing with thousands of 'pre-Truce' claims.[23] The Shaw Commission's expenditure was apportioned between the two states; the British and Irish Governments compensated their own 'supporters' and split the cost 'where the injured person was a neutral in the Anglo-Irish conflict'.[24] Establishing the allegiance of the injured party involved a protracted 'correspondence war' between the Ministry of Defence, Irish Office and applicants' solicitors.[25]

Civil War compensation should have been less complicated because the British Government did not have the same degree of legal responsibility for injuries sustained after the Truce.[26] However, to 'alleviate . . . hardship' arising out of any delay in the assessment and payment of compensation in the Free State,[27] the British Government offered its own assistance to victims of Irish violence. The Irish Distress Committee was set up in May 1922 to assist refugees from Ireland through grants, loans and advances on compensation payments made under Free State law. The increasing pressure of migration saw the Distress Committee reconvene in October 1926 as the IGC, the records of which were researched for this book. The arrival, on British shores, of 'as many as 20,000 people, some with their entire families', forced government to

23 R. Fanning, *The Irish Department of Finance, 1922–58* (Dublin: Institute of Public Administration, 1978); its records are located at The National Archives (TNA), CO 905 (Records of the Colonial Office, Records of the Irish Office, Compensation [Ireland] Commission [Shaw and Wood-Renton Commission]: Registers, Indexes and Papers).

24 NAI, FIN 1/3103.

25 N. Brennan, 'A political minefield: Southern Loyalists, the Irish Grants Committee and the British Government, 1922–31', *Irish Historical Studies* 30, no. 119 (May 1997), 406–19 at 409–10.

26 Fanning, *Irish Department of Finance*, 139: the question of liability for compensation for property damaged and injuries suffered during 1919–21 was formally recognized in the Heads of the Working Arrangements for implementing the Treaty, but not mentioned in Treaty; compensation remained, however, 'undeniably the most complex and sensitive of the post-Treaty problems to be resolved in Anglo-Irish financial relations'.

27 'Irish Free State. Compensation for injury to persons and property. Memorandum', p. 7, 1923, Cmd 1844, XVIII.115.

Table 1. *Compensation claims received and total IGC recommendations*

Outside scope	895	
No recommendation made	900	
Grants recommended	2,237	
TOTAL	4,032	Total amount recommended: £2,188,549

Source: End of Committee report (TNA, CO 762/212).

acknowledge its responsibility to these disbanded members of the Royal Irish Constabulary (RIC), ex-Servicemen and civilians 'believed to have been loyal to the British regime in Ireland'.[28] Between October 1926 and February 1930, the IGC sat twenty-nine times to deal with cases of hardship endured by southern Irish Loyalists between 11 July 1921 and 12 May 1923. Grants were made in more than 55 per cent of the claims; see Table 1.

It was not strictly IGC policy to review inadequate Free State payments; independent Ireland had fiscal autonomy. Whilst the compensation process in the Free State began when the war was barely over, however, the IGC operated later, and for longer, providing victims with an additional avenue of redress. In a number of cases, appeals were made to both governments for the same incident.[29] Robert Otway-Ruthven applied to the British Government for compensation because he had received from the Free State only enough for partial reinstatement of Castle Otway, Templederry, Co. Tipperary, and nothing for the furniture and ornaments looted from the mansion before it was burned.[30] Less wealthy claimants, such as John Gleeson of Templemore, Co. Tipperary, were also aware that dual claims could be made. From a 'family of RIC men', Gleeson was certain of the motive behind the malicious burning of his hay; he did not have to feign loyalty to either government to receive two awards.[31] Anna H.G. Clarke, wife of a British Army Major, believed her award from the Free State to be inadequate, and she asked the IGC for extra help. After ninety tonnes of her hay were burned, Clarke told the Committee, it was impossible to carry on 'usual farming operations', and it was years before the income from her farm

28 Brennan, 'A political minefield', *IHS*, 406.

29 In researching this book, I collated compensation data from both governments; calculations and conclusions take the 'overlapping' cases into account.

30 TNA, CO 762/78/12: Otway, Tipperary (Records of the Colonial Office, Records of the Irish Office, Irish Grants Committee: Files and Minutes).

31 NAI, 401/4 and TNA, CO 762/64/11: Gleeson, Tipperary.

in Kildimo, Co. Limerick, reached pre-1921 levels.[32] Clarke's second lot of compensation was subsequently paid by the IGC.

Clarke's claim was bold, but she believed herself (probably rightly) to be wholly deserving of compensation. The Ministry of Finance and IGC also made judgements on this score. Blatant opportunists were weeded out, for one. Richard Burke's claim to the IGC was rejected on the evidence of Rev. G. McKinley:

> He finds himself now in a poor way because he drank and gambled . . . he never suffered because he was a loyalist, and whatever loss his business has sustained he himself was the cause of it.[33]

The IGC likewise believed John O'Connell of Rockchapel (near Abbeyfeale, Co. Limerick) to be pushing his luck in trying to connect, with the Civil War, the theft from his home of money, coats and boots. The forty-two-year-old postman applied for compensation on 11 February 1927, writing that a 'party of Irregulars . . . came specially [sic] to my house', on the night 24 January 1923, 'having me down as a marked man for being a strong supporter of the Government'. But the Committee found 'no corroboration of the story and nothing to show any pre-Truce support' of the UK; a letter to the applicant on 28 September 1928 advised O'Connell that only in 'exceptional circumstances', and when 'complete proof is furnished', was compensation paid for stolen money.[34] O'Connell argued that he had no proof of the incident because he was scared to tell anyone at the time: 'I was afraid to open my lips about it . . . even when the Free State came into operation'. The IGC nonetheless remained unconvinced that the claimant had 'suffered my part from the Republican party'. 'ARJ' (presumably Committee secretary, Alexander Reid-Jamieson) judged this case a straightforward raid for loot and made 'no recommendation'. Ex-constable Thomas Roulston moved to Joseph Street, Limerick, after alleged raids on his Kilkenny home, and claimed to have been prevented from finding a new job because employers of 'ex-policemen before the Irish trouble' were intimidated. However, not only was Roulston's case for loss of employment 'unsustainable', given his fairly generous RIC pension and the lack of evidence that he had actually sought work since retiring, the Committee also believed him an unreliable applicant. The former policeman had 'lent his name as a reference to several doubtful County Clare cases'.[35]

32 NAI, 392/254 and TNA, CO 762/71/17: Clarke, Limerick.
33 TNA, CO 762/82/6: Burke, Tipperary.
34 TNA, CO 762/104/1: O'Connell, Limerick.
35 TNA, CO 762/134/14: Roulston, Limerick.

An honest, 'poor person' claim, by contrast, such John O'Brien's, was given a more compassionate hearing. O'Brien, of Mary Street, Limerick, had been a night watchman for Limerick Co. Borough Council, but was dismissed after the Truce because of his service during World War I. He was deprived of a pension and his health suffered because of the 'vendetta' against him in the years that followed. The IGC deemed his claim 'too high' and saw no direct causal link between O'Brien's anxiety over the local hostility against him and medical complaints including 'heart affection'.[36] Nevertheless, 'despite reservations the case appears to be one of some hardship, and is, therefore, left for the Committee's consideration'. O'Brien asked for £1,000 and was awarded £400 (£17,800 in today's money).[37]

Awards were not necessarily commensurate to the claimant's need. Class-based judgements on victim deservedness were in evidence in the decision-making process in both countries. In the case of John Crowe, a draper from Kilcommon, Co. Tipperary, who was targeted by the republicans because he had supplied the Free State Army, the Irish Ministry of Finance called into question the evidence of Colonel-Commandant Prout because 'though an Officer, he was of the servant, rather than the farmer class'.[38] Snobbery is most obvious, though, in the records of the IGC; the British Government generously compensated those better able to articulate their cause or provide references from a respected community figure. Edward Scales's claim, for example, seemed exaggerated at first glance, given the size of his stationmaster's cottage in Foynes (burned on 29 June 1922). However, statements from clergymen and a British Army Major attested to Scales's honesty, good character and genuine difficultly.[39] He was 'badly in need of funds' to refurbish his house; the Scales family was living in a disused rectory at the time of Edward's application for compensation. One witness had 'never heard of a more deserving case'.[40]

[36] See Chapter 4 on practical difficulties in measuring (and compensating victims of) psychological trauma.

[37] TNA, CO 762/141/13: O'Brien, Limerick. See Glossary for the formula used to calculate the current value of compensation payments.

[38] NAI, 401/1085, 1585, 1771: Crowe, Tipperary. John T. Prout (1880–1969), born in Tipperary, had fought with the Tipperary Third Brigade during the War of Independence, but – after the split – he joined the National Army and in July 1922 and led a 450-strong command to recapture the city of Waterford from the republicans. On what the accusations of Prout's lower-class status were based is unclear, but Prout's Command did have a bad reputation, receiving the 'worst publicity' of all the pro-Treaty commands during the first half of the war; see Hopkinson, *Green against green*, 209.

[39] NAI, 392/522: Scales, Limerick.

[40] TNA, CO 762/138/10: Scales, Limerick.

Railway worker Scales was not able to return to normality after the war; he did not possess the assets and connections in England that big house owners and other wealthy claimants could turn to in difficult times. Sir John Keane, for example, admitted his claim for the burning of Cappoquin was not based 'on the exigencies of my financial position'.[41] And the IGC rejected Alvary Gascoigne's claim because 'it does not appear to be a case of extreme hardship'. Buildings owned by Gascoigne, in Kilfinane, Co. Limerick, had been used by the RIC and were consequently burned down 'by Irregulars' on 24 July 1922. 'On the balance of probability', decided the IGC, the burning took place during a conflict between National Troops and the anti-Treaty IRA, and no special injury was directed against Gascoigne 'who, in fact, does not appear to be himself resident in Ireland'.[42] Gascoigne was living in Bath, England, when he submitted his claim; he was not, like John O'Brien or Edward Scales, struggling to survive in Ireland. And Gascoigne had lost just a few years' rental income, not his whole livelihood. 'In the course of political upheaval', observed the IGC, 'the whole community suffers and it is not unreasonable the burden of insignificant losses and losses of articles of luxury, when sustained by well to do people, should rest where it falls'.[43]

Major Rose's claim was rejected because his home, Boskell Hall, was burned during a conflict between Free State and anti-Treaty troops and the 'claimant cannot say that this injury was directed against him on account of his support of the British Government prior to the Truce'. The decision was legitimate within the rules of the Committee. Rose was not personally targeted; the fire and bomb damage to Boskell clearly was sustained 'in the course of a conflict between the Irish Regular and Irregular Forces'. However, there was a lack of sympathy in the administration of Rose's case. The ex-Major claimed to have been greatly upset by the burning; he had 'not been out to the place because he does not wish to see the ruins'. But, in handwritten comments on Rose's file, Reid-Jamieson judged the alleged suffering 'absolutely farcical'. There had been 'no molestation' since the destruction of Boskell House, 'no evidence of active hostility or threat' and 'no evidence of active loyalty' on the part of 'Major' Rose, whose personal credibility was attacked in remarks that his was 'only a courtesy title'.[44] Over the water, the Free State did pay Rose compensation, but only £3,250 of the projected £13,000 to rebuild.[45]

41 TNA, CO 762/82/11: Keane, Waterford; see Chapter 3.
42 TNA, CO 762/87/14: Gascoigne, Limerick.
43 TNA, CO 762/212: 'End of Committee Report'.
44 TNA, CO 762/41/2: Rose, Limerick.
45 NAI, 392/537: Rose, Limerick.

The financial stringency displayed in these high-profile cases was driven in part by economics. By the end of the war, the Dáil faced a 'financial crisis' and 'colossal' housing problem;[46] spending large amounts on the rebuilding of damaged mansions would have been wasteful. Compensation understandably was a matter of huge public and political interest. Early Free State estimates put the material cost of the Civil War at £50 million; and, as late as 1927, compensation absorbed 6 per cent of national expenditure.[47] Little more could be squeezed from the ratepayer: taxes were already 'too high for a poor country' like Ireland.[48] The financial picture was not quite so gloomy in the UK, but the British Government also had to consider the taxpayer before committing public money to compensation schemes. A new political system – which saw the decline of the Liberal tradition and would witness the first Labour Government – was settling down by 1924, but the British economy was less robust than a decade before.[49] Compensation for victims of Irish violence came fairly low on a priority list that included unemployment, pensions, reform of the Poor Law and local government, and a large Empire.[50]

2. British 'Loyalty'

a) *Definitions*

There were clear fiscal constraints on the compensation process in both countries. The often unsympathetic handling of the claims of landlords and contrasting displays of generosity by both Governments, in what were perceived as more worthy cases involving small farmers, also reveals broader attitudinal shifts. An unwillingness to accommodate the landowning ascendancy is perhaps unsurprising in Ireland, where landlordism was such a controversial and historically charged issue.[51] The Free State Government did not condone land redistribution outside the official channels and the remaining Munster landlords were treated fairly

46 *Dáil Éireann Debates*, iii, 4 May 1923.

47 T. Garvin, *1922: The birth of Irish democracy* (Dublin: Gill and Macmillan, 1996), 164; Hopkinson, *Green against green*, 273.

48 *Church of Ireland Gazette*, 13 April 1923.

49 P.F. Clarke, *Hope and glory: Britain 1900–1990* (London: Penguin, 1997), 119, 128.

50 Clarke, *Hope and glory*, 135–8.

51 More surprising, as this book shows, is the apparent ambivalence of the British Government towards this group. See Chapter 3 on the treatment of big house owners whose homes were destroyed by arson and Chapter 4, Section 5, on the 'historical problem' of land.

sympathetically, especially by Continental standards.[52] Land hunger nonetheless drove hundreds of acts of violence and intimidation in Cos. Limerick, Tipperary and Waterford, and the independent Irish Government was mindful of its duty to the landless and rural poor; these issues are explored in detail in Chapter 4, Section 5. Land was not, of course, the sole defining issue at the birth of the new state. 'Loyalist' was as condemnatory as 'landowner' in marking out victims of violence within the local community, and the treatment of Loyalists by administrators and politicians is an important indicator of changing state priorities.

'Loyalist' was an identity label in regular contemporary usage during the war. George Moynan's 'motor and cycle' business, for example, was boycotted 'by all but Loyalists', and the leader of the band of '40 armed and masked men', who carried out the first raid on his premises in August 1920, 'said that he had orders to put out all Loyalists, and the North of Ireland was my proper place'. Moynan had 'always assisted' the RIC and was a friend of Detective Inspector (DI) W.H. Wilson, murdered in Templemore in 1920.[53] Moynan, like all applicants to the IGC, was required to justify his Britishness: help was granted in cases where the 'loss or injury described was occasioned in respect or on account of' the claimant's 'allegiance to the Government of the United Kingdom' prior to independence.[54] But what exactly did 'allegiance' to Britain involve? Did 'loyalty' have meaning beyond the Terms of Reference of a government committee? Was it a causal factor in wartime violence?

The accounts of everyday violence set out in Chapters 3 through 5 are undoubtedly shaped by the IGC source material; incidents of arson, intimidation and harm often are explained in terms of the victim's 'loyalty'. Because compensation was awarded on proof of allegiance to the UK, it is to be expected that applicants would frame their application in these terms. Claimants often offer only a generic declaration of loyalty. 'Republicans' burned Caroline Fairholme's Comeragh House, Co. Waterford, for example, because her family had 'by tradition and practice . . . been avowed and consistent supporters of the British Crown'.[55] Compensation for British supporters in Ireland was not a new phenomenon. Historians have used the claims of 'suffering loyalists' to measure victimization during the 1798 Rebellion.[56] How quickly individuals became familiar with the 1920s compensation process and were able to express their appeal in the language of loyalty may only prove their cynical

[52] See Chapter 4.
[53] TNA, CO 762/197/33: Moynan, Tipperary.
[54] Terms of Reference printed on all IGC compensation forms.
[55] TNA, CO 762/94/3: Fairholme, Waterford.
[56] T. Bartlett (ed.), *1798: A bicentenary perspective* (Dublin: Four Courts Press, 2003), 480.

financial ambition.[57] In their claims to the IGC, Limerick farmers Denis Hickey and John Coleman offer identical explanations for the harassment and damage to their lands they experienced during the Civil War.[58] With Caherass and Croom just one mile apart, the victims may have known each other, but whether they simply worked together on their application forms, or sought advice from the same solicitor, the template answers to the Committee's questions had a clear, common objective: emphasize one's allegiance to Britain so as to secure financial reward.

Victims were keen to make use of the channels open to them and, during the years of IGC operation, a sense of entitlement developed amongst compensation claimants. On 28 March 1928, Maurice Lynch wrote to the Committee to hurry along his application, attaching a newspaper article on speculation that the IGC was going to consider injuries that took place after 12 May 1923 (Lynch's suggestion being that his pre-Truce case should also be considered more leniently).[59] John Power's cattle were seized by republicans and a levy demanded for their return. He was not entitled to repayment of the £50 under the Free State's Damage to Property Act and demanded help from the IGC instead, encouraged, it seems, by the large amounts awarded to Senator Bagwell of Marlfield, Co. Tipperary, and others 'in my District'.[60]

In Co. Waterford, Thomas Kennedy's claim for the driving of his cattle was rejected because it was a 'neighbour dispute . . . to be resolved by the County Court'.[61] Arguments between neighbours – over trespass, for example – intended for resolution in the Petty Sessions, did spill over into violence during these years.[62] However, cases like Kennedy's did not fall under the Terms of Reference of the IGC having, in its eyes, nothing to do with the actual war. This, however, did not stop Kennedy trying to couch his claim in the terms required for financial remuneration. To Question Five on the compensation form, whether the 'loss or injury described was occasioned in respect or on account of . . . allegiance to the Government' of the UK prior to the Truce, the claimant responded: 'The only answer I can give to this is that the defendant's son came to my Solicitor's Offices and said that anyone should not take up the case as

57 See Chapter 4: one ex-constable, for example, put an exact price of £300 on his 'right' to live in Ireland.

58 NAI, 392/24: Coleman, Limerick; 392/29, 31: Hickey, Limerick.

59 TNA, CO 762/80/1: Lynch, Limerick; see Chapter 4.

60 TNA, CO 762/68/16: Power, Tipperary.

61 TNA, CO 762/65/8: Kennedy, Waterford. See Glossary and Chapter 4, Section 3: 'Cattle Driving'.

62 See also: NAI, 392/466: Hanley, Limerick; 402/106: Power, Waterford. Chapter 4 suggests certain types of violence and intimidation (such as animal maiming) were more intimate and better suited to the settling of personal disputes over trespass.

I was a bloody Orangeman'.[63] I was unable to verify Kennedy's religion in the Census, or any other source and, whilst sectarian undercurrents cannot totally be dismissed in this case, perhaps the claimant said simply what he believed the IGC wanted to hear.

Some were, by contrast, able to recall a more convincing, specific act of loyalty that had singled them out for attack. Dairy farmer Herbert Sullivan's substantial residence, Curramore House in Broadford, Co. Limerick (Figure 1), was burned down on 11 August 1922. The Protestant 'gentleman farmer'[64] was forced to leave Ireland for a much smaller house in Devon, England. Perhaps Sullivan's past service as a Justice of the Peace (JP) and, in 1889, High Sheriff for Co. Limerick, already had marked him out as a British Loyalist in the eyes of his attackers.[65] But Sullivan himself believed that it was his overt demonstration of solidarity with British troops during World War I that accounted for the ill-feeling towards him:

> When Troops were quartered near me I used to entertain some Officers.... On one occasion in the summer of 1917 as a small detachment was passing Curramore... I asked them all in... gave two Officers and the Sergeant Major lunch, and supplied milk for their men. For doing this I was very much disliked and was much abused afterwards.[66]

The fact that Sullivan, and many IGC applicants, had fled to Great Britain or Northern Ireland by the time they made their claim, also suggests that whilst the British connection may have been exaggerated in certain cases, for many it was more deep-rooted than something manufactured for the purposes of compensation. There is a batch of claims, for example, from the 'garden city' of Letchworth, Hertfordshire, where a 'little colony' of around fifty ex-constables and their families formed from 1922.[67] Britain was seen as a refuge for these people and its government was expected to provide support.

Maurice O'Brien, for example, had high hopes of his new home. The pig and cattle dealer was forced out of Co. Limerick 'on threat of death': after the departure of British forces, 'armed Republicans had possession'

63 TNA, CO 762/65/8: Kennedy, Waterford.

64 Occupation given by Sullivan in his Census return (NAI, Returns of the Census of Ireland, 1911, http://www.census.nationalarchives.ie/ [online database]).

65 Public Record Office of Northern Ireland (PRONI), D/989/B/2/9: 'Irish Claims Compensation Association Report to the House of Lords: Statement of the injustices suffered by Irish Loyalists' (Papers of the Irish Unionist Alliance, Papers of the Southern Irish Loyalist Relief Association, Case Papers).

66 TNA, CO 762/87/4: Sullivan, Limerick.

67 *Clonmel Chronicle*, 16 December 1922; see, e.g., ex-constable James Coogan, from Waterford (Chapter 4).

(a)

(b)

Figure 1a and b. Curramore House, Broadford, Co. Limerick, was burned because its 'gentleman farmer' owner had served milk to British troops during World War I.

of his father Michael's house and, on receiving a 'notice to clear out', on 22 May 1922, O'Brien took the cattle ten miles to Limerick for sale, for the final time. He then fled to England, knowing that 'several men who had failed to leave were murdered'.[68] Maurice was particularly fearful for his own life following the murders of an 'ex-Sergeant Welsh [sic] RIC and an ex-Soldier named Gallaher [sic]', who were both 'shot dead' in Newport, Co. Tipperary, just a couple of miles from O'Brien's home village of Ashroe, Co. Limerick.[69] Advised, 'as all loyalists were', to take any kind of job, Maurice found work as a general labourer in Kent and, though 'the promises of His Majesty's Ministers, before and after the Treaty, led us to believe that all loyalists would be adequately compensated', he struggled on 'a weekly wage' and £75 compensation. In Ireland, Maurice had made a 'handsome profit' from 'jobbing cattle' on behalf of his father; in England, he had 'no spare money' and was 'anxious' for a small grant from the IGC to 'give me a start' in the cattle business once again.[70] Maurice's expectations of the British Government were rooted in his strong Loyalist identity. He told the IGC, in November 1926:

> It will not be possible for me to give any [references] in the Co. Limerick for the following reason – all my neighbours were, and still are, Republicans except those, who, like myself, were driven out and their places burned. I have not had any correspondence with anyone in the neighbourhood since I left five years ago. All the old Loyalists, Magistrates, Ladies and Gents who knew me and my family have left the county long ago. My old clergyman and school teacher has died. I have my ex Police brothers available.[71]

b) Help for Loyalists

SILRA agreed that the British Government had neglected O'Brien and thousands like him. The Association aimed to 'draw the attention of the public to the treatment by HM's Government of those Southern Irish Loyalists who suffered injuries' between the Truce and the end of

68 TNA, CO 762/59/2: Maurice O'Brien, Limerick. Maurice's father, Michael O'Brien, was granted £400 compensation in his own right, for intimidation suffered in his position as 'chauffeur and handyman' for J.B. Barrington: CO 762/59/3 (Michael O'Brien, Limerick).

69 NAI, FIN 1/1082: 'Victimised Loyalists: Maurice and Michael O'Brien'; see Chapter 5 on the deaths of a Sgt. Walshe and ex-soldier, Patrick Galligan, in Newport, Co. Tipperary.

70 TNA, CO 762/59/2: Maurice O'Brien, Limerick.

71 CO 762/59/2: Maurice O'Brien, Limerick. Maurice had three brothers who had served in the RIC. The claimant did not state his religion on the compensation form, but he was probably a Catholic (every 'Maurice O'Brien' in Co. Limerick in 1911, as recorded in the Census, described himself as 'Roman Catholic').

the Civil War, because 'it constitutes not merely a cruel injustice but a direct breach of faith'. SILRA reported that neither government had abided by the principles of 'fair compensation' laid out in the Working Arrangements for implementing the Treaty. The Free State had adopted a 'wholly different' and 'greatly restricted' standard of compensation in the form of the Damage to Property Act (1923) and, whilst the British Government's Dunedin Report of October 1926 had set up a new IGC, to acknowledge the 'distress' caused to 'Loyalists in Ireland . . . due to their hasty abandonment by the Government in 1921', the 'changing basis of compensation' in practice (placing limits on awards, for example) was a 'cruel deception of the Loyalists, many of whom are on the verge of bankruptcy'.[72] The Association did not completely criticize IGC provision, admitting the 'large farmer' had 'got onto firmer ground through . . . compensation'. SILRA also made use of these official channels on its clients' behalf: by 4 October 1928, 437 claims had been presented and £240,585 compensation paid by IGC 'through the efforts of the Association'.[73] However, the 'limitations' of British Government relief were recognized regularly in SILRA meetings;[74] help in the form of loans, donations, food, clothing and seeds for poor farmers, was handed out to plug the gap.

Neediness or 'suffering' was at the heart of the contemporary conception of Loyalist identity; SILRA defined 'Loyalists' as those who lost out when British rule in Ireland came to end (farmers with small holdings, and widows and families of ex-RIC personnel and ex-Servicemen).[75] Before disbandment, the armed forces spent approximately £2 million yearly in Ireland and some shops and businesses, especially those in garrison towns, were hurt as much by a diminishing customer base as by deliberate intimidation and boycotting.[76] Even by March 1929, when Relief Secretary I.H.G. White conducted his visit to Ireland on behalf of SILRA, there remained a 'poorer class of loyalist sufferers' with 'no resources to fall back on'.[77] The 'plight of many of these people, *through no fault of their own* [my emphasis], is really pitiful'.[78] Loyalty here is portrayed not as something positively asserted, but rather as a condition acquired simply through circumstance or career choice. Men who 'loyally

72 PRONI, D/989/B/5/3 (Papers of the SILRA, Memos, Reports, etc.).
73 PRONI, D/989/B/5/2.
74 PRONI, D/989/B/1/2 (Papers of the SILRA, Minutes).
75 PRONI, D/989/B/5/2.
76 See Chapter 4, Section 6.
77 PRONI, D/989/B/5/2. SILRA continued to provide information and raise funds and awareness into the 1950s.
78 PRONI, D/989/B/5/2.

served' in the RIC or the armed forces were, post-independence, obvious and unwanted reminders of British law and order in Ireland, but it was 'no fault' of theirs that, during the revolution of 1916–23, their position became untenable.

The dilemma is captured in fiction. After returning from World War I, the protagonist in Sebastian Barry's *The Whereabouts of Eneas McNulty* joined first the merchant navy for an adventure and then the RIC for a steady job. 'I did what I did, and I was trying to make my way, just like you', he explained to Jonno, his former best friend, who had taken the alternative path and joined the IRA.[79] Catholic Eneas had not made a conscious, political decision to separate himself from the community where he grew up, but, because of his 'time in the peelers', he was marked out 'as a traitor and a betrayer of your brothers'.[80] Eneas's flight from Sligo and attempts, in various parts of the world, to come to terms with his Irish identity, is the subject of Barry's novel. Real-life RIC county inspector in Limerick, John M. Regan, whose memoirs were published in 2007, was also a Catholic and, after 1921, had to reconsider not only his place in the force, but also his complex set of allegiances in independent Ireland.[81]

The question of agency is important: both (the real and fictional) policemen, Regan and McNulty, suffered for their perceived allegiance to Britain. Whether they had acted consciously in a 'loyal' way, out of some kind of devotion to the British state, is more difficult to ascertain. 'The problem of ex-Service men in Southern Ireland' was 'one peculiar to that country':

> Every man was a volunteer and went under special promises of his future care made by the British Government. These promises have almost entirely remained unfulfilled.... In addition when the British Government left Southern Ireland they left these men and their families to the mercy of those who were their bitterest enemies.[82]

There were, of course, specific pension arrangements for ex-RIC and retired armed forces,[83] as well as charitable 'soldiers and sailors' organizations.[84] When considering claims from RIC personnel, the IGC 'took serious account' of the additional help to which policemen were

[79] S. Barry, *The whereabouts of Eneas McNulty* (London: Pan Macmillan, 1998), 81.

[80] Barry, *Whereabouts of Eneas McNulty*, 81, 104.

[81] J.M. Regan and Augusteijn (ed.), *The memoirs of John M. Regan: A Catholic officer in the RIC and RUC, 1909–1948* (Dublin: Four Courts Press, 2007).

[82] PRONI, D/989/B/5/2.

[83] 'Irish Free State. Compensation for injury to persons and property. Memorandum', p. 6, 1923, Cmd 1844, XVIII.115.

[84] PRONI, D/989/B/1/2.

entitled, or may have received already, under the Constabulary (Ireland) Act (1922): compensation allowance, disturbance allowance, free travelling warrants and separation allowance.[85] Yet, whilst some financial assistance was available, political changes at home in Ireland made it very difficult more generally for veterans and law forces to 'pick up the pieces of their civilian lives'.[86] Just as demobilized soldiers of the Habsburg armies saw the order they had fought for 'evaporate' after the war, the sacrifice of the male Irish appeared futile when the 'British Army turned against their country' during the War of Independence.[87] Ex-soldiers and policemen became targets, within their own communities, of arson, intimidation, murder and maiming. During the Civil War, these men (and their families) were left feeling isolated and betrayed not only by their Irish attackers, but also by the British Government they once served. Patrick Maher, Co. Tipperary, was caught in this awkward position. The father of a 'spy' (his son allegedly had given information to the RIC during the War of Independence), during the Civil War Maher was driven from his job in Thurles and no longer felt welcome in his local community. Yet help was not forthcoming from outside: 'I was a British Soldier myself for some time', Maher explained to the IGC, 'but I have nothing out of them'.[88]

Not only was British allegiance (in the form of armed service) poorly rewarded in Maher's case, then, but also his remarks do not convey feelings of pride towards Britain, nor a bond of responsibility between the UK Government and its loyal servants. The *Church of Ireland Gazette* called British Loyalty 'an affair of the heart', but such positive, emotional ties largely were absent in the Munster communities I studied.[89] The term 'Loyalist' may more usefully be analyzed, by contrast, as a label stamped on individuals by outsiders, whether perpetrators of attacks looking for convenient identifiers and justifications for violence, or the government committees and charitable organizations charged with picking up the pieces of war. Pressure groups and support agencies such as SILRA and the ICCA served a particular kind of 'Loyalist' defined by his financial circumstances as much as by his religion or politics. The first objective of SILRA, as outlined in its constitution, was:

85 TNA, CO 762/212: the RIC Tribunal dealt with 4,000 applications between April 1922 and spring 1924, awarding 1,990 grants totalling £119,234.
86 C. Fischer, *Europe between democracy and dictatorship: 1900–1945* (Chichester: Wiley-Blackwell, 2011), 102.
87 Fischer, *Europe between democracy and dictatorship*, 102–03.
88 TNA, CO 762/55/14: Maher, Tipperary; see Chapter 5.
89 *Church of Ireland Gazette*, 21 September 1923.

> [t]o keep before the Public *without distinction of Party or Religion* [my emphasis] the great hardships endured by Loyalists and ex-Service men under conditions in Southern Ireland, and to take steps to minimise their sufferings.[90]

In practice, of course, most of those helped were Protestants, and SILRA cooperated with charities such as the Protestants' Orphans Society. There may have been 'no stranger sight', in the words of Eneas McNulty, than the 'fallen' Protestant 'with no money or land',[91] but the impoverished Protestant was a very real, if problematic, figure in Irish society. The notion of 'universal Protestant wealth' is indeed one of the 'pivotal misperceptions' of the minority denomination challenged by Heather Crawford in her 2010 study of 'Protestants and Irishness'. She argues that an 'emotional legacy of past wrongs' shaped Catholic-Protestant tensions well into the twentieth century.[92] The seizure, occupation and exploitation of land by Protestant settlers and the elite position of the Protestant landowning elite during the eighteenth and nineteenth centuries fostered long-held resentments of Protestant economic dominance and unfair privilege.[93] It is true that Catholics had made 'considerable headway by 1922' in overcoming their subordinate economic position.[94] The middle-class, Catholic farmer or 'grazier', who had done well out of land-purchase legislation and had high hopes for prosperity in independent Ireland, is one of this book's key characters.[95] The 'change in the balance' did not, however, diminish anger at perceived Protestant affluence.[96] That there was no such thing as a poor Protestant was a myth that could not easily be shifted.

The Association for the Relief of Distressed Protestants (ARDP, founded in 1836) also complained of the lack of awareness, amongst well-off Protestants, of the extreme poverty and distress that existed within their own community.[97] The ARDP focused on urban poverty and was largely Dublin-centred in its operations (although, it should be noted, the Civil War was in fact a relatively quiet time for the Association; 1923 was noted for the 'steady progress' of the Protestant poor, before the return

90 PRONI, D/989/B/5/6.
91 Barry, *Whereabouts of Eneas McNulty*, 100.
92 H.K. Crawford, *Outside the glow: Protestants and Irishness in independent Ireland* (Dublin: University College Dublin Press, 2010), 22.
93 Crawford, *Outside the glow*, 23.
94 Crawford, *Outside the glow*, 146.
95 See Chapter 4, Sections 3 and 5, in particular.
96 Crawford, *Outside the glow*, 146.
97 M. Maguire, 'A socio-economic analysis of the Dublin Protestant working class, 1870–1926', *Irish Economic and Social History* 20 (1993), 35–61 at 36.

of unemployment and hardship in the 1930s).[98] Yet, whilst Protestant poverty was something of a cultural anomaly, 'needy' and 'Protestant' were nonetheless key aspects of Loyalist identity, and had been so for a number of years. During the crisis over the third Home Rule Bill of 1912, Conservative groups in England rallied in support of Protestants of all classes who, they feared, would be forced out of Ulster by the imposition of Home Rule on the whole island. By April 1914, the Women's Amalgamated Unionist and Tariff Reform Association (WUTRA) had received £12,000 cash and the promise of hospitality for 5,000 refugees 'in the event of the government using force to coerce Ulster into accepting the authority of a Dublin parliament'.[99] Middle- and upper-class women in rural Sussex, for example, were prepared to house Irish refugees facing 'bloodshed, dislocation and starvation' – that is, in the words of the 'Help the Ulster Women and Children' campaign literature.[100] World War I, of course, put Home Rule on ice and, by the Easter Rising (1916) and Sinn Féin's electoral victory two years later, the moderate, constitutional nationalism of the IPP had been eclipsed by something much more radical and republican – and the Partition of Ireland looked to be unavoidable. However, concern remained for "those who love the Union Jack" and, whilst the withdrawal of British forces did not precipitate the religious 'civil war' predicted by some Conservative voices,[101] British Loyalty retained a distinctly denominational tinge during 1922–3.

3. Religion

a) National and International Trends

The swift and substantial decline of the 'minority' population in southern Ireland between 1911 and 1926 is well acknowledged.[102] The reasons for and precise timing of the change are more difficult to determine because of the long interval between the two censuses and the controversial nature of the relationship between migration and persecution on religious or political grounds. Interpretations depend, for one, on the meaning of 'minority'. The term can be used loosely to cover all

98 K. Milne, *Protestant aid 1836–1986: A history of the Association for the Relief of Distressed Protestants* (Dublin: Protestant Aid, 1989), 18.

99 D. Thackeray, 'Home and politics: Women and Conservative activism in early twentieth century Britain', *Journal of British Studies* 49, no. 4 (October 2010), 826–48 at 832.

100 Thackeray, 'Home and politics', *JBS*, 832, 834.

101 Thackeray, 'Home and politics', *JBS*, 832.

102 E. Delaney, *Demography, state and society: Irish migration to Britain, 1921–1971* (Liverpool: Liverpool University Press, 2000), 72.

ex-Unionists, the British army and public servants in Ireland, but is often equated simply with the Protestant community.[103] Some historians avoid these definitional issues by focusing explicitly on the religious minority. Dooley, for example, tackles the 'plight of the Monaghan Protestants' during 1912–26.[104] A victim's denomination is something (generally) unchanging that can be fairly easily traced; 'Unionism', by contrast, especially outside Ulster, may have only ever been a 'passive, unexpressed preference'.[105] Unionists in Munster, in particular, did not possess the numerical strength, social networks and opportunities for political action enjoyed by Protestants and Unionists in border counties such as Monaghan and Sligo.[106] In researching violence in Munster, I excluded preconceived categories relating to religious and political affiliations from my methodology; this book examines violence by type (boycott, attacks on animals, land seizure and others) and not according to the victim's denomination. This is not a history of the plight (or otherwise) of Protestants and Unionists in the Irish Free State. My analysis of the Civil War nonetheless highlights an inescapable trend: Protestants and those with a connection with the British administration in Ireland were targeted with violence and intimidation, resulting in significant departures from independent Ireland.

Between 1911 and 1926, the Irish Protestant population, of the twenty-six counties that became the Free State, fell by 33 per cent (compared with a total population decline of 5 per cent). 'Protestant' here includes Episcopalians (or Anglicans), Presbyterians, Methodists and Baptists, and excludes any other sect. Enda Delaney favours a long-term interpretation of the phenomenon: the departure of Protestants was a trend already established before independence, influenced by economic and social factors, including the departure of the British administration and armed forces, and the decline of the landlord class. He nonetheless concedes that, of a total decrease of around 100,000 in the population of minority religions in Ireland – in the twenty-six counties, between 1911 and 1926 – only one quarter of departures was ex-British army, police or their dependents. 'At the very least over 60,000 Protestants who were not directly connected with the British administration left southern Ireland between 1911 and 1926'.[107] This does not mean, of course, that

[103] D. Kennedy, *The widening gulf: Northern attitudes to the independent Irish state, 1919–49* (Belfast: Blackstaff Press, 1988), 151.
[104] Dooley, *Plight of the Monaghan Protestants*.
[105] Hart, *IRA at war*, 229.
[106] Dooley, *Plight of the Monaghan Protestants*; Farry, *Aftermath of revolution*.
[107] Delaney, *Demography, state and society*, 71–2.

60,000 Protestants were forced out of Ireland by violence. Andy Bielenberg estimates all identifiable causes of the Protestant 'exodus', leaving a residual range of 2,000–16,000 whose leaving cannot be attributed to economic and voluntary emigration, the British withdrawal or death during World War I.[108] Thus, whilst Bielenberg concludes that 'revolutionary terror' accounted for a 'relatively small share' of total Protestant departures, he simultaneously provides convincing quantitative and qualitative evidence that shootings, burnings and expulsion orders played a role in the removal of Protestants from the south.[109] Bielenberg also agrees with Peter Hart that the timing of the exodus is key to understanding the relative importance of its numerous causes. The 'period of the nationalist revolution', 1920–3, was the 'most intense phase of permanent emigration in the years between 1911 and 1926, while the impact of the First World War was far more temporary'.[110] Hart pushes further the connection between mass departures and violence against Protestants: 'the 'suddenness and scale of this movement eliminates any long-term demographic explanations'. For him, 1921–3 were the 'crucial years' for the purging of the religious minority from West Cork, and it was violence and intimidation, not social and economic factors, that drove these Protestants out of Ireland:

> Munster, Leinster, and Connaught can take their place with fellow imperial provinces, Silesia, Galicia, and Bosnia, as part of the post-war 'un-mixing of peoples' in post-war Europe.[111]

As a term, 'ethnic cleansing' gained wide currency in 1992 during the struggle amongst Serbs, Croats and Bosnian Muslims, in the former Yugoslavia.[112] But the expression first was used at the end of World War II[113] by Poles and Czechs seeking to 'purify' countries of ethnically undesirable elements (Germans and Ukrainians, in the case of Galicia).[114] The repressive actions (deportations, expulsion and genocide) encompassed by this phrase do not describe accurately the fate of Protestants in the twenty-six counties after independence. Hart himself

108 A. Bielenberg, 'Exodus: The emigration of southern Irish Protestants during the Irish War of Independence and the Civil War', *P&P*, no. 218 (February 2013), 199–233 at 223 (table 6).

109 Bielenberg, 'Exodus', *P&P*, 202, 207–12.

110 Bielenberg, 'Exodus', *P&P*, 219.

111 Hart, *IRA at war*, 240.

112 M. Mann, *The dark side of democracy: Explaining ethnic cleansing* (Cambridge: Cambridge University Press, 2005), 356.

113 Mann, *Dark side of democracy*, 17: the term 'ethnic cleansing' was invented in 1944 by Polish lawyer Raphael Lemkin.

114 P. Ther and A. Siljak (eds.), *Redrawing nations: Ethnic cleansing in East-Central Europe, 1944–1948* (Oxford, 2001), 1.

is cautious here: 'We must not exaggerate. The Free State government had no part in persecution'. In southern Ireland, there was 'no plan, no ideology, and no institutional support for continental-style ethnic cleansing'.[115] 'Going over the brink', from ethnic conflict to 'perpetuation of murderous cleansing', does by definition require some 'state coherence and capacity'.[116] And there was no state-sanctioned murder or expulsion of Protestants in Ireland during 1922–3.

A 'campaign of persecution is in progress' against Protestants, reported the *Church of Ireland Gazette*, on 6 October 1922, but it was not, the newspaper stressed, orchestrated by the government, nor supported by the majority of the 'Irish people'. The government reserved the use of violence and repressive legislation for the republican minority – that is, the anti-Treaty army wreaking havoc in the counties. The safety of the religious minority, by contrast, was fairly closely guarded. The Free State was indeed at pains to appear just in their treatment of Protestants; the new government did not want to be judged badly by the outside world. The Free State did, overall, deserve the good press it received for its handling of the minority question.[117] A government report on a flare-up of land agitation in Co. Laois in 1922, for example, emphasized the 'danger that will arise, both in Ulster, and in England, should the impression . . . gain ground' that attacks on the Luggacurran estate were 'influenced by sectarian feeling'.[118] 'What will America think of our using our new found liberty . . . to persecute our fellow countrymen because of their religion', asked the 'Catholic citizens of Ballina' in a petition to Arthur Griffith.[119] The signatories opposed the 'discreditable' campaign of intimidatory notices and 'threatened expulsion' of Protestants in Mayo. They argued not for the special treatment of Protestants, but rather the restoration of law and order, and continued 'goodwill' with their 'decent fellow citizens'.[120] The *Church of Ireland Gazette* echoed this sentiment: Protestants must not expect a 'position of privilege in the Irish Free State'. 'Mr Griffith' and his government, the report claimed further, had delivered what was necessary – a 'square deal' for the

115 Hart, *IRA at war*, 245.

116 Mann, *Dark side of democracy*, 7.

117 Kennedy, *Widening gulf*, 51.

118 NAI, Records of the Department of the Taoiseach, S566: 'Laois Land Agitation, 1922'.

119 Arthur Griffith (1871–1922): Journalist, politician and founder of Sinn Féin; elected president of the Dáil on 10 January 1922 after de Valera resigned; succeeded by Cosgrave. Eamon de Valera (1882–1975): Prominent in the Rising and President of Sinn Féin; sent a delegation to the Treaty negotiations and rejected the outcome, precipitating Civil War; founded Fianna Fáil in 1926, which took power in 1932; President of the Republic and dominated Irish politics until 1959.

120 NAI, S565: 'Petition to Arthur Griffith, 4 May 1922'.

religious minority.[121] Clearly the 'extermination or expatriation of the Irish Protestants' predicted 'a few years' hence from the withdrawal of the RIC and British Army did not take place in the Civil War.[122]

Armenians living in Turkey in 1915–17, and the 1.56 million Greeks and Turks forced to move abroad in 1923, as well as the millions of Central and Eastern European ethnic groups murdered or made refugees by German and Soviet governments during and after World War II, suffered an infinitely more brutal fate, during their respective periods of social and political upheaval. Yet whilst the Irish Revolution is a much scaled-down and less severe instance of the 'un-mixing' process, it can nonetheless be characterized as an ethnic conflict. This book proves that victims of arson, intimidation, assault and murder were not only defined by their religion, but were also marked out by their common descent or culture – what may loosely be called 'ethnicity'. The around 4 to 5 per cent of the population who were Protestants in Cos. Limerick, Tipperary and Waterford[123] were members of a minority group with a meaningful identity in which religion was closely entwined with, for example, social status, land ownership and British service. And they suffered violence and intimidation because of this status.

The human tendency to 'cleave, compare and exaggerate contrasts', leading to conflict with members of a designated out-group, is observable in a number of contexts and countries; this does not make its outcomes any more acceptable, but it does teach us that ethnically targeted violence has an explainable basis in society, and a purpose 'beyond the killing and infliction of hurt'.[124] During the War of Independence, attacks on Protestants could be justified in military terms; minorities were collateral damage in a war against British 'collaborators or informers'. However, the fact that attacks on civilians 'resumed after the Treaty and British withdrawal indicates the salience of religion or ethnicity as a determinant of violence'.[125] House burnings, assaults, boycotts and so on did not serve an obviously military plan; their purpose was to drive away the victim.

Sectarian conflict during the Irish Civil War did not take the form of an 'ethnic riot'; southern Protestants were not subjected to an intense, sudden and lethal (but nonetheless planned and 'patterned') attack

121 *Church of Ireland Gazette*, 13 January 1922. On 18 August 1922, the *Gazette* reported with 'shock' on the death of Arthur Griffith, who was 'regarded by all creeds and classes as the man able to guide' Ireland's destiny.

122 TNA, CO 906/38: *The Weekly Summary*, 20 May 1921.

123 See Table 2. No accurate population data is available for 1922–3.

124 D.L. Horowitz, *The deadly ethnic riot* (London: University of California Press, 2001), 1, 42, 47, 424.

125 Hart, *IRA at war*, 243.

'by civilian members of one ethnic group on civilian members of another ethnic group'.[126] Riotous attacks on Protestants allegedly had occurred in Ireland in 1913. An intriguing, anonymous contemporary text, *Intolerance in Ireland*, recalls one such incident in Limerick city: attendees at a Unionist meeting on land legislation, in the Theatre Royal, were 'stoned and chased by a Catholic mob'. Protestants shops were wrecked, and windows smashed in Protestant churches, halls and schools. 'An Irishman' writes further of the sectarian conspiracy protecting the perpetrators, who 'all got off, as everyone knew they would'.[127] (The acquittal of nine men, accused of assaulting and pelting with stones 'Protestant clergymen and ladies', was indeed received with 'applause' inside the court and by a 'large crowd' gathered outside.[128])

Religious riots did not erupt again in Limerick, or elsewhere in the counties that I studied, during the Civil War. In Northern Ireland, sectarian tensions had since the early 1800s periodically erupted into rioting, and the riots that merged with War of Independence violence and labour tensions of 1919–21, and continued through 1922, claimed more lives than 'all the nineteenth-century riots taken together'.[129] Riots and street violence did not become a regular mode of encounter for Catholics and Protestants in the twenty-six counties. However, what Donald Horowitz identifies as the two 'general aims' of the ethnic riot, 'degradation' and 'homogenization',[130] were at work in other ways during 1922–3. This book shows how violence and intimidation were used, first of all, to degrade the victim, that is, to humiliate or take revenge. Arson and intimidation, explored in Chapters 3 and 4, served to teach a bad employer a lesson, reclaim land from a grabber or grazier, or settle old scores over trespass. Chapter 5, 'Harming Civilians', demonstrates how past service in the RIC or British Army was punished with kidnap, murder and assault. 'Homogenization' approaches 'genocidal aims more closely' and Irish Protestants clearly were not subject to ethnic cleansing. However, perpetrators of everyday violence in Munster did 'want members of the target group' (a group identified by its religious, cultural and political loyalties, that is, Protestants, ex-British Servicemen and landlords) to 'disappear',[131] to die, or at least leave Ireland.[132]

[126] Horowitz, *Deadly ethnic riot*, 1–2.
[127] *Intolerance in Ireland, facts not fiction, by an Irishman* (London, 1913), 114–17.
[128] *The Manchester Guardian*, 4 March 1913, online database (ProQuest Historical Newspapers: *The Guardian* [1821–2003] and *The Observer* [1791–2003]).
[129] Stewart, *The narrow ground*, 141. See Chapter 3, Section 1, on the role of arson in riots and civic unrest in Northern Ireland.
[130] Horowitz, *Deadly ethnic riot*, 424, 430–3.
[131] Horowitz, *Deadly ethnic riot*, 433.
[132] See Chapter 4.

b) *Munster*

Not all historians place religion at the centre of their understanding of the Irish Revolution. Hart's controversial conclusions, for example, have not been borne out by other local studies. These alternative perspectives do not necessarily undermine Hart's bold research: heightened religious tensions are perhaps to be expected in a county that includes a 'sizeable' urban Protestant population, in Cork city.[133] Allegedly the 'most dramatic expulsions of non-Catholics seen in the South', during the Revolution, took place here; Gerard Murphy links directly the 'severe decline' in the Protestant population of the south-east corner of the city, between March and July 1922, with the rounding up and shooting of Protestant teenage 'spies' in this area in 1921.[134] The Protestant experience of the Revolution clearly varied by region. Marie Coleman argues that relations between the Protestant community and republican movement in Co. Longford were reasonably peaceful.[135] And, whilst Protestants in Cos. Monaghan and Sligo suffered in economic boycotts,[136] these counties did not witness the high levels of violence and intimidation that resulted in mass departures in Co. Cork.[137] Dooley argues that 'Protestants . . . living under Dublin rule had less to grieve about than Catholics' in the North,[138] and some local voices in Munster seem to agree. A 'large and representative meeting' of Protestants in Nenagh, Co. Tipperary, on 15 April 1922, for example, condemned the Belfast 'atrocities' (the incursions against Catholics by the security forces of the new Northern Ireland government).[139] Attendees demanded: 'our fellow Roman Catholic countrymen in the Northern Parliament must be treated in the same way as we Southern Protestants'.[140] There were no claims, from this gathering, that the Protestant experience had been anything other than peaceful. The same conciliatory attitude was displayed at a 'special meeting of the Limerick Corporation', on 30 March 1922; delegates discussed the 'position of Belfast Catholics' and denounced

133 Hart, *IRA and its enemies*, 40–1.
134 G. Murphy, *The year of disappearances: Political killings in Cork, 1920–1921* (Dublin: Gill and Macmillan, 2010), 247, 324. However, Bielenberg argues that Protestant decline was actually greater in the north of the city, suggesting that factors other than violence (chiefly the departure of the military garrison) explain this movement; Bielenberg, 'Exodus', *P&P*, 220.
135 M. Coleman, *County Longford and the Irish Revolution, 1910–1923* (Dublin, 2006), 155–7.
136 Farry, *Aftermath of revolution*, 189–90, 206.
137 Hart, *IRA at war*, 223.
138 Dooley, *Plight of the Monaghan Protestants*, 58–9.
139 See Chapter 3, Section 1, on the Belfast pogroms.
140 *Nenagh Guardian*, 15 April 1922.

attacks on Protestants, particularly the burning of the pavilion at the Protestant Young Men's Association Grounds, Limerick city. Alderman Michael Colivet TD also called underhand and 'immoral' the firing into Protestant houses in Limerick.[141] These town meetings probably would have included at least some of the middle-class Protestants and merchants who historically controlled commerce in Munster; whilst those Protestants who retained economic power during the Revolution understandably did not boast about their successes, some minority firms did survive, and thrive, in the new Free State.[142]

How fared conciliatory attitudes and early attempts at religious cooperation once the Civil War began in earnest? In July 1922, the *Church of Ireland Gazette* proclaimed that the 'present is an excellent time for the welding together of those interests in Irish life which, for a hundred years, have been opposed to each other'.[143] The reality, as the war entered its most intensive phase, was somewhat different. Following the confrontation at the Four Courts, in Dublin on 28–30 June 1922, the battle spread to the counties. In July and August 1922, the Free State Army and anti-Treaty IRA clashed in the streets of major towns and in rural ambushes, and vied for control of local barracks. Whilst the Free State Army succeeded, by September 1922, in militarily defeating the republicans, attacks on and against civilians continued until May 1923. And, from these intra-community conflicts in Cos. Limerick, Tipperary and Waterford, there is evidence that targeted violence and intimidation were used to clear out the old Protestant enemy. The downward trend may have been underway before the Civil War, but Munster proved to be particularly 'inhospitable' for Protestants,[144] experiencing the largest percentage drop (45 per cent) in the minority population, of the four provinces, during 1911–26.[145]

There are no precise figures for the Protestant population of the three counties at the outbreak of the Civil War; the demographer's task is complicated by the absence of any data from 1921, when the census was abandoned during the War of Independence.[146] However, the last census

141 *Limerick Leader*, 31 March 1922. The Mid-Limerick Brigade of the IRA also distanced itself from such attacks.

142 See Chapter 4, Section 6b, on urban Protestants' experiences of the Civil War.

143 *Church of Ireland Gazette*, 28 July 1922.

144 K.D. Bowen, *Protestants in a Catholic state: Ireland's privileged minority* (Dublin: McGill-Queen's University Press, 1983), 21.

145 Delaney, *Demography, state and society*, 299, 305. Refers to provinces within the twenty-six counties of the Free State only; Ulster includes Cavan, Donegal and Monaghan in these calculations.

146 A. Mitchell, *Revolutionary government in Ireland: Dáil Éireann, 1919–22* (Dublin: Gill and Macmillan, 1995), 241.

taken before the war (1911) indicates that, even before the Revolution and departure from Ireland of the British administration, Protestants comprised a small minority in Cos. Limerick, Tipperary and Waterford. Protestants historically were urban-based and, in the county boroughs, comprised a relatively large minority (nearly 10 per cent in Limerick co. borough (that is, Limerick city) and 8 per cent in Waterford city, in 1911). But, in the counties, Protestants made up a much smaller, and ever-shrinking, group, and a comparison of Protestant population figures from 1911 with those recorded in the next Census of Ireland (1926) gives some indication of the negative impact this period had on an already small minority; see Table 2.

'Other Religions' in Table 2 encompasses not only Protestants (Episcopalian, Presbyterian, Methodist and Baptist) but also Jews and 'Other' (which includes Quakers, a numerically small group that nonetheless had played a key role in the urban and commercial development of Cos. Waterford, Limerick and Tipperary; see Chapter 4, Section 6b). However, the Free State's non-Catholic or 'minority' population was almost entirely Protestant and, as Table 2 shows, largely Anglican (persons who declared themselves Protestant Episcopalian or Church of Ireland [or England or Scotland] on the Census form).

Between 1911 and 1926, the populations of Cos. Tipperary, Waterford and Limerick fell by 7 per cent, 6 per cent and 2 per cent, respectively.[147] The Protestant population dropped by 46 per cent in Tipperary, 42 per cent in Limerick and 40 per cent in Waterford.[148] Irish Protestants, in other words, were in decline at a much faster rate than were Catholics in the three counties under review. Voluntary migration and death may be as much at the root of this change as enforced flight or cultural pressures: high death rates and low marital fertility, for example, had long affected Protestants.[149] The minority population fall is, in addition, not quite so dramatic if British-born Protestants (namely those Protestants serving in the armed forces in Ireland) are removed from the equation: the Irish-born Protestant population dropped by 29 per cent in Tipperary, 28 per cent in Waterford and 27 per cent in Limerick.[150] It is clear, nevertheless, that a disproportionate number of those leaving Munster during 1911–26 were Protestants; and this does require explanation.

Statements from the communities I studied convey the individual's sense that what they suffered was part of a wider victimization on the

147 Delaney, *Demography, state and society*, 299, 305.
148 Bielenberg, 'Exodus', *P&P*, 205 (Table 3).
149 Delaney, *Demography, state and society*, 295.
150 Bielenberg, 'Exodus', *P&P*, 205 (Table 3).

Table 2. *Populations of the three Munster counties, 1911 and 1926*

			Total Other Religions		Other Religions					
County	Total Persons	Catholics	As Percentage of Total Persons	Actual Numbers	Protestant Episcopalians	Presbyterians	Methodists	Jews	Baptists	Others
Limerick Co. Borough										
1911	38,518	34,865	9.5	3,653	2,316	847	213	119	79	79
1926	39,448	37,640	4.6	1,808	1,285	147	104	30	38	204
Limerick County										
1911	104,551	101,502	2.9	3,049	2,550	136	273	3	17	70
1926	100,895	98,793	2.1	2,102	1,691	65	206	3	10	127
Tipperary County										
1911	152,433	144,156	5.4	8,277	7,221	432	435	7	16	166
1926	141,015	136,564	3.2	4,451	3,747	173	223	7	1	300
Waterford Co. Borough										
1911	27,464	25,331	7.8	2,133	1,530	183	139	62	51	168
1926	26,647	25,466	4.4	1,181	861	124	70	27	20	79
Waterford County										
1911	56,502	54,060	4.3	2,442	2,027	201	122	-	20	72
1926	51,915	50,358	3	1,557	1,253	116	73	-	11	104

Source: Saorstát Éireann: Census of population 1926, vol. 3.[151]

[151] Individual returns from 1926 will not be open to the public until 2027, but the Census data is summarized in the published volumes of the Irish Free State Department of Industry and Commerce's *Saorstát Éireann: Census of population 1926*, ten vols. (Dublin: Stationery Office, 1928). My table is extracted from vol. III, Table 9, 'Number of persons of each religion in each county and county borough in Saorstát Éireann at each census year from 1861, the first year for which the figures are available'.

grounds of religion. 'As a Protestant loyalist', Richard Hughes, of Mullinahone, Co. Tipperary, for example, was harassed, and his home damaged when hay was brought inside and burned. One of the attackers, identified by the victim as 'IRA', told Hughes that he and 'every Protestant Loyalist would soon be cleared out of the Country'.[152] Claimants did not necessarily mention their religion on the compensation form, but Hughes's denomination can be verified in the Census returns: 'Church of Ireland'. In 1911, Hughes, a twenty-three-year-old 'landowner', was resident in Drangan, Co. Tipperary, just two miles from Mullinahone, where the Civil War attacks took place.[153] Arthur Hunt, a Protestant and 'well known' Unionist whose big house, Rockmount, in Kilmacthomas, Co. Waterford, was burned, told the IGC that 'in his district practically all Protestant houses were burnt in a similar way'.[154] Letters in circulation during the Civil War (copies of which are sometimes enclosed in the compensation files) similarly issued threats against entire Protestant communities.[155]

Outside urban centres, Protestants in Cos. Limerick, Tipperary and Waterford comprised a small, dispersed minority of around 3–5 per cent of the total population (see Table 2); it was indeed possible, in Protestant enclaves such as that occupied by Edward Scales, for example, to easily identify and root out virtually the entire minority population. Scales's stationmaster's cottage in Foynes, Co. Limerick, was completely gutted by fire on 29 June 1922. The solicitor investigating Scales's compensation claim, on behalf of the Free State:

> [h]ad been informed by some Catholic clergymen who know the applicant that he . . . suffered a good deal during our own trouble and was apparently singled out specially to be victimised. I may mention that *he is a Protestant and one of the few living in the district* [my emphasis] and one of the Reverend Clergymen . . . said that he believed that had a good deal to do with his being burned out.[156]

The Protestant railway worker had also demonstrated his British loyalty over the years. The neighbour who received the family in the early hours, when Scales's house was 'a mass of flames', recalled:

> I know the Scales were Unionists in politics and that they supplied teas to the soldiers camped at the stations and also that they boarded Naval officers, all of

152 TNA, CO 762/90/6: Hughes, Tipperary.
153 Census of Ireland, 1911 (online database).
154 TNA, CO 762/85/7: Hunt, Waterford.
155 See Chapter 4 for notices received by Protestants, e.g., Willie Roe, Ada Vere-Hunt.
156 NAI, 392/522: Scales, Limerick.

which made them objectionable to the Irregulars and I think this partly accounts for the burning.[157]

The railways were, of course, a particularly dangerous place to work during the war.[158] The burning of the station buildings may have been part of the Irregulars' military plan to sabotage infrastructure and undermine the authority of the Free State, rather than a personal attack on Scales. However, if Scales was already marked out in Foynes as one member of a very small, easily identifiable Protestant community, the destruction of his home and subsequent impoverishment[159] must only have increased his isolation. Indeed, the 1911 Census recorded just thirteen (Church of Ireland) Protestants living in Foynes Town: 'locomotive fireman' (later stationmaster), Edward Scales, lived there with his wife and four children; another (older) Edward Scales headed another family of seven. Births, deaths or children leaving home may have altered these numbers by the time of the Civil War, but railway worker Edward (aged forty-nine, by 1922), and his family, were still living in Foynes up until the fiery attack.[160]

Protestants living, like Scales, in small, isolated communities were vulnerable to attack during the war and were statistically more likely to leave Ireland than were their co-religionists in areas with a stronger non-Catholic presence. During 1911–26, emigration was indeed highest from counties (Galway, Mayo, Roscommon, Kerry and Clare) in which Irish-born Protestants made up less than the 3 per cent of the population; Protestants were less likely to leave areas such as Dublin, Wicklow and counties bordering Northern Ireland, where they constituted a much larger minority.[161] That is not to say that Protestants always found safety in numbers. Protestant shopkeepers and businessmen in Munster's cities and towns, where the minority influence and culture traditionally were strong, were intimidated in large numbers. Boycotts, for example, destroyed minority livelihoods in Lismore, Co. Waterford, and other towns. There is nonetheless an important distinction to be made between the Revolutionary experiences of isolated and endangered Protestants in quiet, rural parts (working-class Protestants in small cottages, as well as the Irish gentry in their big houses) and the strong mercantile

[157] TNA, CO 762/138/10: Scales, Limerick.
[158] See Chapter 3 on damage to the railways and Chapter 5 on attacks on railway workers.
[159] See earlier discussion (Section 1).
[160] Census of Ireland, 1911 (online database).
[161] Bielenberg, 'Exodus', *P&P*, 203, 205 (table 3). In 1911, Protestants made up 30% of the population of Co. Dublin, 23% in Monaghan, 21% in Wicklow and 21% in Donegal; see W.E. Vaughan and A.J. Fitzpatrick (eds.), *Irish historical statistics: Population, 1821–1971* (Dublin: Royal Irish Academy, 1978), 66–8.

and professional Protestants who actually survived – and thrived – in the new Free State.[162]

Certainly there were important interclass distinctions, and regional variations, in the intensity of sectarianism and associated violence, during the Revolution. It was, however, during the Civil War, rather than during earlier periods of conflict, that many Protestants across Munster found their personal, political and religious allegiances called violently into question. Samuel Doupe had worked at Kilboy House, Nenagh, Co. Tipperary for twenty-five years, running the estate in the absence of Lord Dunalley.[163] His loyal service to Dunalley, demonstrated in their personal correspondence,[164] and his symbolic role as guardian of elite advantages, cannot have made Doupe popular locally. With their salaries and free cabins, the 'privileged position' of herdsmen and stewards on big estates had, since the mid-nineteenth century, marked out individuals like Doupe for violent attack,[165] and – as the Irish gentry departed their big houses – many of their Protestant gardeners, woodmen, gamekeepers and other servants lost their jobs and also left for England.[166] 'Devoted servant' Doupe initially stayed behind; it was indeed he who wrote to Dunalley, on 6 August 1922, to break the bad news: 'My Lord, Kilboy is in ruins and the front yard is burned to ashes'. With the farming machinery also destroyed, 'I don't see how we can carry on'. And Doupe knew he was done for without his British protector:

> I suppose I will have to go at once to England as a refugee perhaps you may be able to get me some job . . . its no use I going [sic] to Limerick for it[']s in a state of war.[167]

Returning to the burnt-out house to make arrangements for his departure was 'extremely dangerous'; Doupe already had been shot in the hand during a raid on his own residence, when 'armed men' gave him

162 See Chapter 4, especially Section 6b.

163 The fourth Lord Dunalley (barony cr. 1800) was Henry O'Callaghan Prittie (1851–1927). He was a JP, Lieutenant for Co. Tipperary and a Representative Peer for Ireland since 1891.

164 National Library of Ireland (NLI), MS 29,810 (Dunalley Papers, of the Prittie family Lords Dunalley, 1665–1937).

165 M. Beames, 'Rural conflict in pre–Famine Ireland: Peasant assassinations in Tipperary, 1837–1847', in C.H.E. Philpin, *Nationalism and popular protest in Ireland* (Cambridge, 1987), 264–83 at 274. William McKenna (TNA, CO 762/137/6: McKenna, Co Tipperary), whose wife and son were viciously attacked in August 1922, was a steward at Golden Grove, Co. Tipperary. With his position came a free house, supplies including milk and coal, and a job for his son, together worth around £160 per year. See Chapter 5.

166 Bielenberg, 'Exodus', *P&P*, 233 (Appendix).

167 NLI, MS 29,810(17): 'Correspondence of Lord Dunalley 1922'.

'one month to get out of the place'. The injury to his finger rendered Doupe 'useless for manual labour', but he remained in Nenagh for a few months, attempting to sell off the animals and gather information for Dunalley's compensation claim. But, finally, and in 'fear for my safety', Doupe 'reluctantly' left Tipperary in November 1922 and moved to Fivemiletown, Co. Tyrone.[168] Sectarian language pervades Doupe's account of his departure from Munster: he was 'privately and confidentially informed whilst preparing to leave' not to return 'otherwise I would be shot as I was looked upon as an ultra loyalist'. The raiders 'indicat[ed] that it was in consequence of being a Protestant . . . that I was set upon'.[169] Dunalley verified his steward's statement, and provided references for the compensation claims of his head keeper, William Mollison,[170] and Denis Carroll,[171] a small farmer from nearby Nenagh, whose house was burned and, during the War of Independence, his police constable son, John, murdered.[172]

4. Conclusion

Doupe clearly did not feel secure in the protection offered to the minority religion by the new government. Neither did Charles Bryan, of Co. Waterford. From February 1922, Bryan was repeatedly intimidated, pressed for money and 'threatened with death'. On the night of 14 June 1922, the 'armed men' returned and 'rushed about [the] house with flashlights shouting for me and threatening [my] life'. Bryan, still in his nightclothes, escaped from a window and hid in a field. He spent twenty weeks away from home (hiding first in Glenbeg, near Dungarvan, then in Lismore) and alleged that, whilst he was away, the IRA visited his family and beat his son (who they accused of giving information to British soldiers). The son died in September 1925 and Bryan's wife, who 'never recovered from the shock', died a year later. His attackers told Bryan:

> We want this place for ourselves. Your backers are gone now and you must clear out too as your equals have no right to be in this country.

Bryan, a Protestant, and 'strong supporter' of the British Government throughout 'the period of the trouble', had been left in a vulnerable position by the withdrawal of the RIC and British forces in 1922. He explained that it was after the 'rebels who had been arrested by the British

168 NLI, MS 29,810(17); see Chapter 3.
169 TNA, CO 762/39/10: Doupe, Tipperary.
170 TNA, CO 762/74/3: Mollison, Tipperary.
171 TNA, CO 762/48/9: Carroll, Tipperary.
172 R. Abbott, *Police casualties in Ireland 1919–1922* (Cork: Mercier Press, 2000), 199.

were released' that his family was molested, his wife and son died, and he was left a 'broken man'. Yet Bryan also did not find a new 'backer' in the Free State administration. On the run in June 1922, Bryan claims he went to Dublin and was told by 'some member of the government' that 'I could get no protection'.[173]

W.T. Cosgrave[174] made a national gesture of goodwill to the southern minority via the nomination of high profile Protestants and Ascendancy figures to the Senate. Local meetings of prominent Protestants in the Free State expressed support for troubled Northern Catholics. However, the evidence in this chapter suggests that the rhetoric of religious inclusion was not always turned into action in Munster; see Section 3. Was this indicative of a broader failure, on both sides of the Irish Sea, of government responsibility towards victims of violence? It was the job of British pressure groups to promote the image of the blameless 'Loyalist' and therefore justify their charitable and lobbying roles; see Section 2b. The perspectives of the British and Free State Governments, by contrast, were shaped less by victims' neediness and more by wider economic and political concerns; see Section 1. As a result, it is difficult to prove that certain groups were deliberately treated badly by either government, but the compensation process does reveal certain biases and priorities. SILRA and ICCA believed, with some good reason, that their 'Loyalist' clients often suffered prejudice and were deemed unworthy of assistance, because of who they were. The ICCA's accusation that the Free State evaded payments to certain individuals through 'unjust counter claims' (by deducting 'alleged arrears of Income Tax' from compensation, for example) is borne out in some cases.[175]

Other specific complaints were made about the handling of claims by the Irish courts, the first stage in the compensation process.[176] Gerald Cooney, of Birdhill, Co. Tipperary, was 'forcibly removed' from his home, his animals and possessions destroyed, and 'personal injuries' inflicted on himself, his wife and children. Cooney claimed it was too dangerous to return to Ireland, but the State Solicitor investigating the case commented derisively that it was perfectly safe for Cooney to give

173 TNA, CO 762/111/5: Bryan, Waterford.

174 William Thomas Cosgrave (1880–1965): Succeeded Collins as Chairman and Minister for Finance of the Provisional Government in July 1922, and Arthur Griffith as President of the Dáil in August 1922. In September 1922, he became the first President of the Executive Council of the Irish Free State, that is, the head of government, or prime minister (the Taoiseach replaced this position in 1937).

175 PRONI, D/989/B/2/9. Victims of large income tax deductions and a protracted compensation process included, e.g., Major Morel, whose Tipperary mansion was burned; see Chapter 3.

176 Kennedy, *Widening gulf*, 153.

evidence at the hearing. Cooney understandably did not attend, and, in December 1924, the county court judge dismissed the case altogether.[177] Alice Davis believed the court in Tipperary 'was unsympathetic and even hostile to my claim' for compensation, for the shooting of her constable husband.[178] A particular lack of compassion, it was felt, was displayed in the consideration of claims from large landowners. The ICCA suggested the judge at the local sessions in Co. Tipperary had been deliberately obstinate, for example, in the hearing of Ada Vere-Hunt's case for compensation. He awarded nothing for the attacks on Longfield House (Cashel, Co. Tipperary) and allegedly responded to accusations of cattle driving: 'grass was intended to be eaten by cattle'.[179]

The Vere-Hunts had political, social and cultural roots in Britain and Ireland; during the Civil War, families like theirs were caught more than ever between distinct authorities, neither wishing to accept full responsibility for their well-being. Persecution within the local community and unfavourable treatment at the hands of the new government made the Free State unattractive for the southern minority. But help from their historical protectors, Britain, was not necessarily forthcoming either. The IGC did compensate somewhat begrudgingly the Vere-Hunts, following investigation into the legitimacy of their tenancy and speculation that they had paid money to the IRA to secure protection (not because of threats). In the high-profile cases of John Bagwell and Sir John Keane, whose mansions Marlfield (Co. Tipperary) and Cappoquin (Co. Waterford) were burned, the IGC refused to pay any compensation at all, on the grounds that the Senators' acceptance of a role in independent Ireland was incompatible with their allegiance to Britain.[180] The following chapters analyze these (and many more) cases in depth, illuminating victims' experiences of the war, exploring further notions of British 'Loyalty' and drawing out the function of the violent act.

177 PRONI, D/989/B/2/9.
178 TNA, CO 762/53/6: Davis, Tipperary; see Chapter 5.
179 PRONI, D/989/B/2/9; see Chapter 4 on the intimidation of the Vere-Hunts.
180 See Chapter 3, Section 2b.

3 The Campaign of Fire
Arson during the Irish Civil War

Fire compels and intrigues. In December 1922, railway stores in Waterford went up in a 'mighty blaze . . . seen for miles around' and 'citizens attracted by the brightening flare left their homes and congregated . . . to watch the devastating progress of the fire'.[1] Long the stuff of local fascination and speculation, fire is also one of the 'subjects which seem to engage Irish writers deeply'.[2] The burning of Wildgoose Lodge, for example, was recounted in a 'gothic short story' long before Dooley's history of the gruesome act of revenge against a farmer who had informed on Ribbonmen (agrarian secret society members) in Co. Louth in October 1816.[3] Arson, Colm Tóibín observes, has had a 'distinguished career' in Irish literature:

> From the extraordinary, incandescent prose of William Carleton's *Wildgoose Lodge* . . . to the burning of big houses as the final act in novels (the locals arriving, the odd intimacy between the locals and the quality, the sense of the fire as the end of history) like Elizabeth Bowen's *The Last September*. . . . Prose is attracted to fire.[4]

The burning of the 'big house' has indeed been spectacularly depicted in Irish literature,[5] but there had been little academic analysis of the phenomenon until Dooley's *The Decline of the Big House in Ireland* (Dublin, 2001), which proves there were more big houses burned in every province during the Civil War than during the War of Independence.[6]

1 *Munster Express*, 16 December 1922.

2 C. Tóibín, *The Penguin book of Irish fiction* (London: Viking, 1999), xxi.

3 Dooely, *The murders at Wildgoose Lodge: Agrarian crime and punishment in pre-Famine Ireland* (Dublin: Four Courts Press, 2007). William Carleton's 'The burning of Wildgoose Lodge' was published in *Traits and stories of the Irish peasantry* (Dublin: W. Curry, Jun. and Co., 1840–2).

4 Tóibín, *Penguin book of Irish fiction*, xxi.

5 Big house: the architecturally grand, usually Protestant/Unionist-owned mansion at the heart of the local community and economy; see Section 3, this chapter.

6 Dooley, *Decline of the big house*, 189, 286–7.

Like Dooley's study, this chapter approaches house burning as a historical subject, seeking to build a profile of the type of property and person targeted during the Civil War. My analysis also goes further than the *Decline of the Big House*: I look not only to the great estates, but also to burnt-out homes and businesses belonging to Protestants, Catholics, 'Loyalists' and 'Staters' from across the social spectrum. The question at the heart of the chapter is the question running through the book: What is the function of violence? Here, I ask to what extent arsonists (anti-Treaty IRA or otherwise) pursued new agendas, that is, a military and political campaign to destabilize the Free State in protest against the Treaty and its failure to establish an Irish republic? Or, did the Civil War provide the conditions for the final reckoning of ancient enmities, settling local scores and purging the community of the old enemies – tyrannical landlords, ex-Servicemen, southern Unionists and Protestants?

1. The Importance of Arson

Of the 2,018 compensation claims submitted to the British and Free State Governments from the three Munster counties under review, 1,201 (59 per cent) come from Tipperary, 645 (32 per cent) from Limerick and 172 (9 per cent) from Waterford. Based on recorded incidents, then, Tipperary is obviously the most violent county. The significance of arson, though, is that the prevalence of this violent act is not proportionately diminished in quieter counties, accounting for 18 per cent of claims made for injuries sustained during the Civil War in Co. Limerick, 17 per cent in Tipperary and 12 per cent in Waterford. Arson, in other words, was not simply a by-product of a general atmosphere of disorder and is remarkable for its highly destructive and deliberate nature.

The first famous Civil War fire at the republican-occupied Four Courts on 30 June 1922 was spectacular but accidental. In the process of bombardment by the Free State, the wing housing the Public Records Office was destroyed. Reports of arson attacks made to the compensation bodies of the British and Irish Governments, by contrast, portray arson as a vicious act of violence. Chapter 4 explores the subjectivity of threat: the success of a demand for money, goods, or the individual's removal from the area depended on personal and financial factors, and ultimately if the victim viewed seriously the verbal or written warnings with which he had been served. In Loughill, Co. Limerick, for example, Patrick Courtney was ordered to quit the area or 'suffer the consequences'.[7] In this case,

[7] NAI, 392/18: Courtney, Limerick; see Chapter 4.

though, the ex-policeman felt sufficiently frightened to flee before finding out if 'the consequences' included the burning of his house. Others stayed; violent threats were not always carried through. Arson was far less ambiguous: the permanent destruction of a home, by fire, was a relatively fail-safe method of clearing out the target from the area, either until they could rebuild, or forever.

Fire certainly has both a tremendous destructive power and a symbolically purifying effect; arson removes not only the home, or other target, but also renders almost unrecognizable the signs of life within. In her famous examination of 'religious violence' in sixteenth-century France, Davis describes the ritual violence used by warring Catholic and Protestant crowds to 'purify the religious community and humiliate the enemy':

> The religious significance of destruction by water or fire is clear. . . . The fire that razes the house of a Protestant apothecary in Montpellier leaves behind it not the smell of death, of the heretic whom the crowd had hanged, but of spices, lingering in the air for days, like incense. If Protestants have rejected holy water and incense, they still follow Deuteronomy in accepting fire as a sacred means of purification.[8]

Arson had a similarly 'purifying' effect in Bosnia in the 1990s, and fire played an integral part in ethnic cleansing across the region: Prijedor, for example, was made 'Muslim and Croat free' by the burning of their neighbourhoods and homes.[9]

Munster had seen some spectacular fires in its time: after the battle of the Boyne, Tipperary town was burned down in a clash between William and James in 1690.[10] Crop and outhouse burning was later a key feature of Land War violence in the 1870s and 1880s. Official figures indicate that, unlike 'crude personal violence', which was in decline as a mode of rural protest, the majority of burnings in Ireland at this time could be deemed 'agrarian'.[11] Arson was also a persistent feature of the Irish War of Independence, not only in clashes between the Auxiliaries and Black and Tans, and the local IRA, in the twenty-six counties of what would become the Irish Free State,[12] but also in the republicans' campaign in mainland Britain (see discussion later in this section), as well as in the six counties of partitioned Northern Ireland. Indeed, despite the 'unusual

[8] N.Z. Davis, 'The rites of violence', in *Society and culture in early modern France: Eight essays* (Stanford, CA: Stanford University Press, 1975), 178–9.

[9] A. Stiglmayer (ed.), *Mass rape: The war against women in Bosnia-Herzegovina* (London: University of Nebraska Press, 1994), 86, 89.

[10] M. Hallinan, *Tipperary County: People and places* (Dublin: Kincora Press, 1993), 138.

[11] Townshend, *Political violence in Ireland*, 150–1.

[12] Augusteijn (ed.), *The Irish Revolution, 1913–1923* (Basingstoke: Palgrave, 2002), 156.

circumstances and parochial nature' of the Ulster conflict, it is important nonetheless to relate Northern violence (including arson) to the wider Revolution in Ireland.[13] With the outbreak of the Civil War in June 1922, the IRA's attention and resources were directed away from their campaign in the North, and relative peace was restored in the region.[14] Until this point, however, sectarian rioting and labour tensions merged with the War of Independence to produce a major crisis in Belfast and other parts of Northern Ireland;[15] arson was integral to the violence that unfolded in the North, 1920–2.

The republicans torched big houses and Loyalist business premises (furniture stores and motor works in Belfast, for example, as well as flax mills in rural Ulster),[16] in 'carefully planned' operations that peaked in March–June 1922, after the signing of the Treaty.[17] This was the new state under siege, and incendiarism played a key part in preventing James Craig's government from functioning and undermining Partition.[18] The use of strategic arson in the North in many ways set the terms of future conflict: as the Civil War began, and Northern republicans resorted in desperation to the burning of non-commercial targets, including schools and picture houses,[19] southern units initiated their own highly organized 'campaign of fire' against barracks, infrastructure and potential Loyalist strongholds (see Sections 2 and 3).[20]

That is not to say, of course, that fire starting was the sole preserve of the republicans, during these years of inter-communal warfare in Ulster. The new Northern police force (the Ulster Special Constabulary, or 'Specials')[21] and armed Loyalist groups used arson and

13 A.F. Parkinson, *Belfast's unholy war: The Troubles of the 1920s* (Dublin: Four Courts Press, 2004), 17.

14 A.C. Hepburn, *Catholic Belfast and nationalist Ireland* (Oxford: Oxford University Press, 2008), 240; B.A. Follis, *A state under siege: The establishment of Northern Ireland, 1920–1925* (Oxford: Clarendon Press, 1995), 191–2; and Hopkinson, *Green against green*, 248–52.

15 Belfast was the centre of violence in the Northern troubles; 90% of revolutionary deaths in Northern Ireland took place in the city. See Parkinson, *Belfast's unholy war*, 12; and A. Morgan, *Labour and Partition: The Belfast working class 1905–23* (London: Pluto, 1991), 302.

16 At least five stately homes were damaged or destroyed by fire; see Parkinson, *Belfast's unholy war*, 221; and, on the burning of Shane's Castle, J. McDermott, *Northern Divisions: The old IRA and the Belfast pogroms* (Belfast: Beyond the Pale, 2001), 231.

17 Parkinson, *Belfast's unholy war*, 271.

18 Follis, *A state under siege*, 190. James Craig (1871–1940): Leader of Ulster Unionist opposition to the Third Home Rule Bill and first Prime Minister of Northern Ireland.

19 Parkinson, *Belfast's unholy war*, 273–4.

20 'Campaign of Fire' (the title of this chapter) comes from an ICCA pamphlet published in 1924; see Chapter 1 and Map 2.

21 Garvin, *1922: The birth of Irish democracy*, 51.

other forms of intimidation to terrorize the Catholic population and purge from the North the religious minority.[22] These so-called pogroms included mass expulsions of 'disloyal' (Catholic and socialist) workers from shipyards and engineering works,[23] and the burning of Catholic homes and businesses.[24] 'Vengeful' police forces in the south responded to attacks on their personnel by burning the property of republicans;[25] arson in Northern Ireland followed a similar pattern. The death of a Belfast Special, on 31 May 1922, for example, was immediately avenged: a Loyalist mob burned an entire Catholic street, making homeless eighty-six Catholic families.[26] The IRA retaliated with attacks on the homes and factories of leading Unionists.[27] The unpublished diaries of militant Unionist and gun-runner, Frederic Crawford, who at this time owned a factory in Millfield, West Belfast, describe vividly this process of retaliatory burnings:

> When I came to Boyd Street I saw some RC [Roman Catholic] houses on fire out of which it was alleged for months past sniping had occurred, 14 in all were burned down.[28]

Attention focused naturally on the mass rioting and expulsions in Belfast, but serious arson attacks, fuelled by revenge, occurred outside the city. The burial of the assassinated Divisional Police Commissioner for Munster, Gerard Smyth,[29] at his family plot in Banbridge, Co. Down on 21 July 1920 triggered trouble in the town: crowds burned Catholic pubs and other businesses.[30] Then, in August, the assassination of DI Swanzy, in Lisburn, resulted in reciprocal burnings of large areas of the

[22] M. Farrell, *Northern Ireland: The orange state*, 2nd ed. (London: Pluto Press, 1980), 48–9.

[23] J. Bardon, *A shorter illustrated history of Ulster* (Belfast: Blackstaff Press, 1996), 186.

[24] Between July 1920 and July 1922, nearly one-quarter of Belfast's 93,000 Catholics were put out of their jobs and 23,000 were driven from their homes, and 500 Catholic commercial premises were looted, burned or otherwise wrecked. Of the 453 violent deaths in the city in this period, 257 were Catholic civilians. See Farrell, *Northern Ireland: The orange state*, 62.

[25] D.M. Leeson, *The Black and Tans: British police and Auxiliaries in the Irish War of Independence, 1920–1921* (Oxford: Oxford University Press, 2011), 160–2.

[26] Farrell, *Northern Ireland: The orange state*, 56.

[27] Farrell, *Northern Ireland: The orange state*, 57–60.

[28] PRONI, D/640/11/1: Diary entry, 6 June 1922, 74 (Private papers of Col. F.H. Crawford concerning Unionism, the formation and security of the Government of Northern Ireland).

[29] Abbott, *Police casualties in Ireland*, 96–103.

[30] P. Lawlor, *The Burnings 1920* (Cork: Mercier Press, 2009), 64–78. The violence flared up again in August 1920, following the withdrawal of the military; six Catholic homes were totally destroyed by fire.

Catholic part of the town.[31] The destruction went on for three days.[32] Arson also spread to rural parts. In the village of Roslea, Co. Fermanagh, the shooting and wounding of a Special, shopkeeper George Lester, on 21 February 1921 was avenged by the burning of ten Catholic homes. The IRA responded, one month later, by torching fourteen Protestant farms.[33] And, as a result of 'IRA activities', including the burning of a flax mill in Desertmartin, Co. Londonderry, four Catholics were murdered by 'masked men' and six Catholic-owned buildings were burned down.[34]

Bouts of sectarian violence, reprisals and rioting were thus repeated across the North, in a familiar cycle of violence and counter-violence, attack and revenge.[35] Since the early nineteenth century, sectarian tensions had periodically erupted into rioting and traditional confrontations between Catholics and Protestants were 'reinforced rather than undercut' by the growth of cities (Belfast, Derry) from the 1850s.[36] Arson had historically played a role in this civic unrest. John Darby, for example, includes petrol bombs in the 'endless' and little altered list of the forms of physical harm that occurred during Belfast riots, 1857–1969,[37] although burning did not, it seems, feature as heavily in late-eighteenth- and nineteenth-century clashes in the North, as did arson in early twentieth-century communal and political violence. Protestant 'wrecking gangs' at work during the Armagh expulsions of 1795–6, for example, destroyed property inside the home, but rarely used fire in their attacks on Catholics because, 'contemplating occupation of the vacated holdings', the wreckers did not want to be 'put to the expense of rebuilding sacked domiciles'.[38] Similarly, whilst the recourse of Northern activists during the Revolution does conform somewhat to the historical 'patterns of conflict' identified by A.T.Q. Stewart,[39] the examples of arson to which he refers (particularly in nineteenth-century encounters, such as the Lady Day riots of 1872) do not usually involve the burning of whole minority

31 Hopkinson, *Irish War of Independence*, 156.
32 McDermott, *Northern divisions*, 52.
33 F. McGarry, *Eoin O'Duffy: A self-made hero* (Oxford: Oxford University Press, 2005), 60–1.
34 A. Hezlet, *The 'B' Specials: A history of the Ulster Special Constabulary* (London: Tom Stacey Ltd, 1972), 70–1.
35 Hopkinson, *Irish War of Independence*, 157.
36 T. Wilson, *Frontiers of violence: Conflict and identity in Ulster and Upper Silesia, 1918–1922* (Oxford: Oxford University Press, 2010), 23, 40.
37 J. Darby, *Intimidation and the control of conflict in Northern Ireland* (Dublin: Gill and Macmillan, 1986), 53.
38 S. Farrell, *Rituals and riots: Sectarian violence and political culture in Ulster, 1784–1886* (Lexington, KY: University Press of Kentucky, 2000), 26, 191.
39 Stewart, *The narrow ground*, 137–42.

homes.[40] Instead, furniture was taken out into the street and burned, which drove out the victim but left intact the structure and may suggest the perpetrator's desire to claim the vacated property for his own community.

By the 1920s, however, republicans certainly did not shy away from arson as a tool of total destruction. IRA activities in mainland Britain during 1920–3 are often portrayed as a 'sideshow' of the troubles,[41] but large-scale arson attacks here were effective in focusing public and press attention on Ireland, and generating real alarm in government.[42] Rory O'Connor's planned 'multi-sited catastrophe' did not come to fruition, but – in November 1920 – squads of armed guerrillas burned warehouses in Liverpool, causing hundreds of thousands of pounds worth of damage.[43] The next sustained campaign, during 1921, hit factories and mills in Manchester and its surrounds, as well as private farms in Lancashire, Cheshire, Tyneside and the outskirts of London.[44] Hart argues that these fires were motivated not so much by 'stratagem' as by the 'urge' to retaliate against British violence in Ireland.[45] Arson in Britain does nonetheless evidence a clear strategic preference, on the part of the IRA in these years, for low-technology destruction. The 'basic tools' for arson were 'wirecutters, paraffin, gasoline, and fuses, all easily available'. Explosives and heavier weapons, by contrast, were hardly ever used in the IRA's British campaign, because 'these were needed more urgently in Ireland'.[46]

Given, then, Ireland's historical propensity for arson, and the periodic recourse – north and south – to fire by protestors, criminals and armed groups, it is not inconceivable that, during the Civil War, gangs of arsonists formed almost instinctively, without clear objectives. Subsequently there are, in all three counties, a handful of arson attacks for which compensation was paid for personal squabbles between neighbours over trespass, for example, or eviction.[47] Studies of arson during periods of conflict in nineteenth-century Great Britain, including 'Captain Swing' agitation in East Anglia and the 'Rebecca' riots in Wales,

[40] Stewart, *The narrow ground*, 139. And arson is not mentioned in Stewart's account of the 'fierce riots' that took place in Derry in the 1860s; Stewart, *The narrow ground*, 73–5.
[41] Hart, *IRA at war*, 142.
[42] Hart, *IRA at war*, 177.
[43] Hart, *IRA at war*, 151.
[44] Hart, *IRA at war*, 154, 156.
[45] Hart, *IRA at war*, 176.
[46] Hart, *IRA at war*, 155.
[47] Limerick: NAI, 392/28, 122, 148, 191, 455, 466, 468. Tipperary: 401/329, 409, 756. Waterford: 402/409, 1023.

confirm that private vengeance is a strong motivator for arson,[48] although it is worth mentioning that John Archer also finds evidence of 'collective community displays of protest' in this 'primarily... individual act of hatred and revenge'[49]: until rural conditions in England improved in 1851, unemployment and poverty acted as 'trigger mechanisms' for arson, and crop burning was a 'legitimate weapon of protest' by labourers against, for example, farmers who paid low wages.[50]

Few accounts from Munster tell us much about the men behind the petrol cans in the Irish Civil War. J.A. Burke TD claimed that the thirty- to forty-strong band of armed arsonists that attacked his Co. Tipperary home 'were all under 20'.[51] Local reports suggest that four middle-aged men 'with blackened faces', emerging from Woodrooffe after setting the Tipperary mansion alight, knew the house and surrounding area and may even have had help from the domestic staff. One of the armed men said to owner Major Perry: 'it is queer men you must have; we have been here the whole day'.[52] However, in only a few cases was the victim able, or willing, to identify the perpetrator. The armed men who ordered William Wilson to clear out of Coombawn House, Anglesborough, Co. Limerick, before burning the place, identified themselves as 'Military'; whether they were anti-Treaty forces remains unknown.[53] This was a conflict in which – particularly after September 1922 and the end of the military phase – the 'the torch and petrol tin' substituted the 'rifle' as a popular and accessible means of warfare. 'These weapons', warned Patrick Hogan, Minister for Agriculture, were 'much safer for the people who use them, but are at least as effective and much more dangerous to the civilian population'. Arson in Ireland was not just a republican tactic, but also, according to Hogan, was used to devastating effect by 'a number of gangs, plus a number of individuals, all... with one common bond... a vested interest in anarchy'.[54]

Authorities certainly fear fire as an accessible means of popular violence: arson attacks on Parisian buildings during the final days of the 1871, for example, were blamed on the pétroleuses (female supporters of the

48 Archer, *By a flash and a scare*; D.J.V. Jones, *Rebecca's children: A study of rural society, crime, and protest* (Oxford: Clarendon Press, 1989).

49 Archer, *By a flash and a scare*, 159.

50 Archer, *By a flash and a scare*, 6, 22–3, 132, 147–8, 192, 196.

51 *Nenagh Guardian*, 3, 10 March 1923. Burke may have exaggerated: the *Nenagh Guardian* claimed that Rockforest was visited by *seven* men 'who adopted the usual procedure, and set the floors ablaze'.

52 *Clonmel Chronicle*, 10 February 1923.

53 NAI, 392/318: Wilson, Limerick.

54 *Dáil Éireann Debates* (http://historical-debates.oireachtas.ie), ii, 27 March 1923.

Commune, it was alleged, threw small bottles of kerosene into cellar windows, in a deliberate act of spite against the government).[55] Whether these women were responsible for the acts of which they were accused and, indeed, whether they even existed, was less significant than the huge propaganda value of the female fire-starter: 'the pétroleuse lingered in people's minds, a powerful personification of evil with which to condemn the Commune and to question the very nature of woman'.[56] Indeed, the fact that arsonists cannot always be identified, nor strictly categorized as agents of social, political or criminal violence, does not lessen the impact of arson, nor devalue the study of burning as a wartime occurrence, at least not in Ireland during 1922–3.

Important patterns can be drawn from the collation of compensation data from the Free State and British Governments. The following statistics do not, of course, speak for all acts of arson committed during the Civil War. Instead, Figure 2 relates to the sample of 2,018 compensation claims that were available for study,[57] and provides a breakdown (according to what was burned) of the 108, 164 and 20 cases of arson, in Cos. Limerick, Tipperary and Waterford, respectively.[58]

'Public building or business' includes institutions such as courthouses: 'Murroe Sessions House', for example, was burned in March 1923.[59] Workhouses at Nenagh and Clogheen were also destroyed,[60] leaving 'Borstal boys and staff homeless'.[61] Striking in all three counties is the number of attacks on crops and outhouses serious enough for the victim to lodge a compensation claim with the government. Grazing rights and redistribution were divisive issues during the war; the use of arson to settle old and new land questions is explored in Section 4. The most common type of building burned was, unsurprisingly, the small- to medium-sized private home, although the big house was also disproportionately targeted during the war. Section 3 asks why, particularly during 1922–3, some of Munster's finest Protestant- and Unionist-owned mansions met a fiery end. The next section analyzes arson as a military tactic, focusing first on the burning of public buildings and barracks.

55 G.L. Gullickson, *Unruly women of Paris: Images of the commune* (Ithaca: Cornell University Press, 1996), 13.
56 Gullickson, *Unruly women of Paris*, 159–60.
57 See Chapter 1 on archival exigencies.
58 'Cases of arson' take into account the overlapping compensation claims; i.e., cases in which claims were made to both governments for the same attack.
59 *Nenagh Guardian*, 24 March 1923.
60 *Nenagh Guardian*, 10 February 1923.
61 *Clonmel Chronicle*, 11 November 1922.

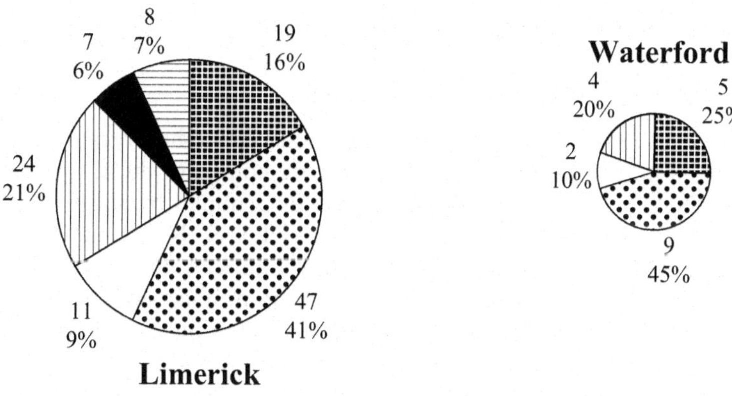

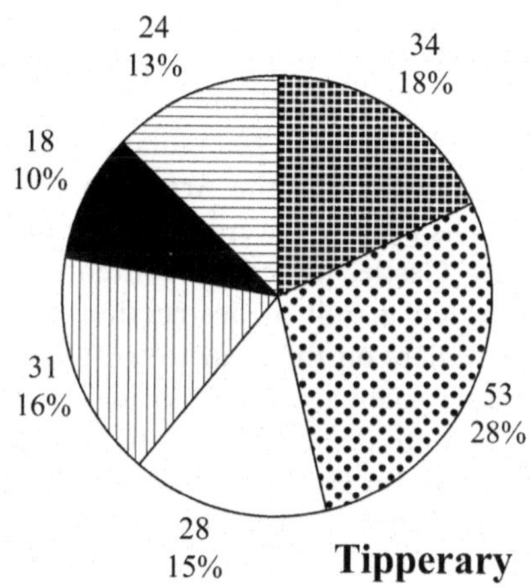

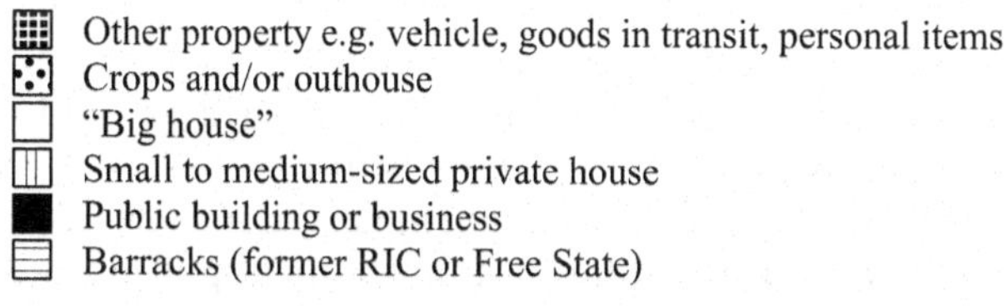

Figure 2. Arson attacks in Cos. Limerick, Tipperary and Waterford, January 1922–May 1923.

2. Arson as a Military Tactic

a) Barracks and Infrastructure

Until September 1922, when the Free State Army had recaptured the key republican-held towns in Munster, the course of the Civil War in Limerick, Tipperary and Waterford was determined by the pattern of barrack occupation by pro- and anti-Treaty forces. Rendering barracks uninhabitable made local Free State control difficult and created logistical problems for the nascent state organization. The torching of Pallas Barracks, Co. Limerick,[62] for example, resulted in the Free State having to accommodate troops in private houses, an undesirable prospect for a new government trying to prove its ability to protect its civilians from the rebels. Just weeks before the burning of Glanduff Castle, Co. Limerick, Commandant O'Sullivan wrote to its tenant, Frances Ievers, apologizing for the sudden occupation of the Castle by National Troops. Intelligence had been received that 'Irregulars were about to take up quarters' and he assured Ievers that the Army would look after her furniture and the estate.[63] His promises were not kept: on 29 June 1922, 200 republicans seized the Castle, looted its contents and set it on fire. Arson attacks like these left a trail of destruction across the province: in November 1922, travellers on the road from Waterford to Clonmel passed a 'mass of burned police barracks'.[64] And, on 15 July 1922, Duncannon Fort – built in 1588 to defend Waterford Harbour from 'Spanish invasion', and used as a base for British forces until the Truce – was left 'a heap of ruins' following occupation and evacuation by republicans.[65]

In Co. Limerick, 7 per cent of arson attacks relate to the burning of permanent or temporary 'barracks', many of which had been occupied by the RIC before the Treaty. William O'Connor's 'two-storey slated dwelling house' in Abbeyfeale was occupied first by the British as a police barracks, then by the IRA, 'until the time of the spilt', and finally by Irregulars, who burned the premises as they left.[66] In Tipperary, 13 per cent of arson attacks relate to the burning of barracks, and more than half of these were formerly occupied by British troops. A *Waterford News* report captures the republicans' delight in ransacking one ex-British stronghold, Kilmacow barracks: a lorry of fifteen men 'pulled up at the former citadel of RIC triumphs, sprinkled the place with petrol and set it

[62] M. O'Dwyer, 'Local happenings, 1922–23', *Oola: Past and Present* 9 (2000), 5.
[63] NAI, 392/274: Ievers, Limerick; see Sections 3 and 4.
[64] *Clonmel Chronicle*, 1 November 1922.
[65] *Munster Express*, 15 July 1922.
[66] NAI, 392/444: O'Connor, Limerick.

ablaze'.[67] Arson was thus a strategic and symbolic act, attacking British rule, Free State authority and the apparently seamless transition between the two that represented everything the Irregulars hated about the Treaty.

There are some seemingly impulsive manifestations of this anti-Treaty feeling in evidence in arson attacks in Co. Limerick. Michael Kennedy had entertained the Free State Army at his farm in Askeaton, Co. Limerick the day before his hay was burned, making him 'unpopular with parties of opposite political views in the locality'.[68] Mary Sidley's sons 'took no part in politics' and her hay 'was maliciously burned' on the night a 'group of Irregulars' raided her neighbours' house for guns.[69] These civilians were punished for their little more than tacit support of the Treaty and the National Troops; the burning of their homes does not seem to fall into an organized military strategy. Across Munster, however, arson was more than a last resort offence or, in other words, a defiant but ultimately futile act by those without a prospect of victory. Hopkinson argues that from January 1923 until the end of the war, the anti-Treaty army could do little of strategic value because local organization had broken down and republican leaders (such as Tipperary Third Brigade's Officer-in-Command [O/C] Denis (Dinny) Lacey and Limerick's anti-Treaty mayor, Stephen O'Mara) were killed or captured.[70] Yet, there is evidence, even during this later period, that burnings were planned and republicans used arson as a deliberate strategy. On 11 December 1922, the Free State Army reported on the 'organised incendiarism which is now the policy of the "Die-Hards"':

> The Irregulars have told farmers in this District, that it will be useless for them to set any corn this coming season, as they intend to set fire to all corn next harvest.[71]

House burnings, especially attacks on large mansions, were executed with military precision. Republicans 'took every precaution against interference' by cutting telephone wires surrounding the house,[72] or placing occupants, domestic staff or passersby under armed guard,[73] to prevent

67 *Waterford News*, 14 July 1922.
68 NAI, 392/105: Kennedy, Limerick.
69 NAI, 392/377: Sidley, Limerick.
70 Hopkinson, *Green against green*.
71 IMA, CW/OPS/1/A; see Chapter 4 on land issues and republican involvement in campaigns for redistribution.
72 *Irish Times*, 15 January 1923: wires cut before the attack on W.T. Cosgrave's 'secluded' home; see discussion later in this section.
73 *Munster Express*, 3 March 1923: Richard O'Shee's gardener and steward were placed under armed guard during the burning of Gardenmorris. See Section 3.

the alarm being raised until the fire was well under way. (Northern republicans had similarly taken steps against interference in their 1920–2 campaign against big houses and Loyalist businesses; firemen attending to the blaze were intimidated by the IRA.[74]) Mansion burning was an exact science and, in a memorable passage from *The Heather Blazing* (which is as much history as fiction; Uncle Tom's experience in this instance is exactly that of Tóibín's own uncle),[75] the Irish writer captures the military process from the initial order from IRA Headquarters to the careful removal of precious books before the fire. Gathered at his grandmother's house, following de Valera's 1951 election speech in Enniscorthy, Eamon Redmond's father and uncle recall the War of Independence:

> "You couldn't just burn a house, you see," Uncle Tom said. "You'd have to get permission from Cathal Brugha in Dublin. You'd have to present him with all the facts; any of the houses that entertained the Black and Tans, had the officers for dinners and parties, they'd be on the list. Your father'd go up, he was young enough and he pretended to spend the day in the National Library, but he'd slip out to see Brugha, or one of Brugha's men, and then permission would come back and then we'd do the job."
>
> "Burn the house?" Eamon asked.
>
> "We gutted a good few of them all right," his uncle sipped his drink. "Wilton, Old Captain Skrine, the Proctors on the Bunclody road, Castleboro. I have a book upstairs I took from Castleboro the night we went out there. They had a great library. It's a pity I didn't have more time. I still have it upstairs. It has a note inside saying '*Ex Libris Lord Carew*'. What's it called? *Cranford* by Mrs Gaskell. I must look for it. I'm sure it's up there somewhere."[76]

Should this highly organized, fiery destruction be interpreted in terms of a broader politico-military strategy on the part of the republicans? The burning of private homes, including Protestant and Loyalist-owned mansions, to prevent future use of the houses as barracks by enemy forces, makes some sense. Arson attacks on a Limerick big house, Glanduff Castle, and a Tipperary mansion, Tullamaine Castle,[77] evidently fall into this category. However, there were also valid, tactical arguments against fires of this kind. Tom Barry, for example, allegedly disagreed with Liam Lynch's policy of burning barracks during the Civil War because, if left intact, these buildings could 'be used to hold prisoners and perhaps hostages since the people were no longer willing to give their houses as they

[74] Parkinson, *Belfast's unholy war*, 273.

[75] Foster, '"A strange and insistent protagonist": Colm Tóibín and Irish history', in P. Delaney (ed.), *Reading Colm Tóibín* (Dublin: Liffey Press, 2008), 21–40 at 31.

[76] Tóibín, *The heather blazing* (London, Picador: 1992), 172.

[77] See following discussion, Section 3.

had done during the War of Independence'.[78] Republicans Liam Deasy and Lacey also complained of the increasing difficulty, since the Civil War began, in securing support and practical help from the local civilian population.[79] Why, then, would a guerrilla army sacrifice potentially valuable shelter and resources by destroying private homes and large mansions? It seems plausible that big houses, such as those explored in detail in Section 3 of this chapter, were destroyed not as potential Free State barracks, then, but as strongholds of British agents, that is, Loyalists left behind by Britain to sabotage independent Ireland once the war was over.

These fears proved to be unfounded. Unlike in post-war Central Europe, where the 'forces of order' eventually succeeded in squashing democracy and containing the 'radical turmoil' that raged in Germany and Austria from the Armistice until Spring 1919,[80] the old political regime in Ireland (Loyalists, landowners and Protestants) did not mount a counter-revolution against Irish independence. Nonetheless, whilst the fighting continued in Ireland, some republicans may have feared a British resurgence. Barry's own account of reprisal burnings during the War of Independence shows the desire of this Munster-based republican, at least, to extirpate the old order and reduce local bastions of British rule to crumbling ruins. Following attacks by the Essex Regiment on houses in the Innishannon district, Co. Cork, the IRA burned 'property of active British supporters'.[81] Then, 'as there were no other active Loyalist homes in that area, we went further afield to teach the British a lesson': the Earl of Bandon's Castle Bernard was burned down during this round of destruction.[82] 'Active' Loyalists or British supporters were not merely those who, in Barry's estimation, 'never considered themselves as Irish', such as Protestants, strong farmers and ex-military officers,[83] but also enemies whose continued presence threatened the republicans' separatist Irishness and whose homes, as a consequence, had to be systematically destroyed. The 'leading British loyalist', in any local community, dwelled in the '"Big House"... secure and affluent in his many acres, enclosed behind demesne walls'.[84] Contemporary military considerations, as well

78 Ryan, *Tom Barry*, 186.

79 See Chapter 5, Section 1.

80 C.S. Maier, *Recasting bourgeois Europe: Stabilization in France, Germany and Italy in the decade after World War I: With a new preface* (Princeton, NJ: Princeton University Press, 1988, c1975), 4. See also J. Joll, *Europe since 1870: An international history*, 4th ed. (Harmondsworth: Penguin, 1990), 239–71.

81 T. Barry, *Guerilla days in Ireland*, 6th ed. (Naas: Anvil Books, 1978), 195.

82 Barry, *Guerilla days in Ireland*, 195.

83 Barry, *Guerilla days in Ireland*, 12.

84 Barry, *Guerilla days in Ireland*, 12.

as the symbolic purging of the historic enemy, explain the destruction of large numbers of these homes during the war.[85]

If the tactical destruction of big houses served a higher republican strategy, arson also granted the anti-Treaty army significant short-term success in preventing the Free State from functioning. The 'principal objects of attack', in this 'campaign . . . which has been devastating the country', were the 'Irish Railways'.[86] These attacks, including the burning of carriages and goods in transit, were 'on a much larger scale than during the Anglo-Irish War' and 'served to demonstrate Free State weakness'.[87] Republicans seized and set fire to a train at Barnagh Station, Co. Limerick, for example, and livestock and food products were destroyed.[88] Tipperary merchants were then forced to use the canals instead, but the supply chain was continually disrupted by arson. In a 'dastardly and inexplicable outrage',[89] goods meant for the railway, and subsequently transferred to the waterways, were destroyed in the burning of Dromineer Harbour stores. Thomas Delaney, secretary of the Grand Canal Company, won compensation from the Free State for this incident.[90] The Great Southern and Western Railway Company (GSWRC) also put forward 'enormous claims', and, together with the destruction of bridges and the crippling of the creamery industry by 'bomb and fire', South Tipperary's 'wreckage bill' grew 'longer day by day'.[91] In other attacks on the network, a train was burned on the way from Kilmeaden to Waterford,[92] Mallow station and stationmaster's residence were 'maliciously' destroyed by fire,[93] and Birdhill signal cabin was burned.[94] The 'war on the railways'[95] also had a human cost: Edward Scales, from Co. Limerick, was made homeless by the burning of his stationmaster's cottage in Foynes,[96] stationmaster Power's dwelling house

[85] See following discussion, Section 3.
[86] *Church of Ireland Gazette*, 2 March 1923.
[87] Hopkinson, 'The Civil War from the pro-Treaty perspective', *Irish Sword* 20, no. 82 (1997), 287–92 at 291.
[88] A number of farmers' and merchants' goods were destroyed in this attack: NAI, 392/82: Mangan, Limerick, 392/87: Talbot, Limerick, 392/376: Roche, Limerick, 392/399: O'Connor, Limerick, 392/409: Slattery, Limerick.
[89] *Limerick Leader*, 4 November 1922.
[90] NAI, 401/160: Delaney, Waterford.
[91] *Nenagh Guardian*, 3 February 1923.
[92] *Munster Express*, 23 December 1922.
[93] *Limerick Leader*, 1 November 1922.
[94] *Nenagh Guardian*, 26 September 1922.
[95] *Waterford News*, 15 December 1922.
[96] See Chapter 2.

and furniture were destroyed in the fire at Grange station,[97] and railway workers were subject to physical assault.[98]

Kevin O'Higgins, Minister for Home Affairs, certainly saw arson as part of a campaign to undermine the authority of the new government:

> A conspiracy has existed against this State for ten months. Its methods are open and apparent – arson, assassination, general sabotage, war on the economic life of the country, the burning of commercial vans, the mining of picture-houses, and attempting to blow up business establishments.[99]

How serious was this 'conspiracy' of arson? Oliver Coogan believes not very: he distinguishes between the 'series of pointless and often mindless acts of destruction' against transport, communications and public buildings, and the 'more serious' attacks on private houses.[100] I reject this distinction and indeed the very idea of 'mindless' violence; this chapter shows that arsonists did not commit burnings on a whim. However, Coogan's analysis is a useful reminder that the campaign of fire was limited neither to the public nor private spheres. And, in the burning of Senators' homes, lies a particularly interesting intersection of the personal and political. As upholders of the Treaty and symbols of Free State authority, Senators were obvious targets for political violence. In reprisal for the executions of republicans under the Free State's 'Public Safety' legislation, IRA Chief of Staff Liam Lynch promised to adopt 'very drastic measures' against persons and property of all pro-government supporters,[101] including the burning of TD and Senators' homes.[102]

Deputy Burke's home in Roscrea, Co. Tipperary, was one casualty of this policy; see earlier discussion, Section 1.[103] The family of Daniel Joseph Byrne TD, of the Farmers' Party in the Dáil,[104] was ordered out of his residence in Mullinahone, Co. Tipperary, 'at the point of a

97 *Munster Express*, 3 March 1923.

98 See Chapter 5 on two serious assaults on GSWRC employees.

99 *Dáil Éireann Debates*, iii, 25 April 1923.

100 O. Coogan, *Politics and war in Meath, 1913–23* (Dublin: Folens, 1983), 286–7.

101 Ryan, *The real chief: Liam Lynch* (Cork: Mercier Press, 2005, first published as *Liam Lynch, the real chief*, 1986), 163.

102 E. O'Halpin, *Defending Ireland: The Irish state and its enemies since 1922* (Oxford: Oxford University Press, 1999), 27, 34–5.

103 *Nenagh Guardian*, 3, 10 March 1923: Rockforest was burned in March 1923, two months after the destruction of Burke's Co. Kildare residence.

104 The Farmers' Party (the political wing of the Irish Farmers' Union, set up in 1919) was a pro-Treaty, agrarian political party representing rural interests, in operation between 1922 and 1932 (although it lost much of its support base to Cumann na nGaedheal in 1927). The Party won seven seats in Dáil Éireann in the general election of June 1922, increasing that total to fifteen in 1923; see Hopkinson, *Green against green*, 262.

revolver'.[105] Contemporary accounts disagree on whether or not Burke and Byrne were home at the time; either way, these attacks must have been frightening and it is worth noting that Byrne did not stand in the 1923 election. The burning of one Deputy's home claimed a life: seven-year-old Emmet McGarry, son of John McGarry TD, was 'badly burned' when 'armed incendiaries' set fire to his father's house. He died in hospital.[106] Marie Coleman believes that the intensification of arson attacks on politicians' homes, during January to March 1923, was a reaction to the increased number of executions in this period.[107] It was in January 1923 that Cosgrave's own Beech Park House, Ballyboden – with its grand piano, furniture and 'many valuable Irish books' – was burned.[108] Then, when Stephen Gwynn praised the toughness of the Free State Government in the *Observer*, in February 1923, his house and library were burned down in retaliation.[109] However, the high profile burnings of Senators' homes in Munster suggest a more complex rationale behind these ostensibly military and strategic burnings.

b) Senators under Attack

Cosgrave's choice of members for Seanad Éireann returned a significant Anglo-Irish contingent, including Sir John Keane, whose country seat at Cappoquin, Co. Waterford, was burned in February 1923. In his claim to the IGC,[110] Keane outlined his 'natural' association 'with the British connection, having served for twenty years in the British Army', been a Justice of the Peace and had 'social intimacy' with British officers quartered in Ireland.[111] He 'was, and am still, a Senator of the Irish Free State', but did not see conflict between his British and Irish commitments. However, the Committee's reply to Keane suggests the establishment of the Free State had created new political loyalties that complicated the issue of motivation:

> Having regard to the number of outrages directed against members of the Irish Free State about the same date . . . your mansion was destroyed, the destruction

105 *Clonmel Chronicle*, 24 March 1923. Byrne's premises were visited again later (14 April 1923) and his hay shed burned.
106 *Clonmel Chronicle*, 16 December 1922.
107 M. Coleman, *County Longford and the Irish Revolution, 1910–1923* (Dublin, 2006), 145.
108 *Irish Times*, 15 January 1923.
109 P. Bew, *Ireland: The politics of enmity, 1789–2006* (Oxford: Oxford University Press, 2007), 440.
110 See Chapter 2 on compensation procedure.
111 TNA, CO 762/82/11: Keane, Waterford.

in your case may be attributable to a motive other that the record of the public services to which you refer.

Keane withdrew his claim. His acceptance of the Senate nomination, in order to 'represent minority interests',[112] shows he located himself cautiously within the new society, but nonetheless he took up the post and pledged allegiance to the Irish Government. Senator James Douglas expressed similar reservations, but ultimately fulfilled his duty: 'whilst I might not agree with everything that they [the Free State] had done, I regarded them as the government and must be loyal to them. . . . My personal opinions were of no importance'.[113] Fortunately for Douglas, he did not join the twenty-one Senators – including Keane and John Bagwell – who suffered an 'outrage' during the war. Five other mansions, besides Cappoquin and Bagwell's Marlfield, were burned,[114] and Dr George Sigerson resigned from the Senate 'owing to threats against his house'.[115]

In the early hours of 8 January 1923, Marlfield, near Clonmel, Co. Tipperary, was 'broken into by a number of armed men who ordered the occupants out and having sprinkled the contents with petrol set fire to the same and withdrew'.[116] The twenty- to forty-man band said that 'they had orders to burn the house, as Mr. Bagwell was a member of the Free State Senate'. The 'imposing mansion, picturesquely situated', was completely gutted save for the servants' wing.[117] The destruction of furniture, paintings, and a valuable library belonging to his historian father, Richard Bagwell (a 'great Irish authority' on the Tudors),[118] incurred a loss of nearly £15,000 (£667,000 in today's terms; see Glossary).[119] The arsonists at Marlfield, it seems, showed less concern than Tóibín's uncle would have done for the literary stock inside.[120] John's family were at home at the time of the attack: the Senator's young sons helped their mother Louisa by grabbing a few possessions, including family paintings; his daughter, Lilla, rushed to set the horses free from the burning stables. Mrs Bagwell wrote to her mother-in-law Harriet the day after the attack: 'The Republicans . . . said it was because Jack had joined the Senate; they

112 TNA, CO 762/82/11: Keane, Waterford.
113 J. Gaughan (ed.), *Memoirs of Senator James G. Douglas* (Dublin: University College Dublin Press, 1998), 98.
114 D.J. O'Sullivan, *The Irish Free State and its Senate* (London: Faber and Faber, 1940), 102–7.
115 *Nenagh Guardian*, 10 February 1922.
116 NAI, 401/744: Bagwell, Tipperary.
117 *Irish Times*, 10 January 1923.
118 *Church of Ireland Gazette*, 12 January 1923.
119 NAI, 401/744: Bagwell, Tipperary.
120 Section 2a.

asked first thing for him; we were so thankful he was not here'.[121] She was right to fear for her husband's safety; later that month, the IRA kidnapped Bagwell (he escaped unharmed after a couple of days).[122]

The county court judge considering John's compensation claim to the Free State said the whole court 'knew the reason [for the attack] was that Senator Bagwell was trying to do his best for the country, and the reward he got was that his residence was burned'.[123] Unfortunately for Bagwell, however, acceptance of the Senate seat did not entitle him to relief as a British Loyalist. The payment from the Irish Ministry of Finance, with its strict 'reinstatement clause',[124] fell far short of Bagwell's expectations and he no doubt felt well within his rights to make a separate claim to the IGC.[125] Culturally, Bagwell had all the attributes of a prominent southern Unionist. His family were landowners: the Bagwells acquired Marlfield in 1775. John had proved his military allegiance as a Deputy Lieutenant and held 'an important place in the industrial life' of Ireland as a railway manager.[126] His pre-Treaty connection with Britain was undeniable, yet, in October 1928, the IGC finally rejected his claim:

> Mr. Bagwell agrees his house was destroyed because he had accepted nomination as a Senator in the Irish Free State. He suggests, however, that his action in allowing himself to be nominated was the act of a Loyalist determined to support the new Government placed in power on the withdrawal of the British Government from Ireland. It is debateable whether this claim could be admitted in view of the Terms of Reference.

Bagwell believed it was 'the duty of anyone owing allegiance to the Government of the Free State' to accept the Senate nomination, which he did in December 1922.[127] He had performed 'an act of the highest patriotism',[128] but this was the flaw in his case: his actions demonstrated loyalty to the Free State Government, not the Government of the United Kingdom.

Financial considerations undoubtedly shaped the IGC judgement. With its 'art treasures and ... historic records which can never be replaced',[129] full compensation for this fantastic mansion would have

121 NLI, MS 32,617 (History of the Bagwell family by Harriet Bagwell).
122 *The Times*, 31 January 1923.
123 *Cork Examiner*, 26 July 1924.
124 See Section 3.
125 TNA, CO 762/95/19: Bagwell, Tipperary.
126 *Church of Ireland Gazette*, 12 January 1923.
127 TNA, CO 762/95/19: Bagwell, Tipperary.
128 *Church of Ireland Gazette*, 12 January 1923.
129 *Munster Express*, 27 January 1923.

been impossibly expensive. The IGC did acknowledge Bagwell's modesty in making a relatively small claim (for the jewellery not covered by Irish compensation law), given the huge losses and personal distress he had suffered, not only in the burning of his home, but also during his kidnap by republicans. However, the 'real point for consideration' by the IGC was not the size of the claim, but the '*reason* for the destruction'.[130] Bagwell had, consciously or not, repudiated his British ties by accepting a political role in autonomous Ireland, allowing the IGC, as a British Government body, to absolve itself of responsibility for his loss.

Keane and Bagwell were from a class with economic, social and cultural roots in both Ireland and Britain. Peter Martin believes that the Revolution forced these people 'to choose to be Irish or British and it is not surprising that many of them found the New Ireland insufficiently attractive to keep them'.[131] The compensation evidence suggests it was in fact the British Government who made the choice on their behalf. By refusing to pay compensation, the IGC forced Keane and Bagwell to accept the legal and financial consequences of taking a role in independent Ireland. Persecution within their local community may have made the 'New Ireland' (in Martin's words) unattractive for the southern minority, but their link with and dependence on Britain was also under review. Keane and Bagwell's class, religion and political allegiance (demonstrated by past service in the British Army and now their Senate seat) had marked them out from their local community; after the Civil War, administrators were using these same identifiers to justify – and refuse – compensation payments for their loss. To prevent their future use as barracks, or as part of the republicans' 'reprisal' policy, the burning of big houses may have been sound military strategy. However, a study of arson attacks on the largely Protestant and Unionist owned mansions, such as Marlfield and Cappoquin, invites broader speculation on intra-community relations and the use of violence, in the three chosen counties, to settle more ancient scores.

3. Targeting Big Houses

J.G. Farrell's novel is set not in the Civil War, but the earlier '*Troubles*' of 1919–21. The Majestic Hotel, as much the heart of the story as the protagonist, Major Brendan Archer, met its fiery fate in a passage that is a powerful reminder of the destructive capacity of arson:

130 TNA, CO 762/95/19: Bagwell, Tipperary.

131 P. Martin, 'Unionism: the Irish nobility and Revolution, 1919–23', in Augusteijn, *Irish Revolution 1913–1923*, 151–64 at 164.

By the time the inhabitants of Kilnalough had noticed the glow in the sky and motored, ridden or walked out to the hotel, the Majestic was an inferno. Streams of fire the size of oak trees blossomed out of the windows of the upper storeys. Caterpillars of flame wriggled their way down the . . . carpets and sucked at the banisters and panelling until all the public rooms were ablaze.[132]

After the fire, Archer made an emotional return to the 'charred rubble' of what had been a (wonderfully bizarre and increasingly dilapidated) refuge for its guests from the 'Shinners' in Co. Wexford:

The Major stepped from one blackened compartment to another trying to orientate himself and saying: 'I'm standing in the residents' lounge, in the corridor, in the writing-room.' Now that these rooms were open to the mild Irish sky they all seemed much smaller – in fact, quite insignificant.[133]

The notion that – once exposed to the elements – this emblem of Anglo-Irish privilege was nothing but a pile of ruins, illustrates the power of arson to engage with the Irish landscape and challenge the place of a building and its occupants in the community. Land purchase legislation had chipped away, since the early twentieth century, at their great estates, and many mansion owners and members of the Ascendancy had chosen to flee Ireland before the Civil War began in earnest. The *Munster Express* reported on 7 January 1922, for example, that Killinane Castle, Co. Tipperary – with its 'hundreds of acres' – was the 'thirtieth Irish mansion to be sold since August'. Still, the big house had continued, into 1922–3, to provide a refuge from the outside world for Irish landlords. The symbolic destruction of these great homes by fire was a direct challenge to their social and economic standing in the local community – and to their outmoded way of life. Accounts of big house burnings in the local press gave readers an insight into an exclusive and privileged world. Tullamaine Castle, near Fethard, with its square, battlemented tower, turrets and long hall, was 'one of the finest private mansions in Tipperary'.[134] Past occupant, John Maher, MP for Tipperary, kept a 'regal style' at Tullamaine and the current owner, Major Morel, had 'fitted out the place regardless of expense'. Modernizations carried out by the ex-Master of the Tipperary Foxhounds included the building of kennels, and a 'point to point' hunt was held in the Castle grounds. Morel had been resident in the 'beautiful and extensive residence' until a few months prior to its occupation by Irregulars, who burned the place as National Troops approached.[135]

132 J.G. Farrell, *Troubles* (London: Jonathan Cape, 1970), 443.
133 Farrell, *Troubles*, 446.
134 *Nenagh Guardian*, 28 October 1922.
135 *Clonmel Chronicle*, 25 October 1922.

Major Perry, a 'large landholder and a representative of a family long associated with the life of South Tipperary' (he was a cousin of John Bagwell and took in the family the night after the burning of Marlfield), also enjoyed fox hunting and horse racing.[136] He was in the smoking room at Woodrooffe, on a Wednesday evening in February 1923, when his daughter ran in saying the stables were on fire. Then, after 'firing the stables', the four armed men 'got into the house, and going upstairs sprinkled the top rooms with petrol and started a fire which soon gutted the whole house'.[137] Flanked by square courts with cupolas, this had been a grand home; now little remained of the eighteenth-century mansion. The demesne had also been the location, earlier in the war, of some intense encounters between the Free State Army and republicans, and it was reported that Perry's compensation claim for the destruction of the mansion would include prior attempts to seize the land and house.[138]

The Perry family, like the Bagwells, were Cromwellian arrivals to Munster.[139] English settlers had imposed themselves, literally, on the Irish landscape through the construction of huge residences. Architecturally varied, what all Irish country houses had in common was their size. Even the more modest 'big' houses were magnified by the wide, open spaces around them.[140] If the construction of the big house was part of the civilizing process of Plantation, then, arson was its symbolically uncivilized end. Replacing deference for the old order with defiance was indeed a key part of the IRA campaign of 1916–23. Violence was liberating in this respect; Ernie O'Malley believed that physical force could free the Irish of their 'slave-mindedness'.[141] The physical dismantling of the traditional British power base, the big house, through fire, was the logical development of O'Malley's War of Independence training: in 1918 he 'made the men manoeuvre in demesne land to rid them of their inherent respect for the owners. Even yet their fathers touched their hats to the gentry'.[142] For the emboldened republican, arson was the spectacular next step: fire ripped off the roof, blackened the walls and literally opened the house to the outside, reclaiming the landscape from the

136 *Munster Express*, 17 February 1923.

137 *Munster Express*, 17 February 1923.

138 *Munster Express*, 17 February 1923. See Chapter 5 on deadly ambushes near the demesne.

139 Hallinan, *Tales from the Deise* (Dublin: Kincora Press, 1996), 37: the townlands Clashganny West, Kilnacarriga and Middlequarter were in the Perrys' possession from 1719 to 1928, when the lands were acquired by the Land Commission. The family also had a 'great house' in Newcastle, Co. Tipperary, burned down by the IRA in 1921.

140 Dooley, *Decline of the big house*, 42.

141 R. English, *Ernie O'Malley: IRA intellectual* (Oxford: Clarendon Press, 1998), 84.

142 English, *Ernie O'Malley*, 84.

(a)

(b)

Figure 3a, 3b and 3c. Graiguenoe Park before and after the burning. The ruins stood until the 1960s, when they were levelled.

(c)

Figure 3a, 3b and 3c (*continued*)

landlord. Charles Clarke's Graiguenoe Park was reduced from a huge, richly decorated home to a burnt-out shell in a matter of hours; see Figure 3. Elizabeth Bowen described the 'hollow of land' left after Bowen's Court was demolished in 1960: 'One cannot say that the space is empty. More, it is as it was – with no house there'.[143]

As an already small southern Protestant minority adjusted to 'numerical decline' and 'radically reduced circumstances', a lingering 'nostalgia' for 'ascendancy' living is understandable;[144] more surprising is the fairly widespread, civilian regret at the burning of the big house. The local press recorded with sadness the transformation of many homes from 'beautiful'[145] residence to 'blackened ruin'.[146] 'Another Tipperary Mansion Gone' proclaimed the *Nenagh Guardian* about Ballinacourty, the 'picturesque residence... of Robert Sanders'.[147] Ireland could 'ill-afford' the loss of more fine houses 'as we had a surplus of ruins handed

143 E. Bowen, *Bowen's Court; & Seven winters: Memories of a Dublin childhood* (London: Vintage, 1999), 457–8.

144 M. Busteed, F. Neal and J. Tonge (eds.), *Irish Protestant identities* (Manchester: Manchester University Press, 2008), 2.

145 See, for example, reports on the burnings of Rockmount and Caroline Fairholme's Comeragh House, both in Co. Waterford (*Munster Express*, 24 February 1923).

146 Ludlow Jones' 'fine residence' Knocknacree, near Borrisokane, Co. Tipperary (*Nenagh Guardian*, 10 February 1923), for example, and Bagwell's Marlfield (*Clonmel Chronicle*, 10 January 1923), both met this fate.

147 *Nenagh Guardian*, 28 October 1922. See Section 5b on the burnings on Sanders' estate.

down from past conflicts'.[148] Indeed, whilst sites of conflagrations may have attracted onlookers, and in some cases arsonists were known locally, burnings did not demand the complicity of the wider community, which was required in successful boycotts or other campaigns of intimidation. Villagers near Rapla House, for example, did not glory in its destruction. Rapla, a local resident recalled, was 'in my youth . . . a very nice place . . . [a]t the entrance to the avenue leading up to the Big House, as I called it, was a beautiful gate-lodge'.[149] Big houses were important local landmarks: sports days were held at Rapla and a dance was in progress when armed men entered and set the place alight on 4 February 1923.[150] And whilst Marlfield village, with its distillery and corn mills, had ceased to be 'an important centre of manufacturing industry', the Bagwells remained a 'resident' family on good terms with the locals. When John's father, Richard Bagwell, inherited Marlfield in 1886, John's mother, Harriet, made life 'more civilised' for the workers: she added gardens to their houses, a 'cooking school, Penny Club . . . tea house', and founded 'Marlfield Embroideries', to give employment to girls and women.[151] By the 1920s, the master of the house was often away in Dublin on business, but John 'looked forward to the time' when the whole family would permanently reside at their country seat. Nineteenth-century tradition seemingly lingered here: just one week before the mansion was burned, 100 estate employees and their families gathered for a party for the Senator's son, presenting a birthday gift 'as testimony' of their 'good feeling and loyalty'.[152]

However, whilst the 'interesting historical associations'[153] of burnt-out buildings (and their 'good landlords'[154]) were celebrated in the local press, nostalgia for the big house was very much absent in government discussion of their fate. Dooley argues, for example, that Irish compensation law was particularly 'ominous' for mansion owners.[155] The Damage to Property Act stipulated, first of all, that judges could consider 'the steps taken or which might reasonably have been taken' by the owner of

[148] O'Dwyer, 'Local happenings, 1922–23', *Oola: Past and Present*, 4.
[149] M. Elebert, 'Recollections of Rapla', *Cloughjordan Heritage* 1 (1985), 9.
[150] *Nenagh Guardian*, 10 February 1923. The resident confirmed these reports in his compensation claim: NAI, 401/856: Maloney, Tipperary.
[151] NLI, MS 32,617.
[152] *Clonmel Chronicle*, 3 January 1923.
[153] See for example, reports on the burning of Rapla House (*Nenagh Guardian*, 17 February 1923) and Duncannon Fort (*Munster Express*, 15 July 1922).
[154] *Clonmel Chronicle*, 3 March 1923: employees of the Earl of Bessborough sent a 'resolution of sympathy' following the burning of his mansion near Pilltown, South Kilkenny.
[155] Dooley, *Decline of the big house*, 201.

the property to prevent the injury.[156] The fact that many big houses were vacant when looted, damaged or burned, or in the care of a few domestic staff, meant that it was highly unlikely that any resistance could have been forthcoming. Just four servant girls occupied Graiguenoe Park, for example, at the time of the burning on 28 February 1923.[157] Clarke, who had added a wing to his grandfather's already huge house in 1903, claimed he was only away on a 'short visit' and 'had every intention of returning'. The ICCA argued on Clarke's behalf that Graiguenoe had 'never been let and always occupied by Clarke, who was left without a home'.[158] His attachment to his Irish residence may have been genuine, but the Free State's paltry award did not give Clarke the chance to stay in the county and the mansion ruins stood until the 1960s, when they were levelled. An 'elderly landlord' of Kilmacthomas, Co. Waterford,[159] Caroline Fairholme, similarly claimed that Comeragh House had been 'constantly inhabited' by her family, for more than a century.[160] However, the place she considered home was taken away, both by the fire 'maliciously' started during an anti-Treaty IRA raid on 18 February 1923, and by the Free State Government, it being 'impossible to rebuild' with the amount of compensation awarded.[161] The reinstated building, the victim complained, was 'vastly inferior' to the original Comeragh House. Between October 1923 and September 1926, Fairholme made eighteen journeys between England and Waterford to settle her affairs. She and two servants travelled 'third class', a detail twice underlined by the applicant on the claims form, as if to highlight the indignity.[162]

Other estates had been leased to large farmers or graziers, but still remained vacant for long periods.[163] Ievers (of Glanduff, mentioned earlier) was the tenant of the Staveley family and even she had 'not resided there permanently for the past 23 years', spending just one week a year in Ireland 'from 1919 until the time the Castle was burned'.[164]

156 The compensation process began at the local sessions; see Chapter 2.

157 *The Nationalist and Munster Advertiser*, 3 March 1923.

158 PRONI, D/989/B/2/9.

159 According to the Census, Caroline would have been sixty-six years old in 1922; Census of Ireland, 1911 (online database).

160 *Munster Express*, 24 February 1923.

161 PRONI, D/989/B/2/9.

162 CO 762/94/3: Fairholme, Waterford.

163 D.S. Jones, 'Land reform legislation and security of tenure in Ireland after independence', *Éire-Ireland* 32, no. 4 and 33, nos. 1 and 2 (1998), 116–143 at 118.

164 NAI, 392/274: Ievers, Limerick. The Free State advised Ada M.T. Staveley's agent that it was the tenant (Ievers), not the owner (Staveley), who was entitled to compensation: NAI, 392/358: Welply, Limerick. The IGC also dismissed the owner's claim: TNA, CO 762/114/24: Staveley, Limerick.

The alleged meagreness of Free State compensation and the difficult prospect of finding new tenants for a place that had been violently attacked meant that many big houses, such as Rapla, were not reoccupied and fell into total disrepair; see Figure 4. And if victims were afraid even to return to their burnt-out homes, the Damage to Property Act's stipulation that compensation be used to rebuild on the same site doubtless encouraged the likes of Clarke and Fairholme to cut their losses and retreat to smaller premises in England, or at least downscale their way of life in Ireland. The Earl of Devon claimed £30,300 for his mansion at Newcastle West, Co. Limerick, and was awarded £6,293.8.0, pending reinstatement. Some caution should be taken with Devon's description of his mansion, pre-fire. The years had, naturally, taken their toll on the building and, over the centuries, parts of the Castle – with its two great halls – fell into ruin. By the time the 'Devons came here', inheriting Newcastle from the Courtenay family, 'they occupied a long, irregular house'.[165] Yet, whatever their state of repair, the ornate painted ceilings and marble fireplaces of the original Castle were a world away from the proposed reconstruction: a 'plain suburban villa dwelling of no special pretensions'.[166]

The reinstatement clause bound the claimant to the Ministry of Finance's payment schedule, which further encouraged rebuilding on a more modest scale. Reinstatement was also a drawn-out process: the IGC complained that the Free State's Damage to Property Act had 'empowered the courts to clog their awards with reinstatement conditions'.[167] In a violent attack in which the gardener and steward were placed under armed guard, Gardenmorris 'was burned to the ground and all the furniture' destroyed.[168] More than £13,000 of owner Richard O'Shee's particularly large award of £15,609.9.6 was to be released in instalments pending reinstatement, and the Office of Public Works reported to the Ministry of Finance at each stage of the three-year rebuild.[169] Major Morel complained after the burning of his home that 'every inducement' to stay in Ireland was 'taken away' by the Free State Government: it was impossible to rebuild Tullamaine for the amount awarded (Morel was at a £20,000 loss, whilst the Ministry of Finance 'evaded' the £12,824 compensation payment); and, on top of this 'injustice', the Land Commission was beginning to compulsorily acquire his demesne land. Morel's estate

165 M. Bence-Jones, *Burke's guide to country houses*, 3 vols. (London: Burke's Peerage, 1978), vol. I: *Ireland*, 224.
166 NAI, 392/285: Devon, Limerick.
167 TNA, CO 762/212: 'End of Committee Report'.
168 *Munster Express*, 3 March 1923.
169 NAI, 402/240: O'Shee, Waterford.

(a)

(b)

Figures 4a and 4b. Rapla House, Co. Tipperary in 1920, three years before the burning (4a) and in 1984, abandoned, overgrown and beyond repair (4b).

had been attacked before: on 22 May 1922 part of the demesne was seized and cattle taken away.[170] The victim's accusation, though, was that it was not only the locals, but also the Free State Government, that wanted a piece of his 400 acres.

Cosgrave admitted that the Damage to Property Act was 'very tightly drawn', but that the big houses burned were 'property of a description which is largely out of date, and not easily marketable, if at all'.[171] Glanduff Castle, for example, was a 'tremendous' mansion; full restoration of its extensive accommodation, including a wine cellar, gun room and tower, would not only have been difficult, but also inappropriate for the government's purposes. Simple economic necessity does in part explain the Free State Government's reluctance to accommodate former landlords: the break-up of the large estates was well underway before the Civil War and progress on land purchase was crucial to the 'commercial and financial stability' of independent Ireland.[172] However, broader shifts in political priorities accompanied material concerns in the Irish Free State. 'Landlordism', in the words of William Sears TD, 'is now in its final stage'[173] and during the compensation process it was the owners of the small- to medium-sized houses or farms, not the out-dated mansions, who most passionately believed that an independent Irish government should take their side.

Complaints were made, for example, when it appeared that claims from big houses were handled more generously than 'small claims'.[174] A large pay-out to O'Shee, who was able to rebuild his chateau-style Gardenmorris House as it was, omitting a third storey at one end, undoubtedly seemed 'very excessive'.[175] The solicitor for Charles White, whose house (used as a barracks) in Annacarty, South Tipperary, was burned on 3 May 1922, feared that his client, of more modest means, was 'not receiving fair treatment and justice'. White found it 'hard to believe that our own Government would treat a farmer worse than the British Government would have done'.[176] It was normal for the British to protect

170 PRONI, D/989/B/2/9. The burning of Tullamaine was reported in *Clonmel Chronicle*, 25 October 1922; see earlier discussion in this section.

171 Dooley, *Decline of the big house*, 203.

172 TNA, PRO 30/67/50: 'Letter to Michael Collins, 13 June 1922' (Domestic Records of the Public Record Office, Gifts, Deposits, Notes and Transcripts, First Earl Midleton papers).

173 *Dáil Éireann Debates*, iii, 14 June 1923.

174 NAI, 401/305: This compensation file from Co. Tipperary includes a letter from a victim's solicitor dissatisfied with the compensation system and its bias towards owners of big houses.

175 NAI, 401/305.

176 NAI, 401/605: White, Tipperary.

elite interests; it was expected – even demanded – that Free State sympathies would lie with the people. It had long been expected, too, that the large demesnes would become targets for violence in times of political upheaval. A 1913 pamphlet on the Defence of Irish Country Houses provided practical advice on how to protect mansions from fire.[177] Arsonists, it warned, could gain entry with the 'connivance of an inmate', or by 'stratagem' (the admittance of an attacker posing as a 'piano tuner', for example, with 'confederates in ambush close by').[178] General hints were offered: do not leave ladders lying around, barricade doors and windows with non-flammable materials, and 'admit none whose loyalty is not above question'. It was hoped that neighbours would work together in time of attack, using flares to call for help and warn other big houses in the area of fire, and that 'houses whose owners were in special danger should be garrisoned by small military parties . . . as was done in certain counties' during the Land War 'in 1881–82'.[179]

Solicitors for Lord Dunalley of Kilboy House (near Nenagh, Co. Tipperary) clearly anticipated a serious incident at their client's home before the burning and did not believe their concerns were taken seriously by the Free State. Correspondence between 'S. and R.C. Walker and Son, Dublin' and the Ministry of Defence, shows an apparent unwillingness on the part of the Irish Government to afford Dunalley adequate protection from what his representatives rightly saw as the inevitable arson attack ahead. Receiving a telegram from Dunalley, on 19 July 1922, that Kilboy 'was in danger', Walker and co. asked the Ministry for protection:

> Of course we know that it would not be possible to send a guard to every house the owner of which was nervous and feared that it might be attacked, but where there is a particular reason for supposing that a house is to be attacked we take it the position is different. Lord Dunalley's house is of course a large one and a number of people are depending on his establishment being kept up and we are sure that this will have weight with you.[180]

However, perfunctory replies and unhelpful telephone calls suggested Dunalley's fears carried very little weight with the Government. The last letter, dated 2 August 1922, arrived just a couple of days before Kilboy House was burned to the ground (on 6 August 1922); the authorities,

[177] PRONI, D/989/C/1/17: 'Notes on the Defence of Irish Country Houses, 1913' (Papers of the Irish Unionist Alliance, Propaganda Material: Printed Pamphlets and Handbills).

[178] There was a suggestion in some cases, such as the burning of Woodrooffe (discussed earlier), that arsonists did have help on the inside.

[179] PRONI, D/989/C/1/17.

[180] NLI, MS 29,810(17).

it seemed, had merely looked on as another symbol of British rule was destroyed.

The assault on the big house did not, of course, begin with the Civil War. World War I drew questions of loyalty into sharp relief, was the catalyst for the Easter Rising and, in suspending Home Rule indefinitely, paved the way for the replacement of constitutional nationalism by a more radical, separatist politics. Service during the war, or a family connection to an ex-officer, recurs in IGC claims as the alleged motivating factor for Civil War arson attacks. Major Rose, for example, owner of Boskell Hall, which was burned on 12 July 1922, had felt isolated in his local community in Caherconlish, Co. Limerick, since returning from World War I. With the nearest police barracks five miles away, 'no protection was given to me'.[181] Both Anna Clarke, whose hay was burned in Kildimo, Co. Limerick,[182] and Frances Ievers of Glanduff Castle, were wives of British Army Majors – a fact made clear to the IGC. Bowen also identified World War I as the moment the world changed for the Anglo-Irish gentry. The news from Europe broke as the fifteen-year-old Bowen attended a garden party at Mitchelstown Castle, Co. Cork:

> It was . . . a more final scene than we knew. Ten years hence, it was all to seem like a dream – and the Castle itself would be a few bleached stumps on the plateau [Mitchelstown was burned in 1922 and the ruins demolished]. . . . Many of those guests . . . would be scattered, houseless, sonless, or themselves dead.[183]

Bowen's terrible fear that her own home, in Kildorrery, Co. Cork, would also be lost 'in flames' was not realized: Bowen's Court was occupied during the Civil War by 'seventy seven republicans', but they 'did little damage' and left after four days.[184] Her emotional attachment to her own big house is evident in her novels. The houses in *The Last September* are personified: they have people's names (Danielstown, Mount Isabel and Castle Trent) and are killed by the fire. This sentimentality explains why she portrays arsonists as murderers; as they 'slid away' from the burning house, her fictional incendiaries were 'executioners bland from accomplished duty'.[185] However, the idea that there was no emotional and ideological investment in arson on the part of the perpetrators during the Civil War, or desire to achieve social and economic change through the act of burning, is not borne out in the evidence from Cos. Limerick,

[181] TNA, CO 762/41/2: Rose, Limerick; see Chapter 2.
[182] Chapter 2.
[183] Bowen, *Bowen's Court*, 435–6.
[184] Bowen, *Bowen's Court*, 440–3.
[185] Bowen, *The Last september* (London: Constable, 1929), 206.

Tipperary and Waterford. The next section reveals how arson was used as a form of protest – and tool for redistribution – in struggles over land.

4. Land redistribution

William Magan, whose ancestral home, Umma More, escaped the fiery fate suffered by his uncle Middleton Biddulph's mansion, Rathrobin, Co. Offaly, in April 1923, believed the Ascendancy's raison d'être disappeared when it was 'shorn of its estates and the opportunity to serve locally in Ireland in the services of the Crown'.[186] Were these losses part of, or accelerated by, the Civil War specifically? Certainly the departure of the British Army and RIC in 1922 removed the opportunity – for Unionists and the Anglo-Irish – to play a role in Irish public life (although a select few did, of course, serve the independent Irish government through membership of the Seanad). The land question, by contrast, was largely resolved by the time of the Civil War and the break-up of landlords' estates well underway. Insecurity of tenure was addressed by legislation in the late nineteenth century, culminating in the Wyndham Act (1903), under which two-thirds of tenants had become proprietors by 1914.[187] Land purchase did not, of course, dispose of all underlying agrarian grievances. Further redistribution – enacted by Free State, rather than British law – was needed to deal with rural poverty and congestion. The Land Act (1923) consequently empowered the Land Commission to take possession of tenanted lands.[188]

House burning was another way to force the owner from the land and leave it to be shared out, with or without the approval of the Land Commission. Digby H. de Burgh's Dromkeen – a two-storey Georgian construction – was a fairly modest big house.[189] Yet the family had allegedly lived on the site since 1174, and this descendent of Norman (rather than Cromwellian) settlers, whose own son was a Sandhurst cadet, was confident in his British loyalty and sure of the culture to which he belonged. And it was the land surrounding Dromkeen, rather than the house itself, that was at heart of threats made against de Burgh before the burning. In 'most Irish counties . . . some of the best – because un-exhausted and well cared for – land is attached to mansion houses in the shape of house farms and demesnes', observed the 1913 Irish Unionist Alliance

186 W. Magan, *Umma More: The story of an Irish family* (Salisbury, Wiltshire: Element Books, 1983), 381.

187 Dooley, "*The land for the people*", 16.

188 Jones, 'Land reform legislation', *Éire-Ireland*, 116–19.

189 Bence-Jones, *Burke's guide*, 109.

pamphlet on the defence of country houses. Accusations in the pamphlet that these estates had been secretly 'parcelled out for spoil' by the Land League years before, so that 'persons now living know the portions which . . . they expect to receive', after independence,[190] echo myths circulating in Ulster around the time of the first Home Rule Bill. National self-government, it was feared, would mean the expulsion of Unionists and, in the meantime, Catholics held a 'raffle' or 'lottery' for the land that would become theirs, when the time came.[191] Indeed, Unionist predictions that 'greed for land will inevitably cause trouble',[192] were seemingly borne out in the Civil War and certainly this was the case in the targeting of de Burgh's estate. Notices posted before the attack called for 'land for the landless' and warned 'all whom it may concern' to 'keep away from these lands and trees'. De Burgh believed that if the house:

> [h]ad been situated in Great Britain, or in Northern Ireland, no trouble would have arisen. . . . But there was for many years a conspiracy to seize and divide the lands of Loyal men in the South of Ireland. . . . The conspirators were told that the Irish Government would pass a new Land Act which would enable the small farmers and labourers to take the property of the Loyalists.[193]

There is no evidence that the 'conspiracy' against de Burgh extended to direct Free State involvement in the burning of Dromkeen. There are notorious recorded incidents of Free State cruelty, such as the Ballyseedy killings in Co. Kerry,[194] but the 'armed men' and 'Irregulars' identified as perpetrators of arson in victims' testimonies are always assumed to be anti-Treaty forces, rather than National Troops. That is not to say, however, that an enthusiasm for land for the people, stirred by independence, was not felt at government level. Another notice posted on de Burgh's land advertised a 'public meeting' to discuss the division of the estate; P. Clancy TD was billed to speak at the local gathering.[195] Clancy's priorities were clear in the years that followed. In the Dáil, he asked the Minister for Lands and Fisheries 'if it is the intention of the Land Commission to acquire' various estates in Limerick, including Emly and Clarina, 'for division amongst congests and landless men of the district'.[196] In Co. Tipperary, too, public meetings to discuss the division of estates 'amongst the small holders, labourers, representatives

190 PRONI, D/989/C/1/17.
191 Morgan, *Labour and Partition*, 11.
192 PRONI, D/989/C/1/17.
193 TNA, CO 762/37/10: De Burgh, Limerick.
194 See Chapter 1.
195 TNA, CO 762/37/10: De Burgh, Limerick. De Burgh was also physically attacked; see Chapter 5.
196 *Dáil Éireann Debates*, xxxv, 28 May 1930, xxxvii, 19 March 1931.

of evicted tenants and landless men in the district' took place – with the support of local TDs – into 1929.[197]

Land hunger is palpable in many other burnings. Before Glanduff was burned, a local woman told the steward that the 'Old Bitch [Ievers, who was not the owner, but had been the tenant for nearly a quarter of a century] . . . had the place long enough and that it was about time to get it divided up'.[198] Castle Fogarty, near Thurles, Co. Tipperary, was burned on 20 April 1922 'by the local people in the hope that they would get the land attached to it' and Major Valentine Ryan's solicitor advised that, 'until such time as the country settled', he should not rebuild.[199] The ICCA protested, in any case, that the £3,000 compensation offered by the Free State was 'totally inadequate' for the rebuilding of Castle Fogarty (valued by an architect at £20,667).[200] Other matters were at stake in this case: occupying republicans may have burned Fogarty to prevent its use as a barracks by the Free State. However, land was clearly a divisive issue: the burning of Fogarty was accompanied by an attack on the steward in charge of Major Ryan's estate. John Cusack, his wife and daughter 'were in bed, and the raiders, without any warning whatsoever, having fired some shots, proceeded to set fire to the house and its contents. Some of them got on the roof, made holes, and sprinkled petrol all over'. The family made a hasty getaway to Thurles in a trap with a 'few articles of clothing', but the house and furniture were completely destroyed.[201]

It was not just big landowners, then, who were driven away by fire. The main enemy of the landless man, by the 1920s, was not the rack-renting landlord of old, or the estate worker who protected him, but the Catholic, nationalist grazier who had bought his way in to the once Protestant, Unionist club of ownership. So, whilst on the one hand the local big house was targeted as a symbol of Plantation and the past injustices of British rule, arson was also used to redistribute land across the community. The burning of crops and outbuildings – which accounts for 41 per cent of reported incidences of arson in Limerick, 28 per cent in Tipperary and 45 per cent in Waterford – attacked the heart of farm life, made winter feeding impossible and caused real hardship, even for the strong farmer. More than seventy head of cattle belonging to 'extensive

197 W.J. Hayes, G. Cunningham and Moyne-Templetuohy History Group, *Moyne-Templetuohy a life of its own: The story of a Tipperary parish*, 3 vols (Tipperary: Moyne-Templetuohy History Group, 2001), vol. III, 27.

198 TNA, CO 762/185/6: Ievers, Limerick.

199 NAI, 401/363: Ryan, Tipperary.

200 PRONI, D/989/B/2/9. The Castle was not completely destroyed: parts of the exterior and one tower survived.

201 *Clonmel Chronicle*, 21 June 1922.

farmer' and Chairman of the Kilmallock branch of the Irish Farmers' Union (Farmers' Party), John Halpin, for example, were 'left without fodder on Monday morning' after the destruction of his hay barn.[202] Many fires probably went unreported. In his survey of arson in East Anglia, 1815–70, Archer suggests incendiary attacks were not universally reported because newspapers feared publicity led to imitation attacks.[203] In Munster, though, headlines such as 'Kilmallock outrages: More hay burned' were nonetheless very familiar. Crop burnings in this area were condemned from the pulpit, to no avail.[204] Vast quantities of hay were destroyed at a time: 200 tonnes belonging to Michael Ryan, Killaloe, were burned in January 1922.[205]

Faced with ruin on this scale, the burning of crops and buildings drove some farmers out of their home and even out of Munster. Herbert Sullivan, for example, the Limerick dairy farmer who had served milk to a British regiment during World War I, was forced to downsize to a small house in Devon following the burning of Curramore House.[206] A 'contemptuous' award of £1,800 from the Free State – and the government's evasion of payment for a considerable time – did not ease his new situation in the UK.[207] In a different case, John Borland's house and those of his shepherd[208] and housekeeper[209] were set on fire and his land seized for four years. Borland stayed in Scotland for safety and, by the time his farm was relinquished, he had been robbed of annual profits of £500, his flock of 500 sheep and lost thousands on the sale of the land.[210] In events that mirrored the Land War campaigns against those who took up the land of the evicted, or refused to withhold rents or labour from the landlord or agent, the sales of burnt-out houses and their estates were subject to local boycott.[211] One auctioneer, Michael Quirke, even had his own hay burned and a threatening letter, 'which was of an illiterate type . . . signed "Cattle Driver"', posted beforehand.[212]

The lands Quirke was involved with, 'Kiltinian ranches' (belonging to Col. Cooke of Kiltinane Castle, near Fethard, Co. Tipperary), had in

202 *Limerick Leader*, 15 February 1922.
203 Archer, *By a flash and a scare*, 70–1.
204 *Limerick Leader*, 1 February, 8 March 1922.
205 *Limerick Leader*, 30 January 1922.
206 Chapter 2, Section 2a.
207 PRONI, D/989/B/2/9.
208 NAI, 392/318: Wilson, Limerick.
209 NAI, 392/233: Watson, Limerick.
210 NAI, 392/314 and TNA, CO 762/83/1: Borland, Limerick.
211 TNA, CO 762/87/4: Sullivan, Limerick, CO 762/64/11: Gleeson, Tipperary, CO 762/80/20: Carroll, Angas, Scott, Tipperary.
212 *Clonmel Chronicle*, 17 June 1922.

fact already 'been divided into small portions suitable for persons who wanted honestly to acquire land and pay for it'.[213] Arson nevertheless was utilized by those who had missed out on legitimate land purchase and redistribution through the accepted channels. Thus if hay stacks and barns were symbols of wealth, fire was a method of getting even, of disrupting the financial security embodied in the pile of animal fodder. Hay ricks were also popular targets because of relative ease of access (away from the main farm buildings) and, in winter months, when few other materials were as dry, and therefore combustible, as the safely guarded pile of straw, little effort and few tools could produce a spectacular flare up – the 'flash and a scare' referred to by Archer.[214] In this way, arson worked as a powerful psychological weapon as well as a means of disruption and financial inconvenience. The fire publicized the fact that an individual had been singled out for special treatment; the rapid destruction of farm buildings and winter food supplies left little time for reflection on the nature of his transgression (although the threatening notices accompanying some burnings do give some clue to motivation). The burning of houses was most damaging in this respect because the incendiaries would need knowledge of the building before firing. The ease with which arsonists found their way around a house (as they did at Woodrooffe, for example) exposed the particular vulnerability of the owner.

5. Arson: Complex Motivations

a) *Targeting Loyalists*

Who was most vulnerable to arson attacks during this period? I collated the compensation data from both countries, taking into account overlapping claims, where applications were made to both governments, for the same attack; I found that the Loyalist, Protestant minority was disproportionately targeted during the Civil War. Taking the three-county area as a whole, 25 per cent of buildings burned were big houses and 19 per cent of arson attacks were attributable to the claimant's 'allegiance to the United Kingdom'.[215] Many of the barracks burned were also formerly occupied by the British Army. Ex-RIC and Army men, including many who had served in World War I, were targeted, with their

213 *Clonmel Chronicle*, 17 June 1922.
214 Archer, *By a flash and a scare*, 149, 150, 163.
215 IGC Terms of Reference; see Chapter 2 on compensation procedure and British 'Loyalty'.

families, for their overt demonstrations of loyalty to the old regime. The compensation evidence suggests that the sectarianism and conflicts over land that had characterized Irish-British enmity for hundreds of years persisted during the Civil War. The burning of Protestant church buildings, for example, reveals an apparently straightforward expression of the old religious enmities. Methodist minister Rev. James Johnston, with the steward and church member, Arthur Bridge and Arthur Switzer, made a claim to the Free State for the burning, on 28 December 1922, of the chapel at Ballylocknane, also known as Newborough, two and half miles from Adare village, Co. Limerick. The stone chapel was 'lined inside by timber . . . and good timber floor, containing pews, organ, pulpit, all of which was totally destroyed'.[216] Rectories destroyed include Clonbeg, located on Sanders' Glen of Aherlow estate (the site of a great deal of violence and disruption during the war), which was burned in February 1923.[217]

Whilst the 'plea of "military necessity" may be made for the destruction of bridges, the blocking of railways and the looting of provisions shops', the 'damage perpetrated on Protestant Churches' was portrayed as 'gratuitous' and immoral.[218] Attacks on Protestants during the War of Independence in Clare, argues Fitzpatrick, were about more than 'land-hunger and arms-hunger'; 'even less did military motives lead to the burning of Protestant churches in at least three Clare villages'.[219] The *Church of Ireland Gazette* also denounced the 'execrable violation of the churchyard at Kilmacthomas [Co. Waterford] which was visited by a party of men who dug up the tombstones, scattering them about the graveyard'.[220] Indeed, the morality of republican tactics was questioned across the board: sniping at Catholic Free State soldiers on their way to Mass was condemned with as much vigour in the local press as was the burning of Protestant churches in Church of Ireland editorials.[221] There were, however, other motivating factors, besides religion, involved in attacks on churches. Canon Charles Atkinson accounted for the burning of his home, Kilpeacon Rectory, Co. Limerick: it was 'well known' that the ex-Army chaplain was 'loyal to the British Connection'. Atkinson was awarded £100 for personal belongings destroyed in the fire on 28 March 1923:

216 NAI, 392/134: Johnston, Bridge, Switzer, Limerick.
217 NAI, 401/90: Sanders, Tipperary.
218 *Church of Ireland Gazette*, 11 August 1922.
219 Fitzpatrick, *Politics and Irish life*, 78. On the burning of Protestant churches, see also Bielenberg, 'Exodus', *P&P*, 209–10.
220 *Church of Ireland Gazette*, 11 August 1922.
221 Chapter 5, Section 2a.

A party of 20 armed republicans entered my home near midnight, turned me out with my wife and daughter and set fire to it. We were sent under armed guard to a house near by and released after the fire had been in progress for an hour – most of the house was saved but some rooms were gutted.[222]

Indeed, the house was not destroyed and, after the war, life returned to relative normality for this small Church of Ireland community: Atkinson held an organ recital at Kilpeacon that summer.[223] During the war, when tensions temporarily were heightened between representatives of the old regime and republicans in protest against the maintenance of the oath of allegiance to the crown, hostility towards the Atkinsons may be accounted for by their so-called 'British connection', as much as by their (unchanging) Protestantism.

Sisters Caroline Grace and Louisa Margaret Fairholme of Comeragh House (see Section 3) were Protestants. Their solicitor explained:

As a result of violent political and ancestral enmity it is notorious that during the trouble in Ireland the masses of the people were extremely hostile to members of claimant's class.[224]

Did 'class' here refer to the victim's denomination, or to their membership of a social elite? Comeragh is not listed in *Burke's guide*, but contemporary reports suggest that it was not far off a big house: in 1911, the Fairholmes employed three domestic staff and a forester to take care of the estate, and allegations were also made regarding the kidnap of a 'coachman' in their employment. Louisa's claim for £200, for the stamp collection lost in the flames, was rejected by the IGC: the item was evidently not important enough to be mentioned in her sister Caroline's compensation claim relating to the house and furniture and, 'apart from the fact that no claim was made' in the original application, 'it would not appear that this is a case of any hardship'. The sisters moved in fairly privileged circles, but this social grouping was not defined entirely by denomination: their solicitor asked that notice be given to friends – ladies of 'their class', Lady Frances Alice Anderson and Mary Carew, a Catholic – to attend the compensation hearing in support of the Fairholmes.[225]

222 NAI, 392/260 and TNA, CO 762/184/3: Atkinson, Limerick. A separate claim was made by the Representative Church Body for the damage to the building: NAI, 392/411.

223 *Church of Ireland Gazette*, 29 June 1923.

224 TNA, CO 762/94/3: Fairholme, Waterford.

225 Anderson and Carew made their own claim to the IGC for loss of income on farmland seized during the Civil War: TNA, CO 762/89/5: Anderson and Carew, Waterford.

The 'class' tension referred to by the Fairholmes' solicitor, which resulted in the violent attack against their home, clearly was not a straightforward conflict between privileged Protestants and impoverished Catholics. Chapter 4 reveals that a growing Catholic middle class of graziers and large farmers had as much to fear, in terms of intimidation, cattle driving and attacks on their land, as did their former Protestant landlords. 'Intelligent Roman Catholics', suggested the *Church of Ireland Gazette*, saw the danger in land hunger and forced redistribution; those who used crop burning and other methods to 'drive innocent Protestants from their homes are not worthy of the name of Irishman . . . and their work is condemned whole-heartedly by the vast majority of decent Roman Catholics'.[226] The burning of the big house was significant and symbolic: fire reclaimed the landscape from the Protestant planter and opened these symbols of British social and economic power – in the words of Farrell's fictional Major – 'to the Irish sky'.[227] Yet ordinary 'Free Staters' were at the mercy of the arsonists too: more crops and outhouses were lost to the flames than were houses of any size and ownership. In Munster, the conflict over the Treaty was overlaid with old battles between religious enemies *and* newer class tensions and intra-community squabbles over land.

b) 'Labour Takes a Hand in the Game'

There were pockets of industry (copper mining, as well as paper and cotton mills) in the essentially rural counties of Limerick, Tipperary and Waterford, and fears were raised, early in 1922, that 'labour takes a hand in the game'.[228] Local economic activity around Cappoquin, Co. Waterford, for example, was focused not only on Sir John Keane's mansion,[229] but also the sawmills on his estate. Both were burned during the war. A strike by Keane's workmen lasted approximately one month: during summer 1922, work on the estate and sawmills was 'completely suspended' whilst 'strikers and pickets' milked Sir John's cattle and sold the milk themselves to the townspeople.[230] The mills were burned during this occupation, on 16 June 1922.[231] Between May 1922 and January 1923, numerous malicious attacks were made on outhouses and grounds at Golden Grove, Roscrea, Co. Tipperary, including the burning of farm

[226] *Church of Ireland Gazette*, 23 June, 6 October 1922.
[227] Farrell, *Troubles*, 446.
[228] *Church of Ireland Gazette*, 3 February 1922.
[229] Section 2b.
[230] *Clonmel Chronicle*, 28 June, 8 July 1922.
[231] *Clonmel Chronicle*, 17 June 1922.

buildings on 28 July 1922. Compensation eventually was paid by the British Government (nearly half of the £4,000 claimed), but correspondence between the IGC and solicitors for the house-owner, Elizabeth Henrietta Lloyd-Vaughan, evidenced the 'preliminary difficulty of showing that the damage caused' to Golden Grove was a result of the victim's pre-Truce British loyalty.[232] The victim's late husband P.W.H. Lloyd (d. 22 December 1923) had been a JP, Deputy Lieutenant of the county and, so Elizabeth told the IGC, 'always a staunch Loyalist'. However, attempts to drive the couple from their home were attributed by the judge in the Free State compensation hearing, and in Mrs Lloyd-Vaughan's own testimony, to disputes between the couple and labourers on their estate. Alleged attempts to 'reduce the men's wages' were met with a seven week strike: Elizabeth 'took it that [those responsible for the attacks came from] the Transport Union. . . . The object was not to get land. It was simply . . . roughs out of the town'. Judge Roche said of Vaughan's case, at Birr County Court on 7 December 1925:

> It is a sad thing that the people of the locality should indulge in such a debauch of savagery. . . . I have no doubt about it that they were induced to come together and do this thing by one or more acting in the name of the sacred cause of Labour.[233]

The red scare undoubtedly was exaggerated in some reports. The cutting of trees and cattle driving on lands around Kilboy (Lord Dunalley's mansion here was burned in July 1922; see earlier discussion, this chapter), for example, was branded 'sheer Bolshevism' by the local press.[234] Conflicts between employers and workers nonetheless resulted in violence, including arson; clearly not all incendiary gangs were anti-Treaty IRA. The burning of a creamery in Tipperary town, for example, initially blamed on departing republicans was, according to a trade union official, 'most likely' carried out by the occupying 'Soviet'.[235] A spate of fires in Ballinamona, Co. Waterford,[236] was the result of a strike.[237] In Co. Limerick, at least eleven burnings were attributed to disputes with workers.[238] It could be argued, of course, that these conflicts would have happened anyway, and that it was the wartime absence of law and order that simply provided the conditions for protest. Labour trouble during

232 TNA, CO 762/99/3: Lloyd-Vaughan, Tipperary.
233 TNA, CO 762/99/3: Lloyd-Vaughan, Tipperary.
234 *Clonmel Chronicle*, 1 November 1922.
235 C.D. Greaves, *Liam Mellows and the Irish Revolution*, 1st ed. reprinted with a new introduction by Gerry Adams (London: Lawrence and Wishart, 2004), 359–60.
236 NAI, 402/98–104.
237 *Munster Express*, 18 February 1922.
238 NAI, 392/121, 456–64, 467, 509.

the War of Independence was seen as distinct from the national struggle; IRA Volunteers were actually used as strike-breakers in some areas.[239]

Indeed, despite the efforts of trade-unionist-turned-republican-leader Peadar O'Donnell, there was no successful marriage of the republican and socialist causes during this period. In charge of an IRA column in Donegal during War of Independence, O'Donnell saw the 're-ignition of Fenian radicalism on the land', but was frustrated that the IRA was sent to police the agitation and that, through the Dáil land courts, the alternative Sinn Féin government acted in favour of landlords and against those involved in cattle drives and land seizures. O'Donnell took the anti-Treaty side during the Civil War, his position on the settlement with Britain incorporating the 'standard republican emotional revulsion and sense of betrayal into a broader class-based, anti-imperialist analysis'.[240] Arrested on 1 July 1922 following the Four Courts-occupation, O'Donnell was imprisoned in Mountjoy, Dublin, where, according to his prison memoir,[241] he shared comradeship and escape plans with inmates including Liam Mellows – the only other republican to grasp the 'fundamentally plebeian nature of the Irish national struggle'.[242] O'Donnell's horror at the execution of Mellows and three other republican prisoners (Rory O'Connor, Joe McKelvey and Dick Barrett), at Mountjoy on 8 December 1922 is captured in *The Gates Flew Open*,[243] as are his continued frustrations at the new, independent Irish government's neglect of the 'social revolutionary dimension' of the Revolution.[244] Michael Collins, O'Donnell complained, had 'confused the Conquest with the mere occupation of the country with British soldiers'. The departure of the British Army and administration from Ireland did not constitute full freedom, in other words, so long as the 'imperial exploitation' of Ireland continued through the economic system.[245] During his solitary confinement at Finner Camp, Co. Donegal, O'Donnell reflected further on the 'heresy

[239] Foster, *Modern Ireland*, 515.

[240] D. Ó Drisceoil, *Peadar O'Donnell* (Cork: Cork University Press, 2001), 23.

[241] O'Donnell did not in fact escape from prison until March 1924, but his vivid reminiscences record numerous attempts to tunnel free, or at least enjoy the 'marvellous rowdyism' (p. 34) and negotiate with sympathetic officials for some freedom of movement – not only at Mountjoy, but also in prisons and camps across Ireland, over nearly two years in captivity. See P. O'Donnell, *The gates flew open* (London: J. Cape, 1932), 23, 34–5, 62–7, 79, 102, 105–11, 179–83.

[242] Greaves, *Liam Mellows*, 392. See also Chapter 4, Section 5, on Mellows.

[243] O'Donnell, *Gates flew open*, 74–5, 77, 83–9. See earlier, Section 2a, and Chapter 5, Section 2b, on the 'Public Safety' Bill and the republican response to the executions. On the executions: Greaves, *Liam Mellows*, 386–93.

[244] Ó Drisceoil, *Peadar O'Donnell*, 2.

[245] O'Donnell, *Gates flew open*, 31.

of the cult of armed men that brought... us to defeat'. The Revolution, he believed, must involve the 'stubborn splendour of the big mass of the people'.[246]

Events on the ground in Civil War Munster confirm that, O'Donnell's effort to foment rebellion aside, the anti-Treaty campaign was not directed towards social revolution. Republicanism and labour remained separate causes into 1922: when cattle was driven on the lands around Suir Castle, near Golden, and a 'large red flag suspended from a tree', both the Tipperary Transport Workers' Union and the IRA authorities distanced themselves from the matter, the latter promising to 'deal severely' with the perpetrators.[247] And on Robert M.D. Sanders' Glen of Aherlow estate, Ballincourte, in Co. Tipperary, the IRA 'ordered' the self-proclaimed 'Red Army' to evacuate.[248] Some 300 workers seized the estate in May 1922 and reopened the sawmills, which had been closed since Sanders' departure. Sanders had fled to London following an earlier labour dispute at Ballinacourty:[249] in November 1920, tension between Sanders' labourers and Auxiliary RIC and British soldiers, sent to the estate to protect the family from alleged assassination threats, was heightened by accusations that British troops were being used as 'strike-breakers' (carting hay and gathering sheep).[250] The occupation and burning of Sanders' mills and, for example, the Cleeve creameries in Tipperary and Limerick may not have been directly connected to the military conflict over the Treaty; the 'raising of the red flag' at Bruree, and the seizure of control by workers across a number of Cleeve sites,[251] including Carrick-on-Suir,[252] took place in any case before the split in the IRA and official start of the Civil War in June 1922. These attacks were not, however, an irrelevant subplot of the Civil War and were deemed worthy by the British Government of compensation: public limited companies, such as the Cleeve Creamery Co., were not usually awarded damages by the IGC, because business organizations 'possess neither mind nor conscience and can be

246 O'Donnell, *Gates flew open*, 168.

247 *Clonmel Chronicle*, 8 February 1922.

248 NAI, 401/90 and TNA, CO 762/19/1: Sanders, Tipperary.

249 D.R. O'Connor Lysaght, 'County Tipperary: Class struggle and national struggle, 1916–1924', in W. Nolan and T. McGrath (eds.), *Tipperary: History and society: Interdisciplinary essays on the history of an Irish county* (Dublin: Geography Publications, 1985), 394–410 at 404, 407.

250 NLI, MS 33,718/F (184/1–39) (Correspondence re: strike by labourers on the estate of Robert Sanders of Ballinacourty, Co. Tipperary [1920]).

251 *Limerick Leader*, 15, 17 May 1922.

252 Hallinan, *Tipperary County: People and places*, 86: a bitter dispute over wages in the creamery led to a worker takeover, which 'tore Carrick apart'.

neither loyal nor disloyal' but, after 'deep consideration' and a 'protracted hearing',[253] an exception was made in their case.[254]

6. Conclusion

To secure compensation from the Free State, Irish law demanded proof that attacks were directed towards the overthrow of the state. In the main, victims could identify perpetrators as Irregulars or republicans; Section 2a ('Arson as a Military Tactic: Barracks and Infrastructure') demonstrated how the burning of barracks, railway carriages and businesses constituted an anti-Treaty campaign to stop the new government from functioning in the counties. Burnings were not impulsive manifestations of anti-Treaty feeling; arson constituted a deliberate form of tactical destruction. The military rationale for the burning of private homes – and particularly Protestant and Loyalist-owned mansions – is not always obvious. Yet the perpetrators' accounts that do survive (from O'Malley and Barry, for example) capture a strong republican desire to rout potential British strongholds. Thus the burning of the big house served a contemporary politico-military plan, as well as the settling of local scores against an historic enemy. Even after January 1923, when republican organization in the counties had largely broken down, arson made a serious impact on political and military targets, including Senators' homes. Section 2b focused on Tipperary's Bagwell and Waterford's Keane and revealed the interesting intersection of the personal and political, and old and new agendas, in these attacks. Marlfield and Cappoquin were residences of prominent Free Staters, but they were also big houses, that is, traditional symbols of Protestant privilege and British landed interest in Ireland.

This was, indeed, a complex war with a high proportion of non-military targets, both in terms of what was burned (crops and outbuildings) and the type of building (private houses as opposed to barracks); see Figure 2. This chapter's detailed exploration of burnings – from high profile mansions to small hay stacks – has shown that whilst arson was not always carried out by armed men following a military order, it was not random, unorganized criminal activity. Arson was targeted within the local community. The assault on the big house perhaps was to be expected; tightly drawn compensation law, particularly in the Free State, made reinstatement of these tremendous homes difficult and undesirable (see Section

[253] TNA, CO 762/212.
[254] The Cleeves also appealed to the Free State for compensation: NAI, 392/211, 230, 370, 401/382.

3). Local press reports evidenced some regret at the passing of these historical landmarks, but more decisive in the dismantling the old order were the fires that razed some of Munster's finest country houses and reclaimed the charred land on which they stood.

Land hunger was a powerful motivator in Civil War burnings; the most common category of arson attack in all three counties was the burning of crops and outhouses. Section 4 ('Land Redistribution') showed that the firing of hay stacks not only produced an impressive flare-up, but also real hardship consequently ensued from the loss of fodder, even for the strong farmer. In chasing out the victim and freeing up his land, arson must be added to the catalogue of intimidatory actions, explored in Chapter 4, employed directly to advance local redistribution. The havoc wreaked by arson, though, was particularly destructive and highly symbolic. House and crop burning could drive out the victim and purify the community of his presence. The prevalence of arson was not diminished proportionately in quieter counties, such as Waterford; in all three counties arson punished victims for their religion, politics and, above all else, their link with Britain.

Perpetrators of arson included the anti-Treaty IRA, organized labour and 'landless men'; arsonists were drawn from across the community and motivations for fire starting were complex (see Section 5). However, what cannot be denied was the significance of the act as a form of protest. Just before Thomas Power's hay rick was burned, the *Munster Express* reported, one of the Waterford farmer's workers 'said to him: "You are after getting a touch of Home Rule," and then added that the haggard was on fire.' The attack was attributed to Power's earlier dismissal of a worker and did not have 'anything to do with the political trouble'.[255] Nonetheless, the notion that Power had received a 'touch of Home Rule', through the burning of his hay, made a connection between political change (Irish independence) and the realization of social and economic goals; and this arsonist, like many others, did not discount violence as a means to achieve this.

[255] *Munster Express*, 21 January 1922.

4 The Right to Live in My Own Country

Intimidation, Expulsion and Local-Community Conflict

In January 1927, from the safe distance of Letchworth in Hertfordshire, James Coogan completed his application to the IGC.[1] After disbandment from the RIC at Dublin Castle in April 1922,[2] Coogan 'came to London direct, it being unsafe to go to Waterford, where my wife was residing . . . as all the disbanded RIC there had left, having received notices to quit the country or put up with the consequences'.[3] He then joined the 'little colony' of around fifty ex-constables and their families, which had formed in the English 'garden city' since 1922.[4] The IGC took into account allowances already received as an ex-constable and granted Coogan £40 compensation for losses associated with relocation to England. But it is the final claim on Coogan's list that provides the most revealing insight into his situation – and the themes of this chapter:

> I am deprived of living in my own country, where I consider I have just as much right to live as any member of the Irish Free State, this is a right I value very much and for which I at least claim £300.[5]

The placing of such a price tag (£13,300 in today's terms[6]) on the right to live in Ireland that demonstrates, if nothing else, some boldness on Coogan's part. He was not alone, of course, in his strong sense of personal entitlement, nor his attempts to frame the application in the language appropriate for financial reward.[7] But the Committee, unsurprisingly, ignored his claim. Coogan had not provided convincingly concrete evidence of how ill-feeling towards a representative of British rule in Ireland

[1] See Chapter 2 on compensation policy and procedure.

[2] Abbott, *Police casualties in Ireland*, 295: official dismissal and administration of pensions and severance pay took place at the Castle and a number of 'disbandment centres'. See Chapter 5 on the violent fate of some ex-officers.

[3] TNA, CO 762/80/3: Coogan, Waterford.

[4] *Clonmel Chronicle*, 16 December 1922.

[5] TNA, CO 762/80/3: Coogan, Waterford.

[6] See Glossary.

[7] See Chapter 2.

directly resulted, following the departure of the former rulers, in his removal from Waterford.

Intimidation creates a frightening atmosphere that is, by its very nature, hard to define. This chapter shows, however, that the threatening acts prevalent in Cos. Limerick, Tipperary and Waterford during 1922–3 had a very real effect on local life and intra-community relations. Thus Coogan's contemplation of his position in the Free State, whatever its worth in monetary terms, raises important questions. Were ideas of nationality and identity changing during the violent transition to independence? How and why did the threat of physical force, or psychological pressure, lead to the rejection – even 'expulsion' – of certain individuals and families from Ireland? Intimidation must be analyzed not simply as a local by-product of general disorder and the war over the Treaty, but as a symbolic and powerful act resulting not necessarily in injury or death, but, often, in loss of livelihood or the removal of the victim from his home, business or lands. Included in this category are boycott, damage to property, verbal and written threats, cattle driving, animal maiming and the seizure of land.

1. Threat and Flight

Despite its contemporary usage in victims' testimonies and government reports,[8] 'expulsion' remains a problematic term. The word suggests physical compulsion, literally forcing someone out of his home. Murder is the obvious, permanent removal of an enemy from the community; I address this form of violence in Chapter 5. This chapter, however, deals not with violence against the person, but actions that, from the victim's point of view, drove them from Munster.[9] The expulsion of an 'out-group' may be 'partly coerced, partly voluntary'; removal of this kind occurs when a minority reacts to ill-treatment – including cultural suppression, intimidation and physical coercion – by emigrating.[10] Delaney is right that 'threats of intimidation or revolutionary rhetoric did not necessarily lead' to mass emigration of the 'minority' populace (Protestants, Unionists and ex-British Servicemen) in Ireland during the revolutionary

[8] NAI, Records of the Department of the Taoiseach, S565: 'Threatened expulsion of Protestants in Ballina, Co. Mayo'.

[9] There is some overlap between the injuries categorized as 'intimidation' and offences included in Chapter 5, on violence against the person. However, the imposition of a schema which treats three 'types' of violence in three distinct chapters is helpful in imposing some order on the messy, violent behaviour with which we are faced.

[10] Mann, *Dark side of democracy*, 14.

years,[11] and this chapter further explores the dichotomy between choice, or voluntary migration, and expulsion – a contentious issue besetting a number of historical refugee crises.

The question of what turned an estimated 600,000 to 760,000 Palestinian Arabs out of their homes between November 1947 and October 1950, for example, remains a fundamental propaganda issue between the Palestinians and Israelis. Benny Morris challenges both the Arab claim (Jews expelled Palestine's Arabs as part of a systematic, political-military plan) and the official Israeli narrative (Palestinians fled 'voluntarily' or they were ordered to do so by their leaders and the leaders of other Arab states). He instead offers a more subtle analysis of the flight from Palestine, identifying four stages of 'exodus' and tracing the practical, financial and psychological pressures that caused the upper and middle classes – and then the masses – to 'pack up and flee' the Jewish state to be.[12] Events in the Middle East represent, of course, a conflict of a vastly different scale and intensity to the Civil War studied here. However, I argue that intimidation was used deliberately in Munster, as allegedly it was in Palestine, to clear out a target group. This controversial claim is borne out, in Ireland at least, by the compensation evidence I have examined.

In terms of their decision to leave Munster in 1922, Patrick and Marion Courtney look to have had little, reasonable choice in the matter. This former constable of the RIC and his wife suffered no physical injuries in the attacks against them, but were removed from Loughill, Co. Limerick, in what the State Solicitor reviewing the compensation claim for the Free State Government deemed a 'very cruel case'. The perpetrators took 'forcible possession' of the house in May 1922, wrecking its furniture and contents. Courtney described how the intimidation continued as he fled: the attackers 'tried to prevent me [getting] to the Railway Station' and threatening notices were posted on Courtney's land, warning off prospective buyers.[13] The ex-policeman could neither sell the land nor return to it. He was still living in London in February 1927 when, after receipt of compensation from the Free State, he made his application to the IGC.

It is also unlikely that Thomas Hogan – threatened with a gun and 'forced to flee to England' – even contemplated staying in Munster. On 5 April 1922, he was 'compelled to leave my country by Forces of the

[11] Chapter 2, Section 3a.

[12] B. Morris, *The birth of the Palestinian refugee problem revisited*, 2nd ed. (Cambridge, 2004), 591.

[13] NAI, 392/18: Courtney, Limerick (Records of the Ministry of Finance, Un-catalogued compensation files: Series 392 [Limerick], 401 [Tipperary], 402 [Waterford]).

enemy acting in opposition to the Provisional Government of Ireland'. Hogan was living in Belfast when he applied to the IGC for compensation for the loss of his dentistry business in Thomas Street, Limerick, and the 'injury to health' caused by the traumatic episode (Hogan did not in the end receive his award, because he died in May 1927).[14] It is worth noting that migration from the Free State to Northern Ireland, after 1922, was 'not inconsiderable'.[15] However, others were less convinced than Hogan of the imminent danger and need to leave. In Co. Tipperary, William Carey's 'dwelling house' was damaged and his possessions destroyed when a 'party of armed men' fired into the premises with rifles, revolvers and stones, for two hours. The men 'used threats to Claimant regarding land in his possession', but Carey did not surrender his farm.[16] As Darby points out in his study of community relations during the Northern Ireland Troubles, one person's response to intimidation may be explained by his personality or domestic circumstances, as much as by reality itself.[17]

Feelings of unease during the Civil War were no doubt influenced, for example, by previous experiences of rejection or intimidation under British rule. The very terms of reference of the IGC reflect at least the British Government's expectation that ex-Servicemen, constables and other political or cultural 'Loyalists' would be punished, under the new, Irish regime, for their previous loyalty to the crown: claimants had to prove that injury suffered during the Civil War was 'occasioned in respect or on account of... allegiance to the Government of the United Kingdom prior to the Truce of 9 July 1921'.[18] There is no doubt that Constable William Hall, for example, suffered for his pre-independence British allegiance. The stripping of uniforms or military decorations is a 'particularly humiliating experience' for soldiers;[19] in June 1921, in Shanagolden, Hall was stripped of his uniform, which was burned when he refused to resign from the RIC. Hall was on sick leave and had been visiting the local dispensary with another constable, Huckerly, when they were 'surrounded by eight armed men', ordered to take off their 'boots, stockings and caps' and told to return, barefoot, to their native Foynes, Co. Limerick.[20] A

14 TNA, CO 762/66/17: Hogan, Limerick. He also applied directly to Free State Government for help: NAI, Records of the Ministry of Finance, FIN 1/1078: 'Compensation of victimised Loyalists': Thomas D. Hogan.

15 M. Daly, *The slow failure: Population decline and independent Ireland, 1922–1973* (Madison, WI: University of Wisconsin Press, 2006), 6.

16 NAI, 401/1076: Carey, Tipperary.

17 Darby, *Intimidation and the control of conflict in Northern Ireland*, 54–6.

18 IGC Terms of Reference printed on all compensation forms; see Chapter 2.

19 Gerwarth, 'The Central European counter-revolution', *P&P*, 188–9.

20 *Irish Times*, 4 September 1920.

more difficult question to answer, however, is whether it was this earlier, pre-1922 episode, or the arrival of independence and ensuing Civil War, that made Hall leave Ireland. After disbandment, Hall had been due to take up his sister's shop in Foynes, but his wife was 'threatened' there and the couple fled to Essex in May 1922.[21] Their new home, Chadwell Heath, apparently was becoming another Irish 'colony', like Letchworth: the Halls were joined there by, for example, Bridget Meade, who left Limerick city for England in April 1922, after being 'repeatedly insulted and threatened'.[22] Gerard Murphy has located other Irish havens in England. He suggests that Protestants and Loyalists who fled Cork in 1922 'did not move far from where they landed'; small Irish communities formed in Swansea, Bristol, Plymouth and Bournemouth.[23]

The experiences of claimants such as Hall, Meade and Coogan,[24] who also left before the Civil War began in earnest, complicate the notion of 'expulsion'. It is difficult to pinpoint the precise reason why, or moment when, the victim felt sufficiently 'intimidated' to leave his home or job. Surely the intimidated party retained some control over his own destiny? Financial circumstances did play a part. Darby includes 'social class' as a determinant in the effectiveness of intimidation in driving out the sectarian enemy: early evacuees from the Belfast communities he studied often were families with higher incomes, who left behind those locked in an unpleasant environment by their deprivation.[25] And the first to leave Palestine during 1947–50 were the country's urban upper- and middle-class families from towns such as Haifa and Jaffa. These evacuees had 'wealthy relatives and accommodation outside the country' (in Beirut, Cairo and elsewhere) and probably expected to return home before long. Businesses closed and municipal services broke down after their departure; the privileged left behind the poor and unemployed, for whom flight meant instant destitution.[26]

The evidence from the Irish Civil War also suggests it was easier for those already spending time outside Munster, with a safety net in Dublin or England, to flee violence than it was for victims of intimidation whose livelihoods were already precarious and who lacked the capital to set up a new life elsewhere. Both governments lacked sympathy in their handling of the claims of landlords and big house owners,[27] claims in which the

[21] TNA, CO 762/122/7: Hall, Limerick.
[22] TNA, CO 762/120/4: Meade, Limerick.
[23] Murphy, *The year of disappearances*, 326–7.
[24] See earlier discussion and introduction to this chapter.
[25] Darby, *Intimidation and the control of conflict in Northern Ireland*, 89–90.
[26] Morris, *Birth of the Palestinian refugee problem revisited*, 112, 133, 590.
[27] See Chapter 3.

victims' intermittent absence from Ireland before the Civil War somewhat undermined their claims of being 'driven out'. John Fillans Barr, for example, was 'not exempt from responsibility' for the attack against his property, which took place *after* he 'fled to England'. In the 'heaviest claim' considered by the IGC, Barr was awarded £53,600 for the damage inflicted by a 'roving band of Irregulars' to his 'beautiful Georgian mansion', Killineer House, Co. Louth. The victim argued that he was 'so affected by the outrages' against him, which included an attempted assassination in September 1922, that he was 'not fully capable' of protecting himself and 'could not return' to Ireland to make a claim under the Free State Act. He was forced out, in other words. In the IGC's opinion, Barr had more choice in the matter: he was a man of vast resources, with interests in shipbuilding and commerce, but he had failed to take 'adequate steps to protect' his house by, for example, hiring a caretaker.[28]

Both the British and Free State administrations displayed sympathy, on the other hand, in compensating poorer claimants. William Walker, for example, had served thirty-two years in the RIC and, after his death, his widow Rachel was intimidated,[29] having been left, like other ex-police wives, 'at the mercy of those who were their bitterest enemies'.[30] During 'armed raids' in 1922, Walker's crops were destroyed, her gates broken and water supply polluted. The widow could not escape the persecution because her dire financial circumstances forced her to stay put in Adare, Co. Limerick. Walker had no pension and 'no shop will run credit with me',[31] although this may have been as much the result of her social ostracism from the local community as it was to do with her inability to pay. Help came instead from the IGC[32] and SILRA, an organization established to raise awareness and funds for those, such as Walker, who had no choice but to remain in an intimidating environment. 'Open hostility' to the widows and children of RIC men was 'non-evident', reported SILRA, as late as 1929, but 'anyone who knows Ireland can realise the sullen feeling of resentment which exists against them owing to their late husbands' services'.[33]

These 'sullen feelings' did sometimes have a more tangible manifestation during the Civil War but, as this chapter shows, victims did not

28 TNA, CO 762/184/3: Barr, Louth.
29 TNA, CO 762/143/12: Walker, Limerick.
30 PRONI, D/989/B/5/2.
31 TNA, CO 762/143/12: Walker, Limerick.
32 The IGC awarded Walker £150 (£6,670 in today's terms and a generous sum considering she asked for just £50 in her initial claim).
33 PRONI, D/989/B/5/2. See Chapter 2 on SILRA and its work.

have to experience actual physical harm to feel afraid enough to leave. 'Perceived environmental threat' is important in understanding the effects of intimidation.[34] During the early stages of the Palestinian exodus, for example, families did not flee under Jewish orders or direct coercion but, 'as Zionist troops conquered town after town and district after district', the desire to move out of harm's way must have been a powerful motivating factor in their departure. In an atmosphere of 'war-filled chaos', those with the resources to leave understandably did so before suffering violence themselves.[35] In Munster, the 'feeling of unease or impression that intimidation might occur'[36] suffused many local communities during the Civil War. Fear is personal and unquantifiable in any real sense; 'psychological violence may inflict scars as enduring as they are impossible to measure'.[37] The mental trauma experienced by civilians and soldiers during the War of Independence and the Civil War certainly did not emerge in the neat, linear fashion conducive to the operation of government compensation committees with strict terms and dates of reference. To this day, post-combat disorders have the capacity to 'catch both military planners and doctors by surprise'.[38] However, World War I – and growing post-war suspicions that soldiers shot for cowardice and desertion may have been suffering from war neuroses – encouraged a revision of attitudes towards, and improvements in the treatment of, psychological distress. It had become clear, for example, that the 'nervous disorders . . . and hysteria' associated with 'shell shock', a term coined during the American Civil War, originated from other causes than shock from exploding missiles.[39]

In response to claims from victims of the Irish Civil War, the IGC included 'shock' in its definition of 'physical injuries': if a bomb misses the body but wrecks the victim's mind, one 'cannot say he has not been physically injured'. Examples from this category include the 'nervous breakdown' of a woman who had been compelled to witness her husband's murder and the 'insanity' caused by 'persistent nightly raids'. The 'relation between fright and injury to the brain and nervous structure'

[34] Darby, *Intimidation and the control of conflict in Northern Ireland*, 54.

[35] Morris, *Birth of the Palestinian refugee problem revisited*, 589.

[36] Darby, *Intimidation and the control of conflict in Northern Ireland*, 53–4.

[37] L. Perry Curtis, 'Moral and physical force: The language of violence in Irish nationalism', *JBS* 27, no. 2 (1988), 150–89 at 158.

[38] E. Jones, 'Historical approaches to post-combat disorders', *Philosophical Transactions of the Royal Society: Biological Sciences* 361 (2006), 533–42 at 533.

[39] A. Babington, *Shell shock: A history of the changing attitude to war neurosis* (London: Leo Cooper, 1997), 106, 108–09, 122, 127, 136.

could be 'proved with medical and scientific testimony', the End of Committee Report claimed (although medical records were rarely provided in compensation cases, at least not in the claims I studied).[40] Victims also reflected themselves on the effect of repeated intimidation on the psyche. In a handwritten letter to Cosgrave, William Ross asked for £1,000 compensation for the 'shock' sustained by his wife 'owing to explosion and street fighting' in Nenagh between 29 June 1922 and 7 September 1922. The pressure had become too much for the family: forced out of his 'market gardening business', Ross was now struggling to support his family in Eardisley, Herefordshire.[41] Other testimonies, by contrast, made a more direct link between targeted intimidation (as opposed to the general state of war) and psychological trauma. Ex-policeman Thomas Needham, for example, claimed that the 'great mental anxiety that weighed upon' him, following assassination threats received between October 1921 and February 1922, forced him to stay in England until 1923 and caused the illness for which he sought compensation. In the end, the IGC ruled that the injuries described 'must have been sustained whilst on duty with the RIC'; they were not connected with the Civil War and the claim was dismissed as outside the scope of the committee (although Needham may well have taken advantage of the specific compensation, pension arrangements and charitable help available for ex-Servicemen and RIC).[42]

Niamh Brennan has found that whilst a 'substantial proportion' of former officers permanently left Ireland in 1922 and joined police forces in Palestine, Northern Ireland and England, others eventually returned after 1923, 'when political stability restored'.[43] However, Richard Abbott identifies a number of constables who simply 'walked away' from the force without, like Needham, even claiming financial remuneration. Whilst these ex-policemen were not necessarily traumatized by their experiences in Ireland, some undoubtedly felt 'compelled to leave', and leave quickly, 'given the situation in the country'.[44] SILRA presented Catherine Kelly's application to the IGC on her behalf, giving weight to her claim that intimidation had affected her husband so badly that he died

[40] TNA, CO 762/212: 'End of Committee Report'.
[41] NAI, FIN 1/2388: William Ross.
[42] TNA, CO 762/162/4: Needham, Tipperary. See Chapter 2, Section 2b, on help for Loyalists and ex-policemen.
[43] Brennan's unpublished research, based on compensation claims, is referenced in Delaney, *Demography, state and society*.
[44] Abbott, *Police casualties in Ireland*, 295.

in Clonmel Lunatic Asylum in February 1926. Kelly's tailoring business, in Silver Street, Nenagh, was boycotted because her husband had served in the RIC and, in this 'very genuine' case, there was 'no doubt whatever' that the ex-policeman 'became demented . . . owing to the terror under which he lived', including the receipt of threatening letters, 1921–2.[45]

The compensation claims capture the threatening atmosphere in Munster, where a violent undercurrent could become explicit if certain social and political codes were transgressed. It was 'well locally understood', for example, that the purchasers of Denis Murphy's lands in Cashel, Co. Tipperary, 'would be intimidated'. On 8 April 1922, Murphy told the IGC, he was given 'three days to leave Ireland by the IRA'. But he could not sell the house: 'no one will touch it because it once belonged to "spud Murphy"', his nickname as a British Government detective. His letter of October 1927 to the Secretary of the IGC revealed that, seven years after he was first 'blacklisted', Murphy remained a traitor in the eyes of the local community:

> Even should I succeed in repairing and getting a tenant, I would then become an English landlord and get no rent. I found the same old ill-feeling towards me, and actions against 'dead and alive' old Sinn Fein leaders remembered.[46]

There was local appreciation, too, of the danger of informing. Rachel Walker (discussed previously) told the IGC that she did not report the attacks against her, until May 1927, because 'we were warned that if we made any complaint we would be burnt out'.[47] Thus the targeting of individuals needed the cooperation or at least complicity of the community: Walker was injured not merely by the acts of a small gang of the IRA, but was also made to feel unwelcome in a wider context. For intimidation to work, for the victim to be genuinely convinced that reporting the initial attack would result in, for example, the burning of his home, he had to believe that speaking to the authorities would be noted locally. Victims of violence in Munster had to face the 'unpalatable truth' at the heart of civil warfare:[48] former friends and neighbours now condoned attacks against them. In only a few cases were perpetrators of intimidation named by the victim, but ex-policeman Patrick Courtney,[49] for one, claimed that

45 TNA, CO 762/180/16: Kelly, Tipperary.
46 TNA, CO 762/5/6: Murphy, Tipperary. Also made claim as 'Victimised Loyalist' directly to Irish Ministry of Finance: NAI, FIN 1/1086.
47 TNA, CO 762/143/12: Walker, Limerick.
48 Blok, *Honour and violence*, 5.
49 See earlier discussion in this section.

he was forced out by John Griffin, Robert Jones and James and Thomas O'Shaughnessy, 'all in the village of Loughill'.[50]

Armed personnel also recognized the importance of the intra-community dynamics of civil warfare, of the destructive potential of neighbourhood animosities. Indeed, whilst intimidation includes less conventional forms of warfare – threatening notices, attacks on land and animals, and boycotting – it still had military utility. If the Irish people could not be inspired into 'Republican enthusiasm' by great gestures of violence,[51] Ernie O'Malley understood well the usefulness of intimidation in cajoling and controlling the local population. The IRA policy of executing alleged spies and traitors during the War of Independence, for example, served as a warning of the dangers of loose talk. By 1922–3, O'Malley recalled, 'people eventually learned to shut their eyes and close their mouths'. O'Malley himself was engaged in intimidatory tactics. He defied Lynch's order to kill the editors of newspapers (the *Irish Independent* and the *Irish Times*) unsympathetic towards the republicans, but he 'did write intimidatingly' to the press during the Civil War.[52]

2. Written Warnings and Threatening Letters

History taught the recipient of a threatening letter to take this form of intimidation very seriously. The authorities also took heed: a familiar form of rural protest in Britain and Ireland, the posting of intimidating notices was logged as a distinct category of injury in nineteenth-century crime statistics.[53] British Government Intelligence Notes from the early twentieth century catalogued 'threatening letters or notices' as an indictable 'agrarian offence . . . affecting the public peace'.[54] Demands for money, goods, or the recipient's removal from the area, accompanied by warnings of the punishments to be expected for non-compliance, induced extreme anxiety and 'justified forms of paranoia'.[55]

Quasi-legal language framed threatening letters as orders that must be obeyed. It is difficult to ascertain whether the typed sheets contained

50 NAI, 392/18: Courtney, Limerick. See also Chapter 5: some victims of violence against the person knew their attacker.

51 English, *Ernie O'Malley*, 78–9.

52 English, *Ernie O'Malley*, 80.

53 Curtis, 'Moral and physical force', *JBS*, 184.

54 TNA, CO 903/19 (Records of the Colonial Office, Records of the Irish Office: Intelligence notes for the Chief Secretary).

55 Thompson, 'The crime of anonymity', in D. Hay, *Albion's fatal tree: Crime and society in eighteenth-century England* (London: Penguin Books, 1977), 255–308 at 255.

in some compensation files are the actual notices received at the time. However, a number of interesting letters, copies or otherwise, do survive. Retired RIC Sergeant Maurice Reidy, a 'native' of Glin, Co. Limerick, received the following whilst stationed in Co. Galway:

Brigade Head Quarters
East Connemara
30 April 1922

To Mr Reidy,

You and your family are to leave this Divisional Area within 24 hours. If at the expiration of that period you have failed to obey this order you must be prepared to take the consequences.

BY ORDER,
O/C 4th Western Division.

Based on experience and hearsay, Reidy no doubt had his own idea of what 'the consequences' would involve: the burning of his house, assault, perhaps murder? He did not stay to find out, moving to Ballyhahill, Co. Limerick, where, in May 1922, the family was served with a second notice, signed 'J.T. O'C, O/C, IRA Barracks, Foynes'.[56] Again, Reidy took heed of the threat, travelling to and from Dublin and his home in Glin, in fear of being found. His compensation claims to the Free State[57] and IGC relate to the cost of these trips and the damage to furniture in transit.

A straightforward demand had been heeded; a former representative of the British state in Ireland was removed from the community. But why was Reidy so convinced of the threat to his life should he remain at home? Did the letter genuinely draw authority from the IRA? Free State Army reports did identify the posting of threatening notices as an Irregular tactic during the war. Notices served to 'local residents' in parts of South Tipperary and Co. Limerick in March 1923 dictated that anyone found 'aiding or abetting the National Army will be given 12 hours notice to quit the district'.[58] A number of authority figures in Tipperary, including the Chairman of the County Council, the chairman of Cashel Urban Council and sheriff of Clonmel, received

56 TNA, CO 762/144/11: Reidy, Limerick.
57 NAI, 392/451: Reidy, Limerick.
58 IMA, CW/OPS/2/M.

the following, signed by republican leaders Dinny Lacey and William Quirke:

> Should any officer or man of the 3rd Tipp. Brigade Area be executed in or outside the Brigade Area you, and certain members of your Board will be deemed participants in the crime and will be dealt with accordingly. War, Truce, or Peace.[59]

These local threats echo orders issued by IRA Chief-of-Staff Liam Lynch and circulated in the press throughout the war, following the execution of republican prisoners for retaliation killings of government officials and the burning of Senators' homes.[60] Posters put up by 'armed Irregulars' in Glin and Ballylongford, for example, read 'That for every Republican shot, two Staters would fall'.[61] Even relatively minor acts of destruction were accompanied by written warnings. In December 1922, the Free State Army's Limerick Command encountered Irregulars 'affixing up notices to trees which they had felled', in Kanturk, Co. Cork.[62]

Violence was a powerful means of communication and notices or letters reinforced the message of the violent act. Republicans could not defeat the Free State militarily, but they did succeed in inflicting severe blows against infrastructure and undermining the authority of the new government in the localities. Blowing up roads and bridges, and tearing up rails, disrupted communications. The intimidation of postmen through written warnings made sure the mail service was unable to function. Notices posted near Listowel, Co. Kerry, for example, warned postmen that they would be shot if they carried out their duties.[63] The intimidation of jurors during the War of Independence had worked in a similar way: violence weakened the grip of the British state on law and order in Ireland and upheld an alternative system of Dáil courts. Then, during the Civil War, republicans rejected the Free State's new police force, Garda Síochána (the Civic Guard), as a 'continuation of the old RIC'. A 'proclamation' signed by Lacey on 22 November 1922 warned 'members of the "Civic Guard"' that, after 1 December 1922, 'such measures as are deemed necessary will be taken to prevent this body functioning'. Safe passage would be granted to Guards returning to 'civil employment', provided they gave a 'written undertaking not to take up arms against, nor to assist in any way, the enemies of the Republic'.[64]

59 *Clonmel Chronicle*, 7 February, 24 February and 7 March 1923.
60 See Chapter 3, Section 2 and Chapter 5, Section 1.
61 IMA, CW/OPS/3/C.
62 IMA, CW/OPS/2/B.
63 IMA, CW/OPS/3/C.
64 IMA, Captured Documents, Lot No. 110, A/1100.

By communicating in these quasi-official missives, the anti-Treaty IRA was, in a sense, administering an alternative government to the Free State apparatus. The republicans thus distanced themselves from actions that did not help their cause, denying involvement in, for example, the intimidation of 'postal officials' in Limerick in July 1922. 'R.G. Hetherington, P. and J. Waldron and T.J. Phelan' were visited by 'masked and armed men' in their homes and served with 'orders to leave Ireland'. These 'outrages' were attributed 'to personal spite on the part of unauthorised individuals' and Stephen O'Mara, Mayor of Limerick, agreed to an 'inquiry'.[65] Labour disputes seemingly explain this occurrence of intimidation.[66] Irish Government plans to cut postal workers' wages had been causing resentment in the summer of 1922 and a Post Office strike began on 10 September. Services were interrupted across the twenty-six counties until work resumed on 30 September. Limerick was particularly 'hard hit': the city's Chamber of Commerce warned of a collapse of trade and unemployment, should the dispute continue.[67] Intimidation, including threatening notices, was used as a kind of picketing, to deter 'scabs' from returning to work. The *Irish Times* published the Post Office's own list of 'cases of alleged intimidation' of postmen, telephone operators and clerks. The father of one female worker in Waterford, for example, was told 'that if he did not want his little business interrupted in the city, he should keep his daughter at home'.[68] In Dublin, people carrying letters for others were 'stopped and deprived of them'. One woman was 'intimidated' and assaulted, for carrying post in her handbag.[69]

Intimidation was clearly not the sole preserve of the republicans. Historians and social scientists have developed Thompson's 'moral economy' thesis to show how even loosely aligned groups of people use violence to enact social change and uphold collectively held moral codes.[70] Before 'boycott' was even coined as a phrase,[71] election mobs used social ostracism and intimidation to influence public opinion and sway the vote in pre-Reform parliamentary elections.[72] However, even if IRA authorship could not irrefutably be proved, the Civil War's most effective threatening

65 *Limerick Leader*, 3 July 1922.

66 See Chapter 3, Section 5b: disputes between employers and workers also resulted in the burning of crops, creameries and saw mills.

67 *Irish Times*, 15 September 1922.

68 *Irish Times*, 18 September 1922.

69 *Irish Times*, 30 September 1922.

70 See Introduction on definitions of 'social violence'.

71 See Section 6.

72 G.J. Lyne, 'Daniel O'Connell, intimidation and the Kerry elections of 1835', *Journal of the Kerry Archaeological and Historical Society* 4 (1971), 74–97.

notices were those in which, so the recipient believed, an armed power (namely the republicans) lay behind the order to leave the area.

Ada Vere-Hunt of Longfield House, Cashel, Co. Tipperary, received the following unsigned letter, but told the IGC it was Andy Donnelly, the 'officer in charge of the Mid-Tipperary Division' of the IRA, who cleared the family out:

Mrs Hunt,

You bloody Protestant you needn't think the staters are going to get Longfields back for you we will put decent Catholics in your husbands place. We'll give you what we gave Clarke if ye set a foote in it, ye made a dear a bargain when ye kept money from us.[73]

Clarke is the owner of the Tipperary mansion, Graiguenoe Park, burned on 28 February 1923.[74] After two months of serious pressure, including threatening letters, the killing of cattle and raids on their home by a 'large crowd of rebels', Ada and Robert Vere-Hunt were finally driven out of Longfields in June 1922. Two years passed before the couple 'set a foote' on their lands again. They moved into their adjoining property, Ardmayle, near Cashel, until this was no longer safe, and then spent time away from Co. Tipperary and Ireland. Their compensation file records stays in Belgium and at hotels in Dublin and Westport (Co. Mayo). Claims also were made for expenses incurred in sending the Vere-Hunt children away with a nurse, during the more disruptive periods of 1922. A range of tactics had been used to remove this prominent family from the county, and – in their compensation file – we get some insight into the perpetrators' motivations, as well as the convergence of land hunger, sectarianism and anti-British sentiment in this series of attacks. The Vere-Hunts were clearly identifiable as Protestants and 'Loyalists': they had entertained a column of the Lincolnshire Regiment at Longfield House, in early 1921. The threatening letter Ada received is a boast as well as a warning: there is no date, but it sounds as though 'Longfields' had already been seized by the raiders at the time of writing and the Vere-Hunts – along with the new 'stater' government charged with their protection – were helpless to resist the land for the people project. The land was not cleared by Free State troops and possession returned to the family's agent until August 1924. According to this land agent, interviewed during the IGC investigation, the Vere-Hunts' property had

73 TNA, CO 762/5/3: Vere-Hunt, Tipperary.
74 See Chapter 3.

been 'coveted for some years by landless men in the vicinity'. The family took 'Longfields' on a ten-year lease from 1919, an acquisition with which the local IRA were allegedly unhappy; the unpaid money referred to in the letter relates to the frequent, and ignored, demands made of the Vere-Hunts, by the IRA, for a levy on the land.[75]

The relationship between anti-Treaty republicanism and land agitation is contentious.[76] A letter received by Ned Wynne, of Outrath, near Cahir, Co. Tipperary, seems to implicate the republicans in what would otherwise be characterized as a neighbours' squabble over land. A woman, Mrs Mulcahy, was evicted for non-payment of rent in 1893 and the holding in question passed to an agent, before being purchased, through the Land Commission, by Captain Bloomfield in 1908. Wynne bought Bloomfield's share but, when he put the land up for auction in April 1921, the sale was 'rendered abortive' by 'descendents' of the evicted woman, even though Wynne's land agent found no connection between these individuals and the land, reporting that relations were 'friendly' between the owner and Mulcahy. It was 'the IRA', Wynne claimed, that 'put [me] out of my farm', so as to divide the land 'amongst the men who had been "on the run"'. A copy of the letter he received before his departure outlines the republicans' designs on the 212-acre property:

H.Q. Bn. 1
3rd Tipp. Bde.
I.R.A. Barracks, Fethard
22/2/22

To Mr Ned Wynne, Outrath, Cahir.

(1) You will hand over the lands in Outrath held by you at present before March 10th 1922, to Captain J. Longeran, for the I.R.A.
(2) You will remove all your stock by then off the farm.
(3) No Agricultural Impliments [sic] will be removed, or sold, by you unless you get orders from us to do so.

No furniture to be removed unless ordered.

(Signed) J.D.L. Commandant

We assume 'J.D.L' to be Capt J. Longeran, IRA, to whom Wynne was ordered to give up his farm. He did leave on 1 May 1922, losing his land, his 'practically new' machinery and valuable cattle (the young ones, he complained, had cost £34 each). Wynne understood the grants received

[75] TNA, CO 762/5/3: Vere-Hunt, Tipperary.
[76] See Section 5.

from the 'Imperial Government' would be deducted from any compensation received, but hoped the Irish Government would offer a fair award, so he could make a new life in his wife's native Co. Cork.[77]

The warnings received by Wynne, the Vere-Hunts and Reidy look like military orders and the targets responded with due urgency. The communications are also reminiscent of threatening letters received by land agents and shopkeepers during the Land War, or notices posted during earlier, eighteenth-century agrarian agitation. The ICCA (a lobbying group like SILRA) gathered some letters as evidence in support of its statement to the House of Lords. The following was posted on Lord Ashtown's Woodlawn estate (Ballinasloe, Co. Galway):

> I hereby give you notice not to aid or assist in working on the grasslands of Woodlawn as the country wants the same for small tenants and means to fight for them to the bitter end.
>
> Remember this goes from the hillside Committee. Abide by what I have said or the next notice you will get will be powder and led.
>
> Signed,
> Roary of the hill
> who always gives notice
> before he does kill.[78]

'Roary [Rory] of the Hill' succeeded 'Molly Maguire', in the 1870s, as the ubiquitous 'righter of wrongs' in agrarian conflicts.[79] That resistance of oppression or injustice would come from the mountains was constantly referenced in letters from this period. Parnell also appealed to the 'hillside men' in his speeches.[80] The 'hillside committee' in communication with Ashtown appealed to this tradition. Civil War letters borrowed other sinister Land War motifs, such as a hand-drawn coffin containing the recipient's name. Robert Swanton JP and his son George, also a magistrate, received the following, on 31 July 1881:

> One thing more I have to say
> Is to shun those peelers without delay
> And not to give the country say
> That you should be a traitor
> Robert, George, and Daly too!
> Woe be to them, for I am true,
> A Croppy-still for ever.

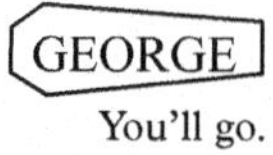

You'll go.

77 NAI, FIN 1/1079: Edward Wynne.
78 PRONI, D/989/B/2/9.
79 W.E. Vaughan, *Landlords and tenants in mid-Victorian Ireland* (Oxford, 1994), 152.
80 D.G. Boyce and A. O'Day, *Parnell in perspective* (London: Routledge, 1991), 4, 300.

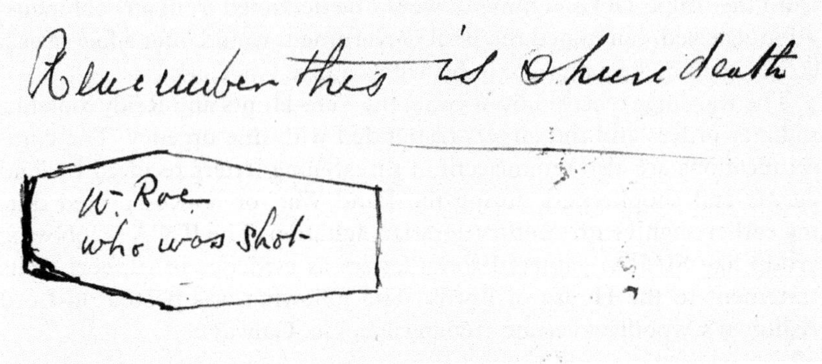

Figure 5. Extract from threatening letter received by Willie Roe, a Protestant shopkeeper in Lismore, Co. Waterford.

Richard Daly, also mentioned in the letter, had his house burned and a notice posted: 'I will stain my hands in your blood. . . . Yours truly, Captain Moonlight'. And 'Croppy' probably harks back to an epithet of the rebels of 1798, who wore their hair cut very short as a sign of sympathy with the French Revolution. 'Despite its crude execution', irregularly written on an old envelope, 'such a notice carried a definitely political message'.[81] Compare with the 'grave warning' received by Protestant shopkeeper, Willie Roe, on 8 May 1922; see Figure 5.[82] Just as the Swantons' role in law enforcement in Ireland, and cooperation with the 'peelers' (RIC), had marked them out for attack some forty years earlier, so Roe's letter, of 1922, rebuked the shopkeeper as an 'informer' of the 'Black and Tans'. Issued by the 'O/C South Battalion' of the IRA at Barrack Street, Cappoquin, Co. Waterford, the letter ordered Roe to 'clear out [or] we will riddle you with bullets when you least expect it'. At the bottom of the page was a final warning, 'Remember this is sure death', and a small drawing of coffin. 'W. Roe, who was shot' was written inside.

Thus whilst many of the letters in circulation during 1922–3 were of a childish, 'illiterate type',[83] and alleged IRA authorship rarely could be proved, the notices made use of historic codes of warning and escalation to make a powerful impact in a modern setting – and were genuinely frightening to recipients such as Roe.

[81] Townshend, *Political violence in Ireland*, 111–12.
[82] See Section 6, for Roe's case in full.
[83] *Clonmel Chronicle* (17 June 1922) describes a letter received by a land auctioneer; see Chapter 3, Section 4.

Indeed, whilst the idea that the Civil War provided the opportunity for airing long-held resentments is appealing, there is also reason to be aware, as ever in the study of the Irish past, of the cleverly rationalized use of history for modern purposes. The profile of those targeted by intimidation reveals that the battle raging in Munster's communities was not a straightforward continuation of the Land War, or expression of anger at the Cromwellian confiscations, but a campaign for redistribution directed, in the main, at the graziers and medium-sized farmers who had recently acquired land, or held more than one, or a larger than average, farm. In the 1870s, reflected D.P. Moran, 'the issue between rack-rented and insecure tenants, and . . . cruel, worthless and foreign landlordism, was fairly clear cut'. At the time of Moran's writing, by contrast, during the Ranch War, land agitation was a more 'complex and more dangerous problem', involving 'neighbour against neighbour, Irishman against Irishman'.[84] Certainly the fight against the grazier could never generate the 'rich popular resonance' of the Land Wars against the landlord. Yet even if, as Paul Bew claims, the historiography has 'exaggerated' the 'extent of anti-grazier hostility' during the early twentieth century,[85] Section 3 demonstrates that in Munster, at least, these tensions ran high well into the Civil War.

3. Cattle Driving

D.J. Corey TD did not think 'the question of ordinary land purchase' would continue to cause problems in Ireland in 1923, but 'ranch breaking will be a troublesome question'.[86] During 1922–3, Munster definitely saw a revival of tactics made famous during the Ranch War. Indeed, amongst the range of violent and threatening acts I have labelled 'intimidation', those associated with the land, including 'ranch breaking' (cattle driving) and the seizure of farms, provided a real opportunity for local involvement. As the 'only equipment needed' for a drive were 'hazel switches, willing hands and, perhaps, a fife and drum band, the activity could be carried out spontaneously and with little organizational structure'.[87] The 'atmosphere of festivity' does not mean that cattle drives

84 P. Bew, *Conflict and conciliation, 1890–1910: Parnellites and radical agrarians* (Oxford: Clarendon Press, 1987), 149.

85 Bew, *Conflict and conciliation*, 208.

86 *Dáil Éireann Debates* (http://historical-debates.oireachtas.ie), ii, 5 January 1923.

87 W. Keaveney, *The land for the people: Robert Henry Johnstone and the United Irish League; A story of land agitation in the early twentieth century* (Dublin: Lios Rua, 2007), 179.

were participated in on a whim,[88] but many local people were willing to condone this form of rural action. It was undoubtedly easier for those who did not usually engage in criminal activity to rationalize participation in a group cattle-drive than in, say, the burning of a big house, which could be difficult and dangerous. Whilst many were tired of the disruption to travel and daily life caused by the fighting, on the other hand a local community's tolerance of some acts of violence and intimidation was an important factor in their persistence.[89] At the heart of cattle driving was the community's desire to regulate access to land and its reoccurrence in this period, in Cos. Limerick, Tipperary and Waterford, reveals the political and socio-economic motivations of those, including non-military personnel, who took violence into their own hands during the Civil War.

On a drive, cattle and sheep were scattered far and wide, causing great trouble for their owner, the hated 'grazier'. The origins of this resentment lie further back but, just as the Land War insult 'land grabber' was employed in contemporary accounts of the Ranch War,[90] so the compensation claims prove that the term 'grazier' had heightened currency as a derogatory label during the Civil War.[91] That Jane Hartigan of Croom, Co. Limerick, had 'let my lands to a Grazer', for example, was crucial evidence in her case: 'the Grazer's Cattle has been driven on several occasions and on the 31st March [1922], his hay was burnt with my out offices on my Lands'.[92] British land legislation had undermined landlordism and enabled tenants to purchase their land, but it did not create tillage for all, nor solve rural poverty. After the Wyndham Act (1903), the decreasing supply of marketable land saw rich farmers and small-town businessmen use the 'eleven month system' to accumulate large ranches of untenanted land.[93] Sixty per cent of the total acreage of Co. Waterford, for example, lay with just 12 per cent of occupiers, by the time of the Civil War.[94] Indeed, the progress of land purchase in the three counties did not compare particularly well with Munster as a

[88] C. Deutsch-Brady, 'The cattle drive of Tulira', *Journal of the Galway Archaeological and Historical Society*, 34 (1974–75), 35–39 at 36.

[89] See Chapter 5: for those who are not normally bloodthirsty, civil war provides opportunities for 'indirect' violence.

[90] Bew, *Conflict and conciliation*, 162.

[91] Persecuted 'graziers' include: TNA, CO 762/49/12: Davern, Limerick; NAI, 392/434: Barrett, Limerick; CO 762/59/18: Wilmott-Smith, Limerick.

[92] NAI, 392/517: Hartigan, Limerick.

[93] Landlords were not legally bound to recognize a tenant's right on land let for eleven months; legislation applied only to yearly tenancies. See Bew, *Conflict and conciliation*, 205, 11. John Bourke's lands were held 'under the eleven month system' and during the Civil War his cattle was driven: NAI, 392/282: Bourke, Limerick.

[94] *Munster Express*, 13 January 1923.

whole, nor with other parts of Ireland: by 1923, 76 per cent of the total acreage of Limerick had been purchased by tenants under the Land Acts of 1881–1909. The figures for Tipperary and Waterford were 61 per cent and 56 per cent respectively.[95] In the eyes of those scraping a living off small plots, particularly in the congested West of Ireland, grazing was a waste of fertile land and untenanted pasture held directly by the landlord a tantalizing prospect. Thus the object of cattle driving, during the Ranch War at least, was to 'harass and demoralise the graziers'.[96] Eventually, it was hoped, these men would surrender their land to the community.

The tactic enjoyed some success during 1904–08: following an intensive campaign of cattle driving and the non-payment of rent in Athenry, Co. Galway, for example, frightened graziers sold their estates, the land was redistributed, and hundreds of viable small farms were created.[97] It was agitation on the ground, Fergus Campbell argues, not high political concerns, that brought Irish land issues to George Wyndham's attention in the first place, resulting in the land purchase Act and later laws. *Land and Revolution* (2005) offers the first full account of the role played by United Irish League land courts in imposing on the government an agrarian agenda and punishing those who did not give up their land to 'the people': Campbell shows that, in Connacht at least, 'the law of the League' replaced the law of the British crown. Whilst peaceful public rallies called for the redistribution of grazing land and on landlords to sell their estates to tenants on fair terms, cattle driving, boycotting, violence and intimidation enforced these demands in the local community.[98]

Animals bore the brunt of the physical violence during a drive,[99] but the sight of the cattle being marched towards his home, accompanied by a large crowd and even a band, was nonetheless a frightening one for the owner.[100] The situation could get out of hand; Free State troops had to be despatched, for example, to deal with the driving off of sixty head of cattle at Mount Russell, in Ardpatrick, east Limerick.[101] This practice of making the target's life a misery and his livelihood difficult, in order to remove the victim and potentially claim his land, recurs in the evidence from the Civil War. Between January and March 1922, fifty-nine cattle were driven from Denis Hickey's land; and twenty-three more

[95] Rumpf and Hepburn, *Nationalism and socialism*, 54.
[96] Bew, *Conflict and conciliation*, 140
[97] Campbell, *Land and revolution*, 183.
[98] On one particularly 'vigorous' campaign of intimidation, in Craughwell, Co. Galway: Campbell, *Land and revolution*, 153–6.
[99] The deliberate harming of stock often took place on a drive as the animals were chased off their grazing land; see NAI, 392/512, 392/454.
[100] Keaveney, *The land for the people*, 180.
[101] *Limerick Leader*, 23 June 1922.

were chased off in attacks on 18–19 May. For Hickey, the perpetrators' motivations were clear:

> Local small holders and landless people were anxious to have the lands of Croom . . . divided up and sold to them, and with that object in view, sought to strip the lands, so as to render same useless to the owner.[102]

The area around Croom was, it seems, at the centre of a spate of driving. Jane Hartigan,[103] had let her lands to a grazier there and Hickey's neighbour, John Coleman,[104] submitted a claim to the Free State almost identical to Hickey's. And, in the early hours of 2 March 1922, 'a hundred head of cattle were driven off lands at Croom and Carrigeen'. 'The motive for the drive', reported the *Limerick Leader*, was 'to focus attention on the need for land by uneconomic holders and labourers in the district'.[105]

Frank Boyle, a farmer from Rath, near Murroe, Co. Limerick, believed that 'local people want to get the land divided', which is why they 'drove my cattle off [and] damaged my farm'. Boyle's fences were cut and his gate and windows smashed in attacks that took place over four days in January 1923.[106] It worked: many graziers like Boyle found it difficult if not impossible to re-let land from which their cattle, or the cattle of the previous tenant, had been driven.[107] Resultant attempts to sell the land were often hindered by local intimidation and the victim incurred a double loss, that is, the value of the land plus the consequential disappearance of his income from it.[108] Cattle drivers were also 'busy' in 'many parts' of South Tipperary in February 1922. As part of a 'campaign to have grazing lands broken up and divided amongst the working classes', drives took place on, amongst others, the parklands of Col. F.S. Lowe, Kilshane House, near Dromline: 150 head of cattle belonging to Daniel Devitt of Cashel were chased off here.[109] Walls surrounding the demesne and a heavy iron gate were pulled down, and notices posted:

> The land for the Irish and the land for the people. These lands are to be for the people, and not for ranches. The cattle were driven off these lands last night.

102 NAI, 392/29, 31: Hickey, Limerick.
103 See earlier discussion in this section.
104 NAI, 392/24: Coleman, Limerick; see Chapter 2, Section 2a.
105 *Limerick Leader*, 3 March 1922.
106 NAI, 392/15: Boyle, Limerick.
107 George Fosberry, for example, suffered this fate: TNA, CO 762/57/5: Fosberry, Limerick.
108 See for example: TNA, CO 762/192/20, CO 762/5/6, CO 762/89/5, CO 762/104/22, NAI, 401/1061.
109 *Clonmel Chronicle*, 8 February 1922.

Anyone found bringing them back or repairing walls or gates will meet with instant death.
(Signed) Captain Moonlight.

The parallels between these notices and letters posted during nineteenth-century rural agitation are clear; if the Land War fell outside Lowe and Devitt's own lifetimes, the fictional signatory undoubtedly evoked frightening folk memories of the 1880s. But 'Captain Moonlight' had now picked up his poisonous pen for a very different kind of conflict: in 1922–3 it was not only landlords of large demesnes like Kilshane who had to fear the landless. Also under attack were middle-class, Catholic farmers, like Devitt,[110] who grazed his cattle on the coveted 'ranches'. In September 1922, for example, 'acts commenced by terror . . . effectual to prevent . . . the user of grazing rights', including cattle driving and tree cutting, drove Jeremiah Casey from a farm he had bought just '3 or 4 years ago'.[111]

Driving intimidated the grazier and caused huge inconvenience and, sometimes, permanent loss. A drive became theft when the animals were not returned to their owner. 'Cattle-stealing' was 'growing around the Thurles and Goold's Cross districts' in May 1922, for example: twenty-eight animals taken off L. Pennefather's lands at Marlow 'cannot be traced', despite the £50 reward offered for the capture of the perpetrators.[112] Although it took much time and effort, the missing livestock usually could be gathered together, unharmed. Following the drives around Croom in March 1922,[113] 'the cattle were found on the roadside and during the day efforts were being made to collect them and put them back on the lands'.[114] Cattle were returned to Lowe's demesne, near Dromline (Co. Tipperary, discussed previously) and the gate replaced. As Thomas Kennedy's cattle were being taken away from lands at Pass, near Clonmel, 'a party of the IRA', acting at this stage as a force for law and order,[115] 'appeared on the scene, and recovered the beasts'.[116] The next section, by contrast, explores those cases in which the cattle, sheep or other animals were deliberately injured or killed.

110 Identity of Daniel Devitt (of Farranamanagh, near Cashel, Co. Tipperary) confirmed in the Census of Ireland, 1911 (online database).
111 NAI, 392/284: Casey, Limerick.
112 *Clonmel Chronicle*, 3 May 1922.
113 See earlier discussion in this section.
114 *Limerick Leader*, 13 March 1922.
115 See Section 5, by contrast, on potential republican involvement in rural violence.
116 *Clonmel Chronicle*, 8 February 1922.

4. Animal Maiming

Kind treatment of animals is a relatively modern concern. In rural societies in the past, men were 'constantly reminded of their dependence on the slaughter of animals, and of the cruelty of animals to each other'.[117] The 'devilish act of cutting out the tongues of horses and cattle' had warranted a statute in England in 1545.[118] Yet, before Martin's 'Humanity' Act (1822), which protected the creature itself from carelessness and cruelty, animals had the status of property and their abuse was an offence against the owner alone.[119] With increased government intervention in health and welfare in the nineteenth century, ideas evolved and humane attitudes became more familiar.[120] Protective legislation was continually renewed. The Munster press reported on 'cruelty to rabbits' in Nottingham: a group of miners at a 'coursing meeting' were fined for failure to comply with a new Act of Parliament.[121] Maiming thus upset and inconvenienced an owner increasingly emotionally attached to – as well as financially dependent on – his animals.

The deliberate injuring and killing of animals became, and apparently remains, an expression of grievance against a person carried out through violence against a living thing cared for and relied on by that person. 'To take it out on an innocent horse was wicked', said Alison Hayes; her pony's nose was cut and 'anti-English' graffiti daubed on her riding stables in west Wales in April 2008.[122] Reports on maimings during the Irish Civil War similarly display bafflement at the 'taking out' of social, political, or personal resentments on a 'harmless' animal:

> It is difficult to establish any connection between dumb beasts and the existence of unrest in the country; but truth nowadays is stranger than fiction. On yesterday evening three donkeys were discovered dead on the roadside at Barne, and on investigation it was found that the poor beasts had been deliberately shot, a label being attached to each inscribed 'Turned their back on Freedom'.[123]

We must wonder whether the targeting in this case of a donkey, a notoriously docile and foolish animal, used in popular culture to satirize incompetent British military leaders, was entirely coincidental. Their owner

[117] B. Harrison, 'Animals and the state in nineteenth century England', *English Historical Review* 88 (1973), 786–820 at 786.

[118] Archer, *By a flash and a scare*, 202.

[119] Archer, *By a flash and a scare*, 199–200.

[120] Harrison, 'Animals and the state', *English Historical Review*, 786–8.

[121] *Clonmel Chronicle*, 18 January 1922.

[122] ''Anti-English attack' hurts horse', *BBC News*, 7 April 2008 (http://news.bbc.co.uk/1/hi/wales/7333435.stm).

[123] *Clonmel Chronicle*, 26 April 1922.

had 'not been disclosed', although we are reminded of the importance of animals to the rural economy and the great losses incurred, and large amounts of compensation consequently sought, following this form of intimidation: the 'rate-paying community will ultimately know to their cost to whom the donkeys belonged'.[124] The labels attached to the dead animals nonetheless hint at a motive,[125] making an – albeit cryptic – connection between this incident and the conflict over the Treaty. Section 2 in this chapter analyzes violence as a means of communication: the posting of notices and threatening letters reinforced the message of the violent act. Thus, whether by (open or implicit) acceptance of the new Free State, past demonstration of British allegiance, or refusal to cooperate with the IRA, the donkeys' owner was deemed to have 'turned their back' on the Irish republic and therefore 'on freedom'. His animals were punished as a result.

Animal maiming could make a powerful public statement. Attacks on livestock by the eighteenth-century 'Houghers' in Connacht were accompanied by proclamations, signed by the fictional 'Ever Joyce', in favour of land redistribution.[126] During the Civil War, particularly gruesome attacks on animals were reported in the press. Yet maiming was also a highly personalized and often secretive attack. The compensation claims suggest this form of intimidation was difficult to trace and perpetrators were rarely prosecuted. Little detail is offered on methods used to disable the beast. Houghing, first recorded in the 1690s as a quick and reliable method of inflicting irreparable damage on animals and humans, was not mentioned by name in the evidence from the Civil War. Cattle, sheep and, in one case,[127] a mare simply were 'seized and killed by Irregulars'.[128] Patrick Maloney, for example, described the attacks against him: 'the Irregulars came to my lands which I hold under the 11 month system... and took the two bullocks mentioned... and had same slaughtered'.[129] Animal deaths could be coincidental with the military conflict: in a number of incidents in Cos. Limerick and Waterford, cattle and a mare were shot during exchanges between Free State and

[124] This attack took place in a county (Longford) outside the remit of this study; the compensation material for this county, which may shed more light on the identity of both victim and perpetrator, has not yet been analyzed.

[125] Compare with labels attached to human corpses; see Chapter 5.

[126] S.J. Connolly, 'The Houghers: Agrarian protest in early eighteenth century Connacht', in C.H.E. Philpin, *Nationalism and popular protest in Ireland* (Cambridge: Cambridge University Press, 1987), 139–62.

[127] NAI, 392/420.

[128] See for example: NAI, 392/488, 392/523. In other cases animals were simply 'killed': NAI, 392/469, TNA, CO 762/14/8.

[129] NAI, 392/5, 6: Maloney, Limerick.

republican troops.[130] Hares were killed in similar circumstances.[131] A bullock owned by James Quinlan, father of a Free State Lieutenant, was shot when his house in Michelstown was fired into on 24 April 1923.[132] In other cases it was difficult to prove any malicious intent: when John Stephenson's gates were pulled down and cattle let off the land, one cow was found dead, 'it is believed from ill treatment as it was a cow in calf', but there were no human witnesses. Richard Crotty's bullock similarly was found dead, reported the Free State Army, but 'it may have been from disease'.[133]

Other attacks were clearly planned and individually targeted: Cornelius Harnett's heifers were 'maliciously drowned'[134] and Philip Heelan's jennet was blinded in a 'wanton and malicious' reprisal over trespass.[135] Retaliation against some perceived wrongdoing is a recurrent feature of these attacks and seemingly motivates attacks on animals to this day: Oxfordshire police believe that a knife attack on a mare in March 2009 was carried out by 'someone out for revenge'.[136] Like a threatening letter, smashed window, or burnt-out haggard, the victim's discovery of a dead or injured animal on his property induced fear and prompted speculation on the intent of the (usually anonymous) perpetrator – and the goodwill of the community at large. Some historians and anthropologists even interpret animal maiming as symbolic murder: 'dead animals meant an act of killing had occurred and it was only a question of time . . . before the maimer turned' on the owner and his family.[137] In Munster, there is no evidence that animal maiming was followed up by the killing, or attempted murder, of its owner. British soldiers in Ireland fell victim to 'houghing' in the eighteenth century,[138] but, even during the bitter Civil War, the mutilation of human bodies, witnessed often in ritual killings on the Continent at this time, was nowhere near as common as was the maiming of animals. Comparing violence in Ulster with another contemporaneous European conflict zone, Tim Wilson notes that the absence of human mutilation in Northern Ireland was 'all the more striking when

130 NAI, 392/161, 392/276, 392/334, 392/505, 392/506, 402/80, 402/89.

131 NAI, 392/126.

132 IMA, CW/OPS/3/C.

133 IMA, CW/OPS/3.

134 NAI, 392/331: Harnett, Limerick.

135 NAI, 402/107: Heelan, Waterford.

136 'Pregnant horse slashed with knife', *BBC News*, 10 March 2009 (http://news.bbc.co.uk/1/hi/england/oxfordshire/7934216.stm). The injuries to its back legs resemble a houghing.

137 Archer, *By a flash and a scare*, 219.

138 M. Powell, 'Ireland's urban houghers: Moral economy and popular protest in the late eighteenth century', in Michael Brown and Sean Donlan (eds.), *Law and the Irish, 1689–1848: Power, privilege and practice* (Ashgate: Aldershot, 2011).

it is remembered that mutilation of animals had long been notorious as a nationalist tactic throughout Ireland'.[139]

The 'element of intimacy' inherent in animal maiming nonetheless makes it a very serious and insidious form of intimidation – and one well suited to the settling of a personal grudge or vendetta.[140] On 22 January 1923, John Bagge carried out the 'malicious maiming' of eleven head of cattle by cutting off their tails with a billhook. It was a fairly gory job; two of the animals were still bleeding the following morning. James Mansfield, a blacksmith from Kilmacthomas, Co. Waterford, owned the cattle, and labourer Bagge was 'on a message' for Thomas Cheasty, on whose land Mansfield's animals had trespassed. Bagge was given whiskey and instructed to 'take a piece off the tails of these cattle', in order to 'quieten Mansfield'. Bagge later told the county sessions that Cheasty also offered him £5 to burn Mansfield's hayrick, though this attack was not carried out. Bagge's movements were far from stealthy: a number of witnesses at Mansfield's forge saw the cattle coming out of Cheasty's yard, followed by the accused in a bloodied shirt. Perpetrators of this typically clandestine crime did, then, sometimes come into contact with the law. Bagge was sentenced to twelve months' hard labour and later summoned from Waterford prison as a witness in Mansfield's damages case against Cheasty.[141] Victims were thus willing to go to the authorities, if not for the abstract notion of justice then at least for financial recompense for the – often large – losses associated with attacks on animals.

In local economies dependent on pasture, the distress caused by missing and injured animals should not be underestimated. A rich seam of pastureland known as the Golden Vale ran through Cos. Limerick and Tipperary and, apart from pockets of small sheep-farms in Co. Limerick, dairy was the main farming type in these counties: 88 per cent (Limerick) and 81 per cent (Tipperary) of all milch cows supplied creameries. Co. Waterford relied more on 'store and fat cattle',[142] but, across Munster, animals were highly profitable commodities. Cows were not the only farm animal targeted during the war. The Free State Army reported one of the more unusual levies extracted by republicans: notices demanded dog licenses be paid to the 'Irish Republic', rather than the appropriate Free State authority. Failure to comply with these demands resulted in the shooting of a number of dogs[143] and the poisoning of seventeen more, including 'valuable greyhounds', in the Old Turnpike locality of

[139] Wilson, *Frontiers of violence*, 123.
[140] Archer, *By a flash and a scare*, 6–7, 218–19.
[141] *Munster Express*, 17 February and 26 May 1923.
[142] Rumpf and Hepburn, *Nationalism and socialism*, 47–8.
[143] IMA, CW/OPS/3/C.

Nenagh, in April 1923.[144] But, more than any other animal, it was cattle that most obviously symbolized the farming system (grazing) that came under renewed attack during 1922–3.

Chapter 3 notes the high incidence of crop and outhouse burning and its long-term economic implications: the destruction of hay made winter feeding impossible and real hardship ensued, even for the strong farmer.[145] Maiming also struck at the heart of farm life by attacking the very thing – animal stock – that generates wealth and sustains the grazing system. The killing and injuring of animals thus complemented cattle driving and hay burning by causing huge disruption and inconvenience for graziers, making their position untenable and their land available for redistribution. However, maiming was also more brutal than the threatening acts explored in Sections 2 and 3 of this chapter. Local rivalries and class conflicts within farming surfaced alongside campaigns for redistribution; bitter, personal scores were settled with the intimate act of maiming. Resentment of horse breeding, for example, is evident in some Civil War attacks. 'Well-known racehorse owner', Major Edwards, was targeted during the war: cattle and horses were driven from Rathduff stud-farm and gates and walls 'thrown down'.[146] Henry Colclough had run his farm at Old Shanbally House, Clogheen, Co. Tipperary, since the eviction of the previous tenant a quarter of a century before. Colclough 'was not seriously inconvenienced' by his possession of an evicted farm and, in the words of the IGC, suffered 'no appreciable loss prior to July 1921'. However, when war broke out in 1922, some members of the local community were less forgiving of his past indiscretion and current good fortune. Until his death just after the end of the Civil War, Colclough earned £400 per year on his farm, an additional £400 profit from horse breeding and around £120 per year in prizes at fairs in Dublin, Clonmel and Kilkenny. His attackers knew exactly how to disable his commercial capacity: on 14 and 16 June 1922, 'twelve Hunters . . . were maliciously injured by their tails being cut, rendering them valueless for Show or Sale purposes'.[147] The manes and tails of three more Hunters were cut in January 1923 and, between March 1922 and February 1923, a 'considerable number' of Colclough's sheep were commandeered. On 30 May 1923, Colclough was shot dead as he put two horses out to graze on a field just a few hundred yards from his house. His wife, Susan, received no compensation for his murder; the attack had occurred after

[144] *Limerick Echo*, 24 April 1923.
[145] See for example: NAI, 402/98, 113, 114.
[146] *Clonmel Chronicle*, 8 February 1922
[147] TNA, CO 762/111/8: Colclough, Tipperary.

the end of the war and fell outside the scope of the IGC. Connections were nonetheless made between his death and the earlier attacks on his land and animals: 'Shocking Crime at Burncourt – Was it agrarian?' speculated the local press.[148]

Deer parks were rare in Ireland; the malicious shooting of forty-two deer between 1 March and 17 December 1922, at Castle Lough, Co. Tipperary, may have been a protest against owner S.G.J. Parker-Hutchinson's use of the land for game. Other attacks on his lands – in 'a somewhat lonely district' near Nenagh – included looting, tree-cutting and driving of cattle and sheep (and ten sheep were killed between June 1922 and January 1923). The claimant and his family moved out of the area in summer 1922, returning to Castle Lough in March 1924 when conditions were 'more settled'. But their position was not one of tremendous hardship: Parker-Hutchinson resided at another of his residences, Timoney Park, near Roscrea, Co. Tipperary, during this period. The victim blamed his 'loyalty' for the attacks: he had been a Deputy-Lieutenant and active in recruiting for the British Army during World War I.[149] The attackers' focus on the parkland and its animals, rather than the house, hints at other motivating factors: this privileged and prominent Protestant[150] had, through his upper-class pastimes, set himself apart from his local community and invited jealousy over land.

5. Land: A Historical Problem

Local resentment of those who had allegedly acquired their holdings unfairly or dishonestly, or laid precious land to waste through grazing, was nothing new.[151] Opportunist looting is a natural part of war and, whilst greed does not necessarily motivate violence on its own, land is finite and may be worth fighting for. Michael Mann's theories apply specifically to ethnic cleansing: possession of the land by one ethnic group excludes others from its use and 'in agrarian societies this is life-threatening'. Colonial settlement has therefore 'produced especially murderous ethnic cleansing over land'.[152] Attacks on the land during the Civil War did not constitute cleansing and involved murder in only a few cases. Yet, whilst the old conflict between Protestant planter and Catholic native had been

[148] Clipping from *Waterford Standard* in Colclough's IGC compensation file.

[149] TNA, CO 762/180/18: Parker-Hutchinson, Tipperary.

[150] *Nenagh Guardian*, 15 April 1922: Parker-Hutchinson was an attendee of the 'large and representative' meeting of his co-religionists in Nenagh, Co. Tipperary, in April 1922, to protest against the possibility of war. See Chapter 2, Section 3b.

[151] Bew, *Conflict and conciliation*, 162.

[152] Mann, *Dark side of democracy*, 31–2.

complicated by land purchase, the heat had not altogether been taken out of the land question.

Leigh-Ann Coffey certainly emphasizes long-standing local land issues in her study of the 'campaign of intimidation' against a group of farmers in Luggacurran, Queen's County, in March 1922. The cattle drives, livestock mutilation and hay burning on this former Lansdowne estate had roots in the landlord's installation of Protestant 'planters' in the place of Catholic tenants in the 1880s. The decision of the evicted to remain in the vicinity 'ensured that the community remained intense and divided'. However, more than any other period of conflict, it was Civil War that provided the 'opportunity for individuals' in Luggacurran 'to act on their long-held resentment'.[153] Their religion had undoubtedly prevented the settlers from integrating fully into the community; Protestants were cast as outsiders and rumours abounded of their Scottish or Ulster origins.[154] Hart also cites land as the 'connecting thread' between the victims of the Dunmanway 'massacre' in Co. Cork in April 1922: none of the fourteen Protestants killed was a landlord, but together they held much valuable property, some of which was confiscated after their deaths.[155] Coffey does not, however, overstate the sectarian dynamic: the 'land committee' formed in Luggacurran in 1922, to 'forcibly evict' the planters and their families, did not have the widespread support of community and the 'decent' Catholics in the area.[156] A government report on the Laois agitation concurred. Protestant farmer John Goucher had bought his holding, near Ballinakill, under the 1909 Land Act,[157] building up forty head of cattle and a 'substantial house' through 'steady hard work'. His neighbours – 'all of whom, with one exception', were Catholics – were 'indignant' at his ill treatment and 'promised to stand by him' after threats were made by the 'Timahoe Land Committee'.[158]

Coffey contends that 'the majority of the Irish population understood the revolution in the context of their own sense of identity and with regards to the interests of their communities'.[159] Religion undoubtedly shaped the construction of this local 'identity' in Luggacurran, but anti-Protestantism was far too entangled with issues of landownership to

153 L. Coffey, *The planters of Luggacurran, County Laois: A Protestant community, 1879–1927* (Dublin: Four Courts Press, 2006), 8, 41–2.
154 Dooley, *Decline of the big house*, 162–3.
155 Hart, *IRA and its enemies*, 286.
156 Coffey, *Planters of Luggacurran*, 57.
157 The estate had been purchased by the Land Commission in 1903. The 'planters', then, were no longer representatives of the local landlord, rather Wyndham and the 1909 Land Act had strengthened their legal hold on the land.
158 NAI, S566: 'Laois land agitation, 1922'.
159 Coffey, *Planters of Luggacurran*, 9.

explain on its own the violence against the planters. It was the historic 'fusion of Protestantism with "usurping settler"', rather than hatred of the minority religion per se, that explains the lingering resentment of Protestants – in this and many other communities.[160] The land hunger stirred by independence in Cos. Limerick, Tipperary and Waterford certainly did not discriminate on national or denominational lines. Persistent intimidation and the seizure of farms were focused not on the lone, Protestant landlord, who had by now largely been bought out, moved away and faded into obscurity. Instead, rural violence targeted farmers of all denominations who had recently acquired land; Catholic David Horgan from Pallaskenry, near Kilcornan, Co. Limerick, was amongst them:

> What is the reason of attacking a poor man like me? I have no quarrel with anybody and stand well with my neighbours. I am a catholic. It is that these ruffians want to steal my land and divide it amongst themselves. We are faced with utter ruin.[161]

The urgency of the land question is palpable in Horgan's testimony. Intimidation was being used in Ireland alongside and instead of the official channels of redistribution: violence drove the owner away, leaving his land to be shared out, with or without the approval of the newly empowered Land Commission.[162] 'But for the driving of [the] Applicant out of the country and keeping him out, these lands would not have been acquired under the . . . 1923 Act in Ireland', read a surveyor's statement in support of the claim of Herbert Sullivan, who fled to Devon from Co. Limerick after the burning of Curramore House in August 1922.[163] In his absence, Sullivan's 240 acres became 'deteriorated' and were compulsorily acquired by the Land Commission in 1924, for less than half their true value.[164]

The Free State did not condone the pursuit of economic and social change through force. Minister for Agriculture, Patrick Hogan, reported to the Dáil on the 'gross intimidation exercised by . . . Evicted Tenants' Associations'.[165] Ireland was home, he calculated, to 'a million and a half landless men, who were "prepared to exercise their claims with gun and

160 Crawford, *Outside the glow*, 16.

161 PRONI, D/989/C/2/21: 'Typescript copy statements and reports about IRA atrocities on loyalist families and confiscation of homes and land etc.' (Papers of the Irish Unionist Alliance, Propaganda material: Government White Papers, printed reports and speeches).

162 Jones, 'Land reform legislation', *Éire-Ireland*, 116–19.

163 See Chapters 2 and 3.

164 TNA, CO 762/87/4: Sullivan, Limerick.

165 *Dáil Éireann Debates*, ii, 27 March 1923.

torch"'.[166] And this 'form of irregularism' had to be 'dealt with along with other aspects of the land question in the forthcoming [1923] Land Bill'.[167] D.J. Gorey TD cautioned:

Land settlement cannot be brought about by the argument of the stick. It is no use to give preference either to the fellow who can cut the biggest stick or to the fellow who can give the biggest shout or to him who uses an amount of intimidation. It must be a legal settlement. It must be a settlement under which every man fit and capable of handling land will have an equal chance with the rest.[168]

However, it was the reality of the land seizures, cattle driving and violent intimidation on the ground in communities in Munster that turned the new government's attention to local grievances in the first place. Gorey may have believed that legislation would satisfy land hunger and consolidate the position of the government in troubled areas. For Dooley, the settlement of the land question from 1923 onwards was 'central to the restoration of law and order in Irish society'.[169] And possibly it was in the interest of government ministers to exaggerate social disorder to justify coercive wartime legislation.[170] Yet my research on intimidation shows that redistribution was enacted not by the politician, but by the 'fellow' with the 'stick' and the 'shout'. The Free State Government, it could be argued, merely looked on, affording large and small farmers alike little protection from the seizure of their land.

Benjamin Schofield made a small claim for the loss of animals and damage caused in February 1923, when his farm in Co. Waterford was seized and 'used as a commonage'.[171] The Westropps, a British Army family from Co. Limerick, owned land across the county.[172] Mountiford Westropp's land at Kildimo was seized and he was forced to sell 'to a "Committee of Farmers at their own price"'.[173] In a separate claim to the Free State, from a location just three and half miles away, Edward

166 Jackson, 'The Two Irelands', in Gerwarth, *Twisted paths*, 70.

167 *Dáil Éireann Debates*, ii, 27 March 1923.

168 *Dáil Éireann Debates*, ii, 5 January 1923.

169 Dooley, 'IRA veterans and land division in independent Ireland 1923–48', in F. McGarry (ed.), *Republicanism in modern Ireland* (Dublin: University College Dublin Press, 2003), 86–107 at 86.

170 O'Halpin, *Defending Ireland*, 33.

171 TNA, CO 762/151/3: Schofield, Waterford.

172 Mountiford's 'father, grandfathers and great-grandfathers' all served in British Army and it is likely that he (and possibly Edward) were related to Colonel George O'Callaghan-Westropp (1864–1944) of Co. Clare, whose colourful career during the War of Independence (and beyond) was noticed by Fitzpatrick. See Fitzpatrick, *Politics and Irish life*, 43–4.

173 TNA, CO 762/98/21: M. Westropp, Limerick.

Westropp recalled how 'local smallholders took forcible possession' of Ballyshonickbane, near Pallaskenry. Edward felt 'powerless' to act against the men who knocked down his fences to make the lands 'a commonage'; the Free State afforded 'no protection'.[174] It was not until June 1923 that the Free State Army 'won back' Joseph Wheeler's farm, in Bottomstown, near Emly, Co. Limerick, which was seized illegally in January 1922 (and only had been acquired by Wheeler in May 1921).[175] Evidence collected by SILRA not only suggests government negligence, but also hints at conspiracy between the Free State soldiers and perpetrators of intimidation. Even in 'quiet parts of the country', at a small farm near Carlow, 'local people' brought in ploughs, turned up grazing land and chased off the stock so as to drive out the farmer and 'split up' the land 'amongst smaller men'. The Civic Guard and National Troops allegedly 'did nothing' in this case because the leader of the 'gang who turned the farmer out of his land was brother to one of the chief officers in command of the Free State Army'.[176]

Prospects were poor for the return of seized land to the owner. Colonel William Fielding, for example, was pessimistic about regaining control of his 690 acres at Baranigue, near Athea, Co. Limerick: 'the Irish Free State Government were repeatedly asked to restore order but were apparently unable to do so and the situation is hopeless now'. In December 1922, Fielding wrote to the Ministry of Finance that 'persons without his authority who cut and disposed of his turf and paid him no rents' had, since January that year, occupied the land, held by his family for seventy years.[177] The non-payment of rents was recognized by SILRA as a pressing issue for landowners in the three counties.[178] The ICCA goes further, suggesting not just a lack of control of the agrarian situation on the part of the Free State, but also the Government's complicity in violent attacks on the land: the newly empowered Land Commission compulsorily purchased Fielding's tenanted lands 'for the benefit of those who illegally disposed the owner'.[179] Of course, enforcing the legitimate transfer of

[174] NAI, 392/227: E. Westropp, Limerick.

[175] TNA, CO 762/31/8: Wheeler, Limerick. The land had been given to Wheeler under the Irish Land (Provision for Sailors and Soldiers) Act of 1919. This legislation extended the benefits of the Land Purchase Acts to men who had served in 'the Naval, Military, or Air Forces of the Crown in the present [First World] war', as if they had been tenants or proprietors; see P. Bull, *Land, politics and nationalism: A study of the Irish land question* (Dublin: Gill and Macmillan, 1996), 200–01.

[176] PRONI, D/989/C/2/24: 'Typed report of the connection between the 'Irregulars' and the 'Free State Army', 1923'.

[177] NAI, 392/305: Fielding, Limerick.

[178] PRONI, D/989/B/1/3.

[179] PRONI, D/989/B/2/9.

land would not have been easy for the wartime government. Prosecution of 'rural violence' – the actions, analyzed in this chapter, resulting in the flight of the owner and seizure of his land – historically was problematic and obtaining information from the public notoriously difficult.[180] During the Land War, landlords expected support from the RIC and protection of the process-server in the execution of his duties. Yet without recourse to unpopular and illiberal legislation, or simply opening fire on unarmed crowds, it was difficult to impose order on collective action on the land. Resident magistrates (RM) in Connaught in the 1880s dealt with rent refusal and repossession of evicted farms by summoning to the petty sessions culprits for 'trespass' or 'forcible entry'.[181] Prosecutions for cattle driving were made under charges of riot, unlawful assembly and conspiracy. Yet, during the land seizures and claiming of turbary that would again torment landlords and graziers in 1922–3, the authorities faced the old problem: 'gangs of 'moonlighters' could march about in broad daylight without the police being able to interfere unless some crime were actually committed in their presence'.[182] During the transfer of authority from the RIC to the Civic Guard, keeping order in the counties was very difficult: armed attacks on Garda stations and patrols continued well into 1923.[183]

Official administration of the land question nevertheless did little to dampen the hopes – held high within rural communities – that a native Irish government would promote the needs of the landless and small farmer over the interests of the landlord and grazier. It was 'fitting', commented William Sears TD, that the 'old brigade should have held out until a National Parliament would dispose of the last remnant of Irish landlordism'.[184] In discussions surrounding the Land Act (1923) he promised:

> This Oireachtas will put an end to a system that was the curse of this country, and I hope we will hear no more of it in that shape.... The announcement that all untenanted land will become the property of the State on an appointed day will go as a message of hope to the people in the West. They have looked upon those

[180] E. Malcolm, 'Investigating the "machinery of murder": Irish detectives and agrarian outrages, 1847–70', *New Hibernia Review* 6, no. 3 (Autumn 2002), 73–91 at 87.

[181] R. Hawkins, 'Liberals, land and coercion in the summer of 1880: The influence of the Carraroe ejectments', *Journal of the Galway Archaeological and Historical Society* 34 (1974–75), 40–57 at 52.

[182] Hawkins, 'Liberals, land and coercion', *Galway Archaeological and Historical Society*, 52.

[183] NAI, Records of the Department of Justice, H 99/109.

[184] *Dáil Éireann Debates*, iii, 28 May 1923.

ranches as their own for generations. They saw bullocks grazing there whilst they were starving on bad land.[185]

Clearly old resentments died hard: Cathal O'Shannon TD recalled there was 'nothing creditable, decent, or serviceable in the whole record of landlordism in Ireland'. His 'congest' constituents had waited a long time for better access to land.[186] And so whatever the reality for the rural poor, under a Land Commission hard pressed to find land for division, the impulse towards 'land for the people' was felt from the ground to the highest government level.[187]

Land agitation in Italy during this period similarly forced legislators to take notice of the rural poor: the Italian Government expropriated the estates of absentee landlords, 'distributing land in small parcels to peasants'.[188] Charles Tilly disputes descriptions of collective rural violence as 'pre-political': the seizure of land and occupation of farms in Soresina and Sicily was as much a part of the 'massive political mobilization' following World War I as was the formation of political parties and rise of Fascism.[189] In Spain, a 'bizarre' landholding structure had long created tension between the absentee landlords of large, extensively cultivated estates ('latifundia'), the seasonal labourers who worked there and the peasants scraping a living off dwarf farms divided into minute plots ('minifundia').[190] Thus attempts by the republican governments of 1931–6 to reform the system – in the name of prosperity and social justice – can also be seen in the context of 'mass politicization'. Mass meetings 'dramatised and publicised' the division between powerful landowners and the poor. The conflict exploded in a 'violent' way in small towns.[191] Ultimately, the expectations of the under-privileged were not satisfied: Spain did not have the financial resources, enjoyed by the British Government in its attempts to solve the Irish land question, to compensate for the expropriation of large landowners. Laws intended to break up the absentee-owned estates in fact 'threatened modest proprietors' and very little land was handed over to peasant settlers.[192] Still, the channelling of social discontent into political movements had proved explosive. From Ireland to the Continent, redistribution of the land of

185 *Dáil Éireann Debates*, iii, 28 May 1923.

186 *Dáil Éireann Debates*, iv, 5 July, 1923. Clancy TD also spoke out for his congested constituents; see Chapter 3, Section 4.

187 Jones, 'Land reform legislation', *Éire-Ireland*, 121.

188 Blok, *Honour and violence*, 4.

189 C. Tilly, *The rebellious century, 1830–1930* (London: Dent, 1975), 168, 170–1, 289.

190 R. Carr, *Modern Spain, 1875–1980* (Oxford: Oxford University Press, 1980), 16–17.

191 Carr, *Modern Spain*, 117.

192 Carr, *Modern Spain*, 126.

the few, in favour of the many, was a powerful and often violent impulse felt across twentieth-century Europe.

However, despite the work of Tilly, Thompson and other analysts of collective violence, some historians continue to distinguish between the social and political (that is, between the local conflicts over land studied in this chapter – what is loosely called 'agrarianism') and the actual war over the Treaty. For Dooley, the Civil War simply created the 'anarchical conditions for agrarian radicals to operate freely' and tenants' associations in the counties lacked central control and clear aims.[193] It is true that, even before Irish independence in 1922, indeed since the Wyndham Act, the land question was no longer bound closely to an overtly political (nationalist) campaign. The leader of the Ranch War, Laurence Ginnell MP, for example, had not enjoyed the support of his colleagues in the IPP. Driving targeted the 'grazier', who was 'typically' an 'ambitious man [and] 'good nationalist'. There was also criticism by some in Sinn Féin of ranch-breaking and even veteran land agitator Michael Davitt debated whether subdivision of grazing lands would lead to any wholesale increase in the area of tillage.[194] 'Society' and 'politics' cannot, of course, be so easily disentangled: Campbell has shown that Sinn Féin's electoral victory (1918) was accompanied by 'tillage agitation' and, whilst the party's leadership was keen that the land issue should not detract from the campaign for independence, local Sinn Féin branches in Galway did support the claims of small farmers.[195]

Neither can the intimidation of landowners and the violent seizure of farms be seen as separate from the wider political and military campaign to undermine the infrastructure and authority of the Irish Free State. The anti-Treaty IRA did not recognize an independent Irish state that was not a republic and, through a range of techniques, mounted a physical and moral challenge to the governing ability of the fledgling state. Ada Vere-Hunt was warned not to call on the 'staters' for help,[196] and the Westropps and Col. Fielding were offered 'no protection' by the new government.[197] Intimidation of non-combatants and attacks on land ridiculed the ability of the Provisional and later Free State Government to perform its function and protect from violence and disorder citizens of all political allegiances and religions. Patrick Hogan agreed that, whilst the conflict surfaced in different ways, with individuals and groups 'all out for different objects . . . using different methods and . . . weapons', all

193 Dooley, *"The land for the people"*, 40–2.
194 Bew, *Conflict and conciliation*, 11, 150–1.
195 Campbell, *Land and revolution*, 242–3.
196 Section 2 in this chapter.
197 See earlier discussion in this section.

forms of violence and disruption constituted a threat to the stability of the Free State:

> You have houses burned, you have banks robbed – sometimes in the name of the Republic and sometimes without any patriotic pretence... you have trains attacked – sometimes in the name of the Republic and sometimes in order to seize goods – you have haggards burned in labour disputes, and you have men murdered for a piece of land. There is no difference in character between any of these episodes. They are simply different phases of what we are fighting.[198]

A pressing question is whether those 'landless men' or 'landless people'[199] identified by victims as the perpetrators of cattle drives and violent land redistribution were the same men as the 'republicans' or 'Irregulars' named in other claims? 'Land grabbing was much too widespread for all of the blame to be laid at the door of the anti-Treatyites'.[200] And there were few overt claims to social revolution from the anti-Treaty IRA. Indeed, the conservative nature of the Irish Revolution (1916–23) – culminating as it did in a Church-backed Irish Free State that left traditional property rights untouched – has become something of an historical truism. This formative period in Ireland's past has been largely viewed through a military history or state-building paradigm; class struggle is downplayed.[201] The biographer of Liam Mellows,[202] the lone 'socialist republican' of the conflict,[203] argues that there was support, on the anti-Treaty side, for social, as well as political, revolution. The Communist Party of Ireland's proposals for the division of the lands of the aristocracy amongst the landless and small farmers, for example, were an attempt to 'present a comprehensive alternative to the kind of Ireland Griffith was determined to create'.[204] In addition, whilst the IRA Council's 'revolutionary' land policy, published in May 1922, was not followed up by immediate action, its instructions to local commandants, to seize lands and hold properties in trust for the Irish people, 'may well have encouraged the land seizures and cattle drives then proceeding' in land-hungry

198 *Dáil Éireann Debates*, ii, 17 January 1923.
199 NAI, 392/214: Dunne, Limerick: 'landless people made an attempt to strip two dwelling houses so as [to] prevent any person working the farm'. Damage to farms in possession of 'a party of landless men': NAI, 392/16: McCoy, Limerick and NAI, 392/19: Liston, Limerick.
200 Dooley, 'IRA veterans and land division', in McGarry (ed.), *Republicanism in modern Ireland*, 170.
201 H. Patterson, *The politics of illusion: A political history of the IRA* (London: Serif, 1997), 25.
202 C.D. Greaves, *Liam Mellows and the Irish Revolution*, 1st ed. reprinted with a new introduction by Gerry Adams (London, 2004).
203 Patterson, *The politics of illusion*, 27.
204 Greaves, *Liam Mellows*, 357.

districts such as Leitrim and Roscommon.[205] However, these ambitions were not widely held beyond Mellows, who was executed by the Free State in December 1922, and Peadar O'Donnell (said to have influenced Mellows' thinking on social policy whilst the two were held by the Free State in Mountjoy Prison, Dublin).[206] Radical land policies, Greaves concedes, were far 'easier formulated than made good'.[207] Henry Patterson also argues that Mellows' programme was not radically left-wing, but rather was an attempt to 'preserve intransigent revolutionary nationalism by tapping into perceived social discontent'.[208]

The anti-Treaty position was indeed given 'social sustenance' by the 'large reservoirs of agrarian discontent'; the small farmers of the congested West, in particular, did support the republicans.[209] The pattern of Treaty support was 'logical enough':

> In Southern and Western areas, with their land-hungry small farmers or large agricultural proletariat based on dairying, the tendency was Republican; in the midland ranching districts where, it is said, 500 acres can be managed by a man with a stick and a dog, it was towards the Provisional Government.[210]

Certainly there lay a 'great deal of potential for social upheaval' amongst the tenant farmers who had not benefited from land purchase legislation and occupied the 'uneconomic' holdings that made up 65 per cent of all agricultural holdings in Ireland in 1922.[211] The Free State Army reported:

> Land hunger plays an important part in Irregularism and the freedom which many have enjoyed for the past few years in regards [to] evasion of payment of... debts weigh much in the desire to postpone the advent of ordered Government.... Until the people are made to realise that they must settle down to normal life again the Irregulars will get some support from a certain class.[212]

The individuals who joined the 'roving bands' of the anti-Treaty IRA, to 'swell the ranks for a day or two', may well have been frustrated small farmers or labourers, willing to engage in violent and destructive acts

205 Greaves, *Liam Mellows*, 313–14, 317.
206 D. Ó Drisceoil, *Peadar O'Donnell* (Cork, 2001), 28. On O'Donnell, see Chapter 3, Section 5b.
207 Greaves, *Liam Mellows*, 314, 357.
208 Patterson, *The politics of illusion*, 27.
209 Patterson, *The politics of illusion*, 24. See also: Jones, 'Land reform legislation', *Éire-Ireland*, 117.
210 Greaves, *Liam Mellows*, 302.
211 'Uneconomic' holdings were made up of less than twenty acres of 'reasonable' land or valued at less than £10. See Dooley, 'IRA veterans and land division', in McGarry (ed.), *Republicanism in modern Ireland*, 86–7.
212 IMA, CW/OPS/2/M.

against suitable targets.[213] Some victims clearly identified the perpetrators of attacks on their property as 'military' men. John Bourke's cattle, for example, were driven by 'armed Irregulars'.[214] One claimant lost three and a half years' rent when a house he owned on Main Street, Rathkeale, Co. Limerick, which he had previously leased to the RIC, was occupied by 'leading Republican' John Hayes, from May 1922 to January 1926.[215] The gradual disintegration of a cohesive, military campaign on the part of the anti-Treaty IRA after September 1922, by which time the Free State had recaptured the majority of republican strongholds in Munster, gave individual republicans freedom from plans and procedure – and the opportunity to settle local scores and agitate on the land.

Earlier in the conflict, by contrast, before the shelling of the Four Courts and the split in the IRA, the propagandists made a clearer distinction between the Army and the 'blackguardly gangs' driving cattle, destroying property and murdering 'for other than political purposes'.[216] When William Kennedy, for example, a 'popular farmer' from the Thurles district, was shot dead near Borrisoleigh, Co. Tipperary, in February 1922, the local IRA investigated the matter and distanced its men from the crime. Kennedy's death instead was 'associated with the trouble about land'.[217] The 'IRA authorities in Tipperary' again repudiated any connection with the murder of an ex-Colonel of the Shropshire Regiment in May 1922, taking 'active steps to apprehend' the men who fired the shots on Higginson.[218] This book considers acts of violence carried out from the ratification of the Treaty in January 1922, that is, before the Civil War began in earnest and during which time – in the absence of the departing British forces or a new Free State Army – IRA brigades took it upon themselves to maintain order in the localities. Cattle drivers on the lands of George Ryan at Inch, near Thurles, Co. Tipperary, for example, were 'fired at by IRA', who took possession of the animals for the owner.[219] The day after Ned Wynne received the 'document . . . requesting him to hand over his farm' to the IRA,[220] the local Anglican vicar, Horace C. Dean, contacted Sean Robinson, IRA, at Clonmel Barracks:

> I write to know if this thing is done with your knowledge and approval. It seems to me to be a most arbitrary and illegal act. . . . I appeal to you to exert your authority

213 IMA, CW/OPS/2/M.
214 NAI, 392/282: Bourke, Limerick.
215 TNA, CO 762/195/22: Latchford, Limerick.
216 *Limerick Leader*, 6 February 1922.
217 *Clonmel Chronicle*, 8 February 1922.
218 *Clonmel Chronicle*, 27 May 1922.
219 *Clonmel Chronicle*, 8 February 1922.
220 Section 2 in this chapter.

and see to it that this man and his family are left in peace and possession of property acquired by them honestly and with the goodwill of their neighbours.[221]

IRA commandant General Brennan called for a 'period of truce to cattle driving and interference with land . . . until there is a settled Government in the country'. Persons engaging with cattle driving, before the 1 August deadline, 'do so at their peril'. Yet, Brennan seemingly expected great things of the Irish administration after this date: 'we pledge our honour to use all our influence with the Ministry of Agriculture to have lands which ought to be the people's property fairly divided'.[222] Thus the commencement of the military conflict on 30 June 1922 did not represent a sudden turning against (and turning out) of the landed, Loyalist enemy from the community. The Civil War instead saw an intensification of campaigns of intimidation and battles over land begun, in some cases, during the War of Independence and Truce period.

6. Boycotting

a) History and development

British police and military forces had 'selected' Nora Heaslip's premises on Barrack Street, Nenagh, for their refreshments and she 'catered for them in the kindliest possible manner'. When Heaslip 'refused to discontinue supplying the "Enemy"', she was 'threatened with all sorts of punishment – even Death to myself and Destruction to all I possessed'. The grocer and confectioner 'thought the campaign against me would gradually cease when the [Truce] was signed in December 1921'. She was wrong: 'when fighting commenced between the divided Irish Forces my persecution was renewed in a most outrageous manner.' The 'campaign of terror' against her included the firing of shots into her home, 'death warrants' posted on her door and raids on her business premises. Customer testimonies, contained in her compensation file, alleged that Heaslip's shop 'was boycotted because it was the favourite house of the British Forces. It was the general rule of campaign to intimidate her customers and frighten them from frequenting her shop'. The IGC had some doubts about this case. There were suggestions, for example, that Heaslip was in difficult financial straits not because of a boycott, but because of the national economic downturn. The dissolution of Heaslip's business partnership with her sister, to whom some customers remained loyal

[221] PRONI, D/989/C/2/21.
[222] *Limerick Leader*, 28 April 1922.

(presumably for other than political reasons), cannot have helped either. But the serious attacks against Nora must account, at least in part, for her four-month flight from Nenagh.[223] Appeals to the IGC had an obvious, financial objective and, in Heaslip's case, there may have been some irregularities. Yet there was also something more at stake than pounds, shillings and pence. Violent threats and intimidation forced victims to consider their national allegiance and decide whether they belonged, and wanted to stay, in the Irish Free State.

The intimidation of customers of an ill-favoured shop, such as Heaslip's, was not unusual. Boycotting was used with particular effectiveness during the Civil War to render unviable and undesirable a victim's livelihood – and ultimately his life in Ireland. 'Boycott' has, of course, a particular association with Irish history and the tactic resurfaced in the late 1950s during an ugly episode in Co. Wexford: in response to a Protestant woman's defiance of church teaching on the education of her Catholic children, Catholics of the village, led by local priests, began a boycott of Protestant-owned shops and farms in Fethard-on-Sea.[224] The term originated in the famous struggle on Lord Erne's Co. Mayo estate (Lough Mask, near Ballinrobe) between Captain Charles Boycott and the local branch of the Land League. Boycott's attempts to serve eviction notices on 22 September 1880 were met with complete aversion by the local community: estate employees, his blacksmith and laundress all refused to serve him, and he no longer received telegrams or provisions from shopkeepers. The Boycotts, who previously had lived comfortably off Charles' commission as a land agent, were left to do their own house- and farm-work. Their land became 'public property' as locals broke gates and chased cattle. If Charles or any member of the household 'set foot outside grounds', they were 'hooted and hissed at and generally derided'. Boycott's young nephew, for example, was intimidated when he attempted to collect the mail abandoned by the usual post boy.[225] And so the familiar rural practice of exclusive dealing, now christened 'boycotting', became widely used against landlords and agents, as well as farmers and shopkeepers.[226]

Boycott was a form of punishment and protest against those whose loyalties or behaviour conflicted with the Land League's campaign for

223 TNA, CO 762/64/2: Heaslip, Tipperary. Heaslip's solicitors provided the IGC with proof that their client had stayed in England for this amount of time.

224 T. Fanning, *The Fethard-on-Sea boycott* (Cork: Collins Press, 2010), 5–6.

225 J. Marlow, *Captain Boycott and the Irish* (London: Deutsch, 1973), 59, 139–41.

226 D. Jordan, 'The Irish National League and the "unwritten law": Rural protest and nation-building in Ireland 1882–1890', *P&P*, no. 158 (February 1998), 146–71 at 165; Curtis, 'Moral and physical force', *JBS*, 181.

reduced rents and tenants' rights. During 1879–82, the League leadership encouraged rent strikes and resisted the evictions of those who could not or would not pay what were considered to be unreasonably high rents. Anyone participating in evictions, or socializing or doing business with anyone who did, was boycotted. League members were placed at the entrance to shops and pubs to ensure that no trade was carried out with boycotted persons.[227] Charles Parnell demanded that 'pressure from public opinion . . . must be brought to bear upon those who are weak and cowardly' – including those who took up a farm from which a tenant had been evicted.[228] He outlined this 'new form of social and moral excommunication' at Ennis on 19 September 1880, giving strict instructions on how a 'land grabber' should be treated: 'you must shun him on the roadside'.[229]

The Land League, then, had a specific idea of the enemy in its midst; commonly held notions of rural society and access to land marked out 'community' from 'pariah'. In one case from nineteenth-century Co. Tipperary, opposition to eviction was powerfully demonstrated when approximately 300 people attended the sheriff's sale of the goods of an insolvent tenant and not a single bid was made.[230] Boycott acted as a sanction against those who held or used land unjustly into the twentieth century.[231] British Government Intelligence Notes on Cos. Limerick, Tipperary and Waterford, during 1915–19, recorded:

> The causes which led to . . . boycotting mainly arose in connexion with the holding of grazing lands, [or] evicted farms, [or the] purchasing of holding land which people in the locality want to get divided.[232]

During 1922–3, Frank Coffey's position as 'caretaker for the plantations' at Kilduff House, Templemore, Co. Tipperary, set him apart from the local community. A letter from SILRA in support of his compensation claim explained: 'In those troubled times any one in Coffey's capacity doing his duty by a landlord would be classed as a "Loyalist"'.[233] He had also in the past 'refused to pay levies to the IRA, and on one occasion gave information to the RIC that an ambush had been prepared', a claim verified by a letter from James Smith, the ex-RIC officer from Templemore who believed Coffey 'saved my life'. As punishment for this

227 Jordan, '"Unwritten law"', *P&P*, 159, 165.
228 Townshend, *Political violence in Ireland*, 117.
229 Marlow, *Captain Boycott and the Irish*, 134.
230 Vaughan, *Landlords and tenants*, 178. The sales of burnt-out houses and their estates (see Chapter 3) were similarly subject to local boycott. See for example: TNA, 762/64/11, CO 762/80/20, CO 762/83/1, CO 762/87/4.
231 *Intolerance in Ireland*, 92–7.
232 TNA, CO 903/19.
233 TNA, CO 762/197/25: Coffey, Tipperary.

betrayal and his privileged position as an estate worker, Coffey could not get a thresher for his crops, the creamery refused to take his milk, and his cattle were driven.[234] Robert Hicks was boycotted from spring 1922 and could not get his tillage done. 'My Loyalist neighbours helped me', Hicks explained, but they had their own work and the crop came in late.[235] The withholding of labour left land untilled and livestock untended, which had dire financial consequences, even for relatively well-off farmers.[236] Hicks was a Protestant and Coffey was a Catholic; religion had little to do with target choice as landlords' stewards and land agents were, like Captain Boycott before them, forced out of their positions by intimidation.[237]

Boycott was an old method that could be fairly easily adapted to new situations; during the Civil War, boycott became a weapon of the town as well as the countryside. The Belfast Boycott a year or so earlier was its first famous application in an urban setting. This boycott of Northern banks, insurance companies and later of all goods distributed from or manufactured in Belfast and other Northern towns was sanctioned, at least at first, by Dáil Éireann and implemented by the County Councils. 'Boycott Committees' kept lists of 'commercial travellers, shops, and factories . . . selling Belfast goods or dealing with firms handling them'.[238] In the end, the boycott only underscored the border, but its purpose was to challenge Partition by illustrating the importance of the south as a market for Northern goods; it enjoyed some success, having a 'significant' effect on the banking community and causing even 'greater harm' to the distributing trade.[239] The IRA helped to implement the boycott,

[234] TNA, CO 762/197/25: Coffey, Tipperary.

[235] TNA, CO 762/94/11: Hicks, Tipperary.

[236] TNA, CO 762/192/14: Moore, Waterford; CO 762/195/20: Shier, Limerick; CO 762/195/15: Sparling, Limerick.

[237] Coffey and Hick's religion verified in the Census (1911). Attacks on estate officers, stewards, etc.: TNA, CO 762/39/5 and D/989/B/2/9: Palfrey, Tipperary (forester on Lady Beatrice Pole-Carew's estate; home raided by masked and armed men on 9 May 1922 and could not return to work until April 1923); CO 762/74/3: Mollison, Tipperary (head keeper to Lord Dunalley, Kilboy; see Chapter 3); CO 762/74/14: Nolan, Tipperary (coachman to Charles Clarke, Graiguenoe Park; see Chapter 3); CO 762/77/10: Bourchier, Tipperary; CO 762/196/11: Hayes, Tipperary; NAI, 401/120: Hamilton, Tipperary (in employment of Victor William Christopher Cavendish, the Duke of Devonshire); CO 762/198/5: Bride, Tipperary (ex-Serviceman granted agricultural training by Ministry of Labour on Devonshire's estate); NAI, FIN 1/2391: John Hurley ('Victimised Loyalist' claim from the gamekeeper for Sir John Keane, Cappoquin, Co. Waterford, who moved to Stratford-on-Avon after being 'compelled to leave Ireland by the republicans' and on the 'point of a revolver').

[238] D.S. Johnson, 'The Belfast Boycott, 1920–1922', in J.M. Goldstrom, *Irish population, economy, and society: Essays in honour of the late K.H. Connell* (Oxford: Clarendon Press, 1981), 287–307 at 291.

[239] Johnson, 'Belfast Boycott', *Irish population*, 287, 299, 306.

'picketing Protestant suppliers of Belfast goods to frighten off Catholic customers'.[240]

The coordination of national and local bodies in evidence during this period, from mid-1920 until June 1922, was not witnessed during the Civil War. Yet, there were ways in which the anti-Treaty IRA, with the support of the local community, could enforce the social and economic ostracism of its targets. Letters or notices posted on business premises marked out the boycotted victim. John Holmes of Galbally, Co. Limerick, was discharged from his court clerkship in December 1922. He then failed to make a living as an auctioneer and land valuer because 'threatening notices, signed by the IRA, warned people to do no business with this 'ex-clerk of Petty Sessions and British Spy'. The 'people' did heed the warnings, and Holmes was boycotted until May 1923. Indeed, for this category of intimidation to work, the local community had to be united in support. Non-combatants usually tolerated what traditionally had been regarded as a morally superior form of protest. Speaking in August 1880, James Redpath, an American journalist with pro-Land League sympathies, called boycotting a 'peaceful war' because it encircled the target with 'scorn and silence' and did not cause physical harm.[241] A boycott could 'quietly ruin a man', saving him, in Michael Davitt's words, 'from becoming the victim of an outrage' like murder.[242] The perpetrator, too, would be saved from the legal recriminations associated with more serious offences.

Holmes himself was sure of the reason for his exclusion from the community: 'I am a member of the Church of Ireland and it was because of [this] and of being loyal to the British Government that I was boycotted'. The IGC was convinced by Holmes's story and he was awarded the £100 compensation he sought.[243] The customers of Clonmel draper William Sweetnam were also 'warned not to buy from us but to support their own people'. Sweetnam knew to which 'people' he belonged: 'we were Protestants and not in sympathy' with the actions of the IRA.[244] The boycott forced the family out of business: on 28 October 1922, Mrs Sweetnam put out a local advert that she was 'leaving and clearing [the] entire stock at cut price'.[245]

240 Dooley, *Plight of the Monaghan Protestants*, 46.
241 G. Moran, 'The origins and development of boycotting', *Journal of the Galway Archaeological and Historical Society*, 40 (1985–86), 49–64 at 50.
242 Jordan, '"Unwritten law"', *P&P*, 167.
243 TNA, CO 762/177/4: Holmes, Limerick.
244 TNA, CO 762/162/1: Sweetnam, Tipperary.
245 *Clonmel Chronicle*, 28 October 1922.

The patronizing of one's co-religionists was not, of course, an unusual practice in Ireland. On return from British service overseas, Eneas McNulty, the unlucky hero of Sebastian Barry's novel,[246] found that:

> Even the Protestant businesses won't touch him, which he tries in the last resort. Not that they would have been likely to employ him in the first place, inclined as they were, and rightly, to see to their own.[247]

Some businesses, then, were hurt not only by an organized boycott, but also by the disappearance of their customer base. Indeed, SILRA helped specifically the 'small farmer [and] shopkeeper . . . who earned their living from the Army, Navy, and Police' and relied on the estimated £2 million spent yearly by the Forces in Ireland.[248] Nenagh, Co. Tipperary, for example, was known as a military town. Since the eighteenth century, soldiers there 'spent freely' in local businesses.[249] Before making awards, the IGC had to consider whether the reported loss of trade was caused by the 'disturbed state of the country',[250] or by a shrinking (Loyalist) customer base. In its final report, the Committee noted the 'failure of applicants', in accounting for the losses sustained by their farm or business, to make 'due allowance for changed economic conditions in Southern Ireland'. The IGC 'could not disregard' the contributory influence of the 'general trade depression' and the loss of purchasing power within the agricultural community in Ireland. However, the IGC was also aware of those 'pitiful instances of shops and small businesses built up before war with energy and thrift, fostered in favouring conditions of war and now ruined as result of post-Truce aggression'.[251] There is, indeed, strong evidence that shopkeepers, hoteliers and others were actively punished during the Civil War for their previous loyalties.[252] Mary Hogan's agricultural goods were boycotted because she used to supply the RIC in Co. Tipperary with horses.[253] Maurice Lynch incurred 'loss of earnings'

246 See Chapter 2, Section 2b.

247 Barry, *Whereabouts of Eneas McNulty*, 54.

248 PRONI, D/989/B/5/2.

249 Hallinan, *Tipperary County: People and places*, 117.

250 TNA, CO 762/135/5: Mulligan, Limerick; his motor business on O'Connell Street, Limerick town, was 'boycotted' during the war.

251 TNA, CO 762/212.

252 TNA, CO 762/50/17: Flynn, Waterford (grocery store boycotted after the withdrawal of the RIC); CO 762/64/16: Allen, Tipperary (boot business boycotted 'after British left'); CO 762/85/3: McConnell, Tipperary (motorcycle dealer forced from premises after RIC withdrawal); CO 762/167/11: Riordan, Tipperary (general merchant still being boycotted in June 1928 because his sons served in World War I); CO 762/194/5: Scales, Tipperary (boycotted because he sold butter to the RIC, prior to their evacuation from Templemore barracks).

253 TNA, CO 762/168/8: Hogan, Tipperary.

as a labourer and his wife's knitting business was boycotted, because of their 'British sympathies'.[254] These 'sympathies' may have been displayed in a number of ways, particularly during World War I: Kathleen and Nicholas Rooney had served Marines in their public house in Ardmore, Co. Waterford, which was subsequently boycotted during the Civil War and compensation awarded by the IGC.[255] Custom was withdrawn from William Quinn's public house in Loughill, Co. Limerick,[256] not merely because of pro-British customers, but also because Quinn himself was ex-RIC.[257] After serving in World War I, Stuart Trainor returned to Co. Limerick, and invested his life savings in a motor business, shop and hotel. Raids on the premises continued until November 1922. A boycott was enforced and the motor and grocery businesses 'completely wiped out'.[258]

In the three Munster counties under review, the long-term effects of a boycott should not be underestimated. Boycotts could last for years, sometimes until the date of application for compensation.[259] On 2 November 1926, the IGC ruled that John Russell's claim was invalid because the boycotting of his wife's business began in 1919, in response to the claimant's involvement in the recruitment for World War I of local mill hands. However, in an appeal of 10 November 1926, Russell stressed that even though the campaign against him began outside the Terms of Reference of a committee focused on Civil War injuries, he had been 'suffering hardship and loss since'. And now he had to support his stepsons who, on returning from World War I, 'have lost all prospects of earning their livelihood in the Irish Free State'.[260]

The onus on claimants to the British Government's IGC was, of course, to prove that the losses suffered through boycott were a result of pre-Truce associations with the UK. Thus it may be that the political or sectarian nature of the attack was exaggerated in some cases. Nonetheless, contemporary victims of boycott did see the departure of Loyalists and Protestants as an emerging trend. Mr and Mrs Cecil Burchett, for

254 TNA, CO 762/80/1: Lynch, Limerick.

255 TNA, CO 762/165/6: Rooney, Waterford. Other boycotted hotels: CO 762/14/20: Murphy, Waterford and CO 762/76/10: Lyons, Tipperary (the Railway Hotel was 'placed out of bounds to Irish' because Lyons had 'traded with the military'; Lyons does not specify, but I assume 'military' in this case means the British Army).

256 Where ex-constable Patrick Courtney lived; see Section 1 in this chapter.

257 TNA, CO 762/84/17: Quinn, Limerick.

258 TNA, CO 762/82/5: Trainor, Limerick.

259 See, for example: TNA, CO 762/167/11: Riordan, Tipperary. Lismore shopkeeper Willie Roe (later in this chapter) claimed that '"anti-British" sentiment' still affected his trade in 1927.

260 TNA, CO 762/14/17: Russell, Tipperary.

example, who ran a shop in Nenagh, Co. Tipperary, complained that 'nearly all the County families who were the back-bone of our business were between 1920 and 1923 driven from the country. This completed our ruin and in 1924 we were compelled to sell the whole property'.[261] The question is if this economic tool, boycott, served a purely sectarian agenda. Or did it have a purpose: the removal of all (financial, social and religious) remnants of British influence in Ireland? The evidence suggests that victims of boycotts, such as shopkeeper Willie Roe, were selected not as the single representative of the minority denomination in a locality, but as one member of a larger class of Protestants that exerted a significant commercial and economic hold on an area. Roe ran a 'Family Grocery and Fancy Stationery Store' on South Mall, Lismore, Co. Waterford and, in February 1927, claimed he was still feeling the effects of the 1919–22 boycotting of his business that followed the departure of the 'loyal gentry and townspeople':

> The "anti-British" sentiment is still a practical factor and influence in this neighbourhood, and trade is placed where that sentiment is acceptable, so that I have lost, and am now still losing, trade.

For an often desperate and under-resourced anti-Treaty army, a shop like Roe's was an obvious target in practical terms. Early in the Civil War it was his 'Bovril, sugar, potatoes, butter' that were demanded in letters from the 'Third Battalion' of the IRA.[262] The relatively ill-equipped Irregulars commandeered a variety of goods for their fight against the Free State.[263] One shopkeeper was forced to supply boots to the IRA in occupation of Roscrea,[264] and, a Limerick draper recalled, 'the Irregulars were in occupation of Askeaton . . . and were supplying themselves with whatever they wanted by seizing same from shopkeepers'.[265] Michael Farry, writing on Sligo during this period, agrees that 'when goods were to be commandeered it made sense for the IRA to take those goods from one who was perceived as "the enemy"'.[266] However, Roe, and others like him, were much more to their attackers than convenient sources of provisions. A more threatening notice, signed 'by order, O.C. South Batallion, IRA', gave Roe and his family thirty-six hours to clear out or be 'shot at sight the lot of you and burned in your house'. A sinister postscript revealed something of the author's wider ambitions: 'We will clear all

261 TNA, CO 762/57/4: Burchett, Tipperary.
262 TNA, CO 762/108/11: Roe, Waterford.
263 See also Chapter 2, Section 1, on looting during the war.
264 TNA, CO 762/57/17: McCorduck, Tipperary.
265 NAI, 392/164: Canty, Limerick.
266 Farry, *Aftermath of revolution*, 193.

the Bloody Protestants out of this town also'. This promise suggests that, in the attacker's eyes, there was a sizeable Protestant contingent in Lismore set apart from the majority by their economic position, as well as their religion. The returns of the 1911 Census demonstrate that, at that time, at least, the family's shop on South Mall would have served a reasonably sized Protestant customer base. Willie was one of only four Methodists in the district in 1911 but, of Lismore's population of 2,402, 9 per cent were Protestants of all denominations.[267] A personal reference from the Dean of Lismore in support of Roe's claim confirmed that the 'smaller folk and casual shoppers' did not deal with Roe, whose 'better class' of shop did not mix 'public house' with 'provision business'. Boycott and violent threats during the Civil War thus reaffirmed the suspicion between the Protestant shopkeepers with their 'gentry' patrons and the rest of the town.[268] Roe can certainly be counted as a member of the 'small Protestant communities in the towns' who had 'developed comparative prosperity' to then be 'considered "fair game"'. According to the *Church of Ireland Gazette*, 'a "bad national record"' became during the war 'a satisfactory cloak to cover sheer covetousness and personal dislike'.[269]

b) *Urban Experiences*

It was not only because of their politics and religion, but also 'by reason of their . . . larger stake in the country', that Protestants had something to fear from the outbreak of Civil War.[270] The *Church of Ireland Gazette* celebrated the 'Southern minority' as 'one of the finest assets of the infant state'. As the people who pay the 'greater share' of Ireland's taxes and were qualified by 'education and upbringing' to take a leading part in the economy, the persecution and emigration of Protestants was detrimental to the whole state: 'it would be a serious matter if their energy and character were eliminated and sent to enrich other countries than their own'.[271] Yet intimidation, via boycotting, often resulted in just that: the financial ruin and departure from Ireland of those Protestants families and firms long prominent in Munster's cities, towns and industrial centres. The Cleeve family, for example, controlled a huge portion of the dairy

267 Census (1911): Lismore Protestants comprised 157 persons belonging to the Church of Ireland, 28 Presbyterian, 18 Church of England, 10 Baptist and 4 Methodist. Roe resided with his (Church of Ireland) wife, son, daughter and a Catholic servant girl.
268 TNA, CO 762/108/11: Roe, Waterford.
269 *Church of Ireland Gazette*, 23 June 1922.
270 P. Buckland, *Irish Unionism, 1885–1922* (London: Historical Association, 1973), 202.
271 *Church of Ireland Gazette*, 23 June and 6 October 1922.

industry in Co. Limerick until a string of their factories and creameries were burned during 1922–3.[272] William Frederick Cleeve recalled:

> During the disturbed period in Ireland notices were posted up that our family had made millions of money and were paying enormous sums to the British Government for income tax . . . and duty. We were held up to public odium.[273]

Not all Protestants made 'millions of money'. However, whilst independent Ireland was largely an agricultural nation and the majority of the population (59 per cent in Munster in 1926) lived in rural areas, the economic resentments described by Cleeve were prominent during the Civil War, particularly in urban areas, where Protestants' continued financial success was most evident. In Co. Waterford, for example, Protestants were 'essentially urban based'.[274] Concentrated along Waterford city's harbour, the smaller mansions of the strong merchant families, such as the Salters and Gallweys (who had risen to dominance by the end of the eighteenth century), were as symbolic of the minority influence in this county as was the traditional big house.[275] Non-Catholics had been central to the development of Munster's urban and industrial landscape. The Quakers, for example, were 'key figures' in Co. Waterford's eighteenth-century trade boom;[276] in Co. Tipperary, too, in the first half of the nineteenth century, cotton magnate Malcolmson was 'one of many' Quaker businessmen in the large market town of Clonmel.[277]

The special influence of this sect had largely waned by the time of the Civil War. The small Quaker community in Limerick, for example, had by the early twentieth century entered 'near fatal decline'; the 'energy and dynamism' of its members, who had played a central role in developing business in the city, was 'kept alive' by a few remaining members,[278] including O'Connell Street grocer and wine and spirit dealer Ernest Bennis, who still appears in the trades register in the civil-war period.[279] However, in terms of Munster's Protestant (Anglican, Presbyterian, Baptist

272 Sir Thomas Cleeve founded the Condensed Milk Co. of Ireland Ltd in 1889, with William Beauchamp and Edmond Russell. Ten claims from Cleeve's descendents (shareholders in the business) were received by the IGC: TNA, CO 762/189/6–16. Claims were also made to the Free State.

273 TNA, CO 762/189/6: W.F. Cleeve, Limerick.

274 Kiely and Nolan, 'Politics, land and rural conflict', in Nolan and Power (eds.), *Waterford: History and society*, 459–94 at 467.

275 Foster, 'Preface', in Nolan and Power (eds.), *Waterford: History and society*, xxi.

276 Foster, 'Preface', in Nolan and Power (eds.), *Waterford: History and society*, xxii.

277 Hallinan, *Tipperary County: People and places*, 97.

278 P. Lovett, 'Quakers in Limerick', *The Old Limerick Journal* 37 (Summer 2001), 3–9 at 9.

279 Limerick City Council, *Limerick City Trades Register 1769–1925* (online database, http://www.limerickcity.ie/webapps/tradesreg/Search.aspx).

and Methodist) community, there were certain areas, such as the towns along the Blackwater Valley, Co. Waterford,[280] where the minority influence and culture remained strong. And, despite enjoying some safety in their relative numbers, these urban Protestants clearly were not exempt from violence and intimidation during the conflict. Hart and Farry agree that religious antagonism in Cos. Cork and Sligo, respectively, was also particularly resonant in areas where the non-Catholic population was comparatively large.[281] In these counties, resentment of the financial control exercised by the religious minority over rural and urban communities (Protestants in Co. Sligo owned the biggest farms and contributed disproportionately to the commercial life of the county) also manifested itself in boycotting.[282] The imposition of the Belfast Boycott in Monaghan similarly had been 'aimed at breaking' the 'economic hold' of the religious group (Protestants) that made up 25 per cent of the county's population.[283]

Attacks displaying elements of sectarianism were not limited, in other words, to lone Protestants living in rural areas. The threats and boycotts explored in this chapter prove that Protestant merchants and businessmen in Munster's cities and towns quite rightly 'feared that they might suffer because of their still considerable wealth'.[284] Many in fact fled Ireland; urban Protestants were more likely to depart the Free State during the Revolution than were their rural counterparts. Between 1911 and 1926, the non-Catholic population in urban districts in the twenty-six counties fell by 38 per cent, and the non-Catholic rural population fell by 28 per cent.[285] In the province of Munster, the contrast is more marked: the minority population declined by 55 per cent in the towns and 33 per cent in rural areas.[286] This does not mean, of course, that towns and cities were a more threatening environment for Protestants than was the countryside; intimidation (boycotts or otherwise) did not necessarily cause the large-scale departures. Andy Bielenberg names 'revolutionary terror' as just one of many causal factors of the urban Protestant outflow.[287] Minority involvement in the armed forces was traditionally high in Ireland; the rural-urban differential is therefore explained partly by the withdrawal of the British military, which was largely stationed in

280 See Willie Roe's experience in Lismore, Section 6a.
281 Farry, *Aftermath of revolution*, 193; Hart, *IRA and its enemies*, 289.
282 Farry, *Aftermath of revolution*, 183–5, 194–5, 198.
283 Dooley, *Plight of the Monaghan Protestants*, 9–10, 45–6.
284 Bowen, *Protestants in a Catholic state*, 196.
285 Bielenberg, 'Exodus', *P&P*, 203 (table 2).
286 Department of Industry and Commerce, *Saorstát Éireann: Census of population 1926*, vol. III, Table 5B.
287 Bielenberg, 'Exodus', *P&P*, 202.

towns and cities.[288] Garrison towns experienced the most notable decline in the minority population. Tipperary town and Clonmel, for example, saw an 89 per cent and 63 per cent decrease in their respective Protestant populations, compared with a county-wide drop of 46 per cent.[289] High minority declines were also recorded in small provincial towns without an army presence. Outside Waterford city, for example, the county traditionally did not have a significant British Army presence;[290] however, whilst Dungarvan and Lismore were not barrack towns, both experienced, between 1911 and 1926, a fall in the non-Catholic population in line with the county average (40 per cent).[291] And there was no pre-war military presence in Carrick-on-Suir, Co. Tipperary, but its non-Catholic population fell by 65 per cent (compared with a county-wide decline of 46 per cent).[292] These departures may well be explained by the general economic unease. 'Urban dwellers are much more subject to fluctuations in fortune', notes a 1928 history of Limerick's 'merchant princes', 'than those who are settled on the land'.[293] Protestants in towns and cities in the south, 1920–3, faced a particularly hard time: a dramatic post-war slump in manufacturing,[294] deepening recession and the 'general disturbance of trade' that comes with war and political upheaval (the Belfast Boycott, for example, 'ruined' many Protestant firms).[295] Indeed, whilst many Protestants farmers and graziers in Munster were intimidated from their land, with local gentry and large landowners being particularly harshly treated during the Civil War, nationally the only occupational categories not to experience decline amongst non-Catholics in this period were farmers and livestock dealers. Middle-class rural Protestants more readily held on to their wealth and position, argues Bielenberg, than did Protestants in construction, industry and the professions.[296]

On the other hand, there were many Protestants who continued to succeed in professional and business life in the new Free State. This group

[288] Bowen, *Protestants in a Catholic state*, 21–2.

[289] Department of Industry and Commerce, *Saorstát Éireann: Census of population 1926*, vol. III, Table 7.

[290] McCarthy, *Waterford and the Irish Revolution 1912–23* (Unpublished manuscript; book forthcoming with Four Courts Press), chapter 1.

[291] Department of Industry and Commerce, *Saorstát Éireann: Census of population 1926*, vol. III, Table 11.

[292] Department of Industry and Commerce, *Saorstát Éireann: Census of population 1926*, vol. III, Table 11; Bielenberg, 'Exodus', *P&P*, 205 (table 3).

[293] A.J. O'Halloran, *The glamour of Limerick* (Dublin and Cork: Talbot Press Ltd, 1928), 57.

[294] E. O'Connor, *A labour history of Waterford* (Naas: Waterford Trades Council, 1989), 165.

[295] Bielenberg, 'Exodus', *P&P*, 214.

[296] Bielenberg, 'Exodus', *P&P*, 233 (appendix).

presents a problem for the historian; the tendency at the time was not to write about the Troubles, and certainly not to draw attention to families who had retained economic power. It is indeed understandable that a small, periodically persecuted minority wanted to keep a low profile following this particularly intense period of political upheaval. It is also beyond the scope of this book, on violence in all its forms, to write the history of a single group (Protestants, urban or otherwise). In contrast to the ubiquitous 'suffering Loyalist', the relative absence from the historical record of the 'successful Protestant' is nonetheless significant. It may evidence Protestants' desire to lie low, or simply prove that, for the middle classes, there was little to complain about. R.B. McDowell argues that life for the 'ex-unionist' in the Free State was not all 'decline and despair'; 'he soon realized that though the Treaty had involved a revolutionary transfer of political power there were remarkably few changes in his own environment'.[297] Journalist Brian Inglis, for one, echoes these sentiments. Inglis recalls his middle-class Protestant childhood in Malahide, Co. Dublin, just after the Revolution: the independence struggle 'made surprisingly little difference to Grandmother and the Unionist set' (the burning of a coast guard station, for example, 'perturbed' but did not put off golfers from their game at 'the Island', the Dublin businessmen's club founded by Inglis's grandfather).[298] And, a year or two after the Treaty, a kind of normality had returned:

> The Unionists closed their depleted ranks; as soon as they found that the new Irish Government could be trusted not to expropriate their land, debase the currency, or make general legislative mayhem, they settled down to ignore its existence.[299]

Other famous Protestant dynasties (Arnott of the Dublin department store, Quaker tea and coffee merchants, the Bewleys, and Cork flour-milling family, the Halls) similarly may be said to have 'settled down', and continued to prosper, under an independent Irish Government. Compensation claims relating to boycott and looting name other large, minority-owned firms that still dominated commerce in Munster. Cork-based grocers and manufacturers of jam and tobacco – Dobbin, Ogilvie and Co., for example – were prominent members of the province's business community in 1918,[300] and were still trading after the Civil War,

297 R.B. McDowell, *Crisis and decline: The fate of the southern Unionists* (Dublin: Lilliput Press, 1997), 166.
298 B. Inglis, *West Briton* (London: Faber and Faber, 1962), 14.
299 B. Inglis, *West Briton* (London: Faber and Faber, 1962), 15.
300 Cork Incorporated Chamber of Commerce and Shipping, *Cork Commercial Handbook* (Cork: Cork Chamber of Commerce, 1919).

when a compensation claim was lodged in Co. Limerick on behalf of the company for stock looted in transit.[301]

There was some continuity, too, in the fortunes of urban Protestants in the three counties studied in this book. Grocery chain L&N Stores, for example, established in the nineteenth century and run by Waterford's (Presbyterian) Torrie family,[302] survived the Troubles, and traded across Munster until the 1980s.[303] Adam F. Torrie was proprietor of the 'London and Newcastle Tea Company' in Broad Street, Waterford city, and owned another store in Tramore. A letter exchanged between Torrie's daughters suggests that the business was largely unaffected by the Civil War. Margaret (Peg) Torrie describes to her sister, Annabel, the siege of Waterford (in July 1922, Prout's Free State command seized back the city from occupying republicans). The violence did not disrupt greatly Peg's summer tennis tournaments:

> Tuesday [18th] was a glorious day, one of the best this year, so we all gathered at the [Tennis] Club. . . . Mrs Haughton and I were playing our Cup Singles, just about 7 o'clock, when we heard shots which came from the other side of the river.

The following day, 19 July 1922, 'rifle shots started at 7am', 'but everybody went to work as usual'. The shelling in the city centre undoubtedly disrupted the working day for some, but perhaps by 'everybody' Peg means her own class, that is, the close-knit, Protestant community of merchants and professionals based along Newtown Road in John's Hill. The Torries saw out the siege gathered with neighbours, including Church of Ireland solicitor, Mr Thornton, and Mr Fudger, a Methodist insurance agent, at the home of Quaker grocer family, the Chapmans.[304] Peg identifies the seriousness of the battle: she and her friends were not 'long in clearing off' the tennis courts when they heard 'the Republicans were mounting a machine gun in Nolan's',[305] and she is sympathetic to the 'poor unfortunate' people who had 'to fly' from the gunfire in Barrack Street, or had their homes taken over by National Troops.[306] Yet, whilst L&N did not escape completely the hands of commandeering soldiers ('[an employee] had to come down one morning at 2 o'clock and hand

301 NAI, 392/475: Dobbin, Ogilvie and Co., Limerick.
302 Census of Ireland (1911), online database.
303 L&N was finally bought out by a supermarket conglomerate in 1995; see 'Online archived obituaries: Robin Torrie', *Munster Express*, 14 November 2007 (http://www.munster-express.ie/archived_obituaries/torrie-robin/).
304 P. Grogan, 'Letter from a war zone', *Decies* 67 (2011), 87–95 at 91. Denominations verified in the Census of Ireland, 1911 (online database).
305 Grogan, 'Letter from a war zone', *Decies*, 90.
306 Grogan, 'Letter from a war zone', *Decies*, 92–3.

out 6 sides of bacon') Peg does not allege that the Torrie family were harmed or specially targeted. Pat McCarthy also does not believe that the Revolution was a particularly difficult or dangerous time for the city's Protestants. Families such as the Strangmans ('prominent merchants' in Waterford since the eighteenth century[307]), the Jacobs, the Goffs and the Harveys remained in business throughout the war. The diaries and memoirs of, for example, Philip and Rosamund Jacob, Emily Ussher and Annabel Goff-Davis, portray the 'life of comfort and leisure' enjoyed by this 'thriving middle class' before 1922, and do not suggest bitterness or trouble afterwards.[308]

The endurance of a small contingent of strong Protestant families that hung on to their wealth and status in the towns is an important trend, but more remarkable are the isolation and sectarian harassment suffered by many of their urban co-religionists. Boycotting is certainly a more subtle form of intimidation than the spectacular conflagrations that cleared out the gentry from their big houses, but the idea that urban Protestants had a significantly better experience of the Civil War than did rural Protestants is not borne out by the evidence from Munster. The urban-rural differential is complicated further by the fact that industry in Munster (copper mines, paper mills and so on[309]) was based chiefly in rural pockets on the large Protestant-owned estates. Power traditionally rested, in other words, not only with Protestant merchants and professionals in the larger towns, but entire local economies were also dependent on big houses and their surrounding industries. In Portlaw, for example, the estate village of the Marquess of Waterford, economic activity was focused on the de la Poer Beresford family's Curraghmore House and the nearby Pouldrew Flour Mills.[310] Henry Pyper lost his job when the anti-Treaty IRA burned down the mills. He could not stay in Munster, or even in Ireland, because his trade was boycotted; when potential Dublin employers 'found out I was a Protestant . . . and son of an RIC Sergeant . . . they said it affected their trade and . . . could not keep me on'.[311] He escaped to England in

307 L.M. Cullen, 'The overseas trade of Waterford as seen from a ledger of Courtenay and Ridgway', *The Journal of the Royal Society of Antiquaries of Ireland* 88, no. 2 (1958), 165–78 at 166.

308 McCarthy, *Waterford and the Irish Revolution 1912–2*, chapter 1.

309 Nolan and Power (eds.), *Waterford: History and society*, xxi, 467.

310 In the nineteenth century, cotton mills owned by the Malcolmson family were another large employer in Portlaw. The 'big-house economy' functioned in other Munster counties. During Clonmel's heyday as a busy market town and milling centre, Marlfield (the 'picturesque' estate village of the Bagwell family) was also of 'considerable importance' to the local Co. Tipperary economy; see Hallinan, *Tipperary County: People and places*, 96.

311 The Census (1911) confirms Pyper (then aged seventeen and a 'chemist's assistant' in Johnstown, Waterford city) belonged to the Church of Ireland and his father was an RIC sergeant.

1924 where, at the time of compensation application, he was living in Luton and making a 'difficult living' as a bus driver on £3 per week.[312]

Pyper's plight is an important reminder, if one were necessary, that not all Protestants resided in the grey towers of Lismore Castle (the home of Waterford's powerful Cavendish family).[313] Whilst violence and intimidation were used to strike against easily identifiable symbols of Protestant influence and British rule in Ireland, boycott also dealt with those who contradicted the received notion of the enemy – that is, working-class Protestants, 'small farmers' (named as a deserving group in a SILRA fundraising pamphlet) and those who ran small shops and public houses, and for whom ostracism by the local community was financially devastating.[314] Presbyterians William and Elizabeth Cordner of 'The Garage', Henrietta Street, Waterford city, for example, owned one of the county's many motor agents, and their businesses was 'completely ruined' by a boycott. They later moved to Belfast; William was a native of Co. Armagh.[315] 'There was no mistaking', said Elizabeth of her previous home in Waterford, 'that we were not the sort of people wanted there'.[316]

7. Conclusion

The anti-Semitic aspect of the Limerick boycott (1904) marks it out as something of a special case, but the episode also illustrates how intimidation works to divide people and how easily a community becomes convinced of the enemy within. In Limerick, in 1904, Fr Creagh's sermons on the Jews' 'nefarious business practices' fuelled popular speculation on the intentions of the new immigrants; a boycott was enforced, which 'dealt a severe blow' to the Jewish community.[317] In Cos. Limerick, Tipperary and Waterford, during the Civil War, rumour and suggestion also played an important role in creating the intimidating atmosphere, 'more subtle and invidious than cruder forms' of violence,[318] in which Protestants and British 'Loyalists' – rather than Jews – were especially targeted. There lurked within Munster's rural and urban communities

312 TNA, CO 762/119/9: Pyper, Waterford.

313 Lismore Castle was damaged and wine and valuable maps stolen, during its occupation, July–August 1922. See NAI, 402/120, 378, 379, 380, 381: Beecher, on behalf of Duke of Devonshire, Waterford.

314 PRONI, D/989/B/5/2.

315 TNA, CO 762/139/3: Cordner, Waterford. Census confirms their religion and in 1911 the household consisted of William, Elizabeth, their son, daughter and a Catholic servant.

316 TNA, CO 762/139/3: Cordner, Waterford.

317 D. Keogh and A. McCartney, *Limerick boycott 1904: Anti-Semitism in Ireland* (Cork: Mercier Press, 2005), xii, 19, 125–6.

318 Darby, *Intimidation and the control of conflict in Northern Ireland*, 97.

a violent undercurrent that became explicit if certain codes – regarding land ownership, religion and political allegiance – were transgressed.

These fearful feelings were all consuming. Individuals and families who had seen their neighbours attacked or received a threatening letter, like those documented in Section 2, did not have to experience actual physical harm to feel frightened enough to leave. Section 1 showed too how personal and financial circumstances, and experiences of persecution under British rule, could determine victims' responses to intimidation. Yet, whilst necessary caution is taken with terms like 'expulsion' and 'cleansing', this chapter proves that intimidation was used in an instrumental way, resulting in significant departures from Munster and Ireland. By collating compensation evidence from both the British and Free State Governments, I draw on the experiences of both permanent migrants and those who were displaced for a number of nights, months or years, but later returned home.

It was certainly the intention of the perpetrators – often identified in warning notices and witness accounts as republicans or military – to clear out the old enemy from the community. Ex-RIC and servicemen and their families, even those with ostensibly tenuous business or social links with the British administration, were punished for their past allegiances (see Section 6 on boycotting). Sectarianism also surfaced in campaigns of intimidation: letters in circulation during the Civil War, including some issued on behalf of the IRA, made specific threats against the Protestant community. Boycotts were enforced on denominational lines, weakening Protestants' commercial hold on an area, particularly in urban communities, where the non-Catholic population and influence was strong. Indeed, whilst a small contingent of Protestant middle-class merchants and professionals continued to thrive in the early Free State, Section 6b challenges the assumption that urban Protestants were less affected by the war than were Protestants in isolated big houses and rural communities.

Nevertheless, attacks on Protestant shops and businesses cannot be seen in isolation from the wider political conflict over the Treaty. Violence and intimidation directed against remnants of British rule in Ireland included not just Protestants, but also 'Staters' of all denominations who, the anti-Treaty army believed, were acquiescing in the maintenance of the British link by accepting the Treaty and the oath of allegiance to the crown. Intimidation of civilians, as well as attacks on public and private property, communications and infrastructure, constituted a serious effort to undermine the authority of the new government.[319] Threats to order

[319] See Chapter 5, Section 4: destruction of property was a powerful tactic and employed more regularly (and with greater efficiency) than was lethal violence against the person, in order to coerce and control the populace.

and stability came from a number of quarters; violence was not the sole preserve of the Free State or republican armed forces. Resolution of land issues was sought through local action as well as legislation: cattle driving, harassment and animal maiming were used to chase away the landowner and re-divide his land (see Sections 3 and 4). This chapter most obviously demonstrates the continued salience and divisive power of the land question across the three Munster counties and particularly in Co. Limerick, which stands out amongst Tipperary and Waterford as a centre for cattle driving and land seizure. And, whilst historical justifications were given and familiar tactics (such as threatening letters) employed, the conflicts witnessed during 1922–3 were not a strict continuation of the Land War struggle against the alien landlord. Former estate-workers and those associated with big house advantages were turned from their homes and jobs, but independence and the Free State's own Land Act (1923) had raised new hopes amongst the landless: the intimidation of farmers in Cos. Limerick, Tipperary and Waterford targeted mainly those who had recently acquired land or held large pastures. There were new scores to be settled: animal maiming (Section 4) emerged as a weapon in bitter personal conflicts over trespass and class rivalries within farming.

The Civil War was a complex conflict in which anti-British hostility, sectarian enmity and local competition over land were bitterly entangled with the war over the Treaty. During the Civil War, observed Eneas McNulty, 'people are choosing who they want in and who they want out'. After service in the British merchant navy and 'my time in the peelers', Eneas had returned to Sligo in 1922 as 'one of the fearing men . . . the boys of the black-list'.[320] Real life Waterford native and Letchworth resident James Coogan called the Irish Free State 'my own country';[321] but, in the violent transition to independence, the place of a Catholic ex-constable was far from secure.[322]

320 Barry, *Whereabouts of Eneas McNulty*, 97, 104, 118.
321 See introduction to this chapter.
322 Coogan's religion verified in the Census: in 1911, thirty-five-year-old, 'Roman Catholic', 'RIC constable' James lived with his wife Nora in Johnstown, Waterford city.

5 Harming Civilians

Killing, Wounding and Sexual Violence in Munster

This book makes use of under-researched sources to capture those violent episodes and experiences that often go unrecorded. Violent death or murder, by contrast, is recognized by historians as an 'unambiguous form of violence that can be measured more reliably' than, say, damage, threats and forcible displacement.[1] Peter Hart measures revolutionary violence in Cork by 'bomb and bullet' for this very reason; death and serious injury caused by guns and explosives are relatively easy to trace.[2] In this chapter, I also look at violence against the person – that is, the infliction of bodily damage and death through physical contact and the use of weapons. My chief focus is violence committed behind the front lines, alongside and away from encounters between the Free State Army and anti-Treaty IRA.

It is possible, as Kalyvas demonstrates in *The Logic of Violence in Civil War* (2006), to make a distinction between violence and the military conflict within which the violence takes place.[3] The violent and intentional victimization of civilians – defined by him as anyone who is not a full-time soldier – is the primary focus of his important work. Drawing on data from conflicts around the world, as well as his own comprehensive research on the wars in Greece (1943–9), Kalyvas explains the 'logic' of civil-war violence: the deliberate infliction of harm by armed political actors on non-combatants is selectively used to maintain or establish control within the contested territory. In communities in Munster, during 1922–3, I also seek 'logic', meaning and purpose in the murder and maiming – largely by armed personnel – of unarmed civilians and those (off-duty soldiers, for example) unable to offer physical resistance at the time of their attack. Chapter 4 reveals how the threat of violence, articulated through written or verbal warnings, was used during the Civil War to drive out

[1] Kalyvas, *Logic of violence*, 20.
[2] Hart, *IRA and its enemies*, 319.
[3] See Chapter 1.

unwanted elements from the local community. In this chapter, I explore those cases in which the ominous promises were followed through.

1. Civilians: Definition and Discussion

Some civilian fatalities can be accounted for as collateral damage of a war played out close to the people: deaths were inevitable as the Free State Army and anti-Treaty IRA vied for control of Limerick's barracks and clashed in the streets of Waterford, Clonmel and other republican-held towns. The compensation claims reveal what happened when non-combatants were caught, literally, in the crossfire of the short, but 'sharp',[4] military phase of the war. Daniel Donovan's claim was rejected by the IGC because he suffered gunshot wounds in an exchange between the Free State and Irregular armies in Limerick city on 19 July 1922; Donovan was injured, in other words, during the course of the fighting and was not targeted for his personal affiliations. As a prison official since 1906, Donovan may have been seen as a representative of the British justice system in Ireland. However, his shooting was deemed non-malicious. For the purposes of compensation, Donovan could not prove that his injuries were sustained on account of 'pre-Truce' British loyalty.[5] George Hehir's daughter, Kathleen, was accidentally shot and killed in Boherboy, near Kilcornan, Co. Limerick, during 'an altercation between officers of the National Army and some civilians', on Christmas Eve 1922. Seventeen-year-old Kathleen had supported her siblings by working as a servant in Limerick city, but the IGC rejected George's claim (£210) for the loss of his daughter's earnings. The grieving father understandably felt hard done by; he had already been disappointed by an 'unjust' award of £40 from the Free State Personal Injuries Committee.[6]

However, whilst George Hehir undoubtedly saw his daughter as an unfortunate bystander, a casualty of a military and political conflict in which she took no part, the intentions and identities of Kathleen's killers were far from clear. Often, the 'killing of civilians is careless or coincidental and not the main purpose of an attack or of the war as a whole'.[7] Kathleen's death would seem to fall in this category. Louise Ryan states that female casualties of the War of Independence were 'usually' those

[4] The local Munster press described a number of 'lively' encounters; see Chapter 1.

[5] TNA, CO 762/79/2: Donovan, Limerick.

[6] See Chapter 2 on the operation of the Compensation (Personal Injuries) Committee.

[7] Slim, *Killing civilians*, 40.

women and girls 'shot in the cross-fire between the British military and the IRA'.[8] However, my research on Munster during 1922–3 complicates the notion of a passive, homogenous public simply waiting to be gunned down by Irregulars or rescued by the Free State. For a start, the shots that killed Kathleen were exchanged between civilians and the National Army, not the republicans. Secondly, just because the casualty was not personally singled out and killed, it does not mean she was entirely uninvolved in civil-war violence. The identity of a civilian may be clear outside war; members of this protected group include unarmed men, women, children, the elderly and medical officials. But, within war, 'harmlessness', or non-combatant status, is ambiguous.[9] The intimidation of shopkeepers and businessmen who had dealt with the British administration in Ireland, or supported the Free State Army in some way, shows that even the seemingly innocuous act of boarding soldiers or dealing with a boycotted farmer linked the 'civilian' victim 'to one side or another'.[10] Notices posted around Newcastle West, Co. Limerick, for example, warned: 'any shops supplying food to the Army will be treated as armed soldiers'. And a number of women (allegedly members of Cumman na mBan) were arrested in Nenagh, Co. Tipperary, after posters making similar threats towards shopkeepers were distributed in Listowel, Co. Kerry.[11]

Neither would have Kathleen Hehir been removed from harm's way by virtue of being a young woman. In traditional representations of the civilian idea, women and children are the 'epitome of innocence in war'.[12] Nationalist accounts of the War of Independence certainly celebrated the heroic deeds of 'brave young men', whilst women were 'contained within the conventional narratives of grieving mothers or passive, nameless victims'.[13] In reality, however, women often share the ideologies of armed groups and, short of participating in the actual fighting, do support militancy. Female couriers, gun runners, cooks and nurses played their role during 1919–21 and involvement continued during the Civil

[8] L. Ryan, '"Drunken Tans": Representations of sex and violence in the Anglo-Irish War, 1919–21', *Feminist Review*, no. 66 (Autumn 2000), 73–94 at 77.

[9] Slim, *Killing civilians*, 204.

[10] IMA, CW/OPS/3/C.

[11] IMA, CW/OPS/3/C. Cumman na mBan: 'the league of women'. Women's auxiliary corps to the Irish Volunteers, founded in 1914; played key supporting role in the 1916 Rising, War of Independence, and Civil War. Most members opposed the Treaty and at least 400 were imprisoned during the Civil War; C. Clear, 'Cumman na mBan', in Connolly, *Oxford companion to Irish history*, 137–8.

[12] Slim, *Killing civilians*, 201.

[13] Ryan, '"Drunken Tans"', *Feminist Review*, 74.

War.[14] Ernie O'Malley certainly had faith in his female comrades in the summer of 1922:

During the Tan war the girls had always helped but they had never sufficient status. Now they were our comrades, loyal, willing and incorruptible comrades. Indefatigable, they put the men to shame by their individual zeal and initiative.[15]

The Free State Army reported on 21 October 1922 that women in Clonmel 'are playing a very important part' in the war, carrying dispatches, bringing clothing and food, and 'assisting' the republicans 'in every possible way'.[16] Amongst the 'commercial travellers, postal, and railway workers carrying' messages for the Irregulars in Limerick City, in April 1923, were many women cyclists.[17] Two 'female "diehards"' were arrested in Lisvarrinane, Co. Tipperary, the same day that local republican Dan Breen and two comrades were captured in a dugout in Aherlow.[18]

The 'identification problem' is particularly pertinent in guerrilla wars: when fighting is conducted amongst or even 'through' the people, it is hard for the incumbent power (the Free State, in the case of the Irish Civil War) to 'tell friend from enemy'.[19] One September evening in 1922, for example, Irregulars in Waterford city 'mixed amongst the crowds leaving the picture theatres and indulged in . . . indiscriminate firing, the object being . . . to hit and wound some of the National soldiers who were amongst the audience'.[20] National Troops also observed that working along 'whole time' anti-Treaty personnel in many areas were 'local men' willing to engage acts of destruction and contribute to 'Irregularism' on a more casual basis. 'In some districts', in Co. Limerick, 'these locals specialize in road, rail and wire destruction and in looting', and were 'responsible for a great amount of the opposition encountered'.[21] By 25 April 1923, 'Irregular organization' within the Limerick Command was at a 'very sorry pitch' but, supporting the '115 whole time column men' active in Glin, Ballyhahill, Askeaton, Foynes and Ballybunnion, were 'a large number of men who might do one day's or rather night's work of destruction in the week'.[22]

As well as tracking IRA personnel, armament levels and the republicans' 'immediate aims', the Free State Army weekly Command reports

[14] Ryan, '"Drunken Tans"', *Feminist Review*, 77.
[15] E. O'Malley, *The singing flame* (Dublin: Anvil Books, 1978), 148.
[16] IMA, CW/OPS/1/A.
[17] IMA, CW/OPS/2/M.
[18] IMA, CW/OPS/3/C.
[19] Kalyvas, *Logic of violence*, 89, 91.
[20] *Waterford News*, 8 September 1922.
[21] IMA, CW/OPS/2/M.
[22] IMA, CW/OPS/3/C.

obsessively attempted to gauge local 'morale': were 'agrarian motives, labour trouble, lawlessness' helping the Irregulars? What were republican 'relations with the people'? The identity of 'the people', though, was fairly simplistically conceived: the assumption was that, save a few misguided rebels, the majority of the population was united on the side of authority. One Intelligence Officer, for example, observed two postmasters in the Waterford area 'with 'strong "Die-Hard" sympathies', but stated these were not widely shared: Williams, the postmaster in Kilmacow, 'is believed to be active, and his Post Office is boycotted at present by the people'.[23] The same 'people', Free State General Brennan commented, 'seem to be getting very tired of this trouble'.[24] It was suggested that supporters of the Irregulars did so under threat of violence: information 'is not received very freely', in the Limerick Command area, 'due to fear of reprisals by Irregulars'.[25] By April 1923, Limerick city columns 'hardly deserve the name of "column"', but, even these relatively weak republican bands were intimidating:

> The people show no love for the Irregulars or their tactics, but nevertheless information is slow in coming in. The reason for this is fear of the Irregulars having reprisals afterwards.[26]

Intelligence on republican movements was highly prized. Indeed, whilst popular 'support' for one side or the other takes many forms, Kalyvas argues that 'malicious denunciation' – civilians informing or 'snitching' on their enemies, by passing information to armed forces – is central to civil war. The war for information and allegiance was certainly closely fought in Munster. 'Spies' and 'traitors' on both sides often met a violent end. Keeping quiet could be as dangerous and divisive as speaking out: a report from a Free State Intelligence Officer hinted at the complicity of civilian funeral-goers in Dungarvan, Co. Waterford in a republican attack on National Troops. On 10 December 1922, about four miles outside the town:

> The Irregulars were laying in wait for the men coming with the car. The car passed the place, but the Irregulars did not fire, as there was a funeral passing at the time. Most of the people at the funeral knew that the Irregulars were there, but they did not tell the officer. They were waiting to see the ambush.[27]

23 IMA, CW/OPS/1/A.
24 IMA, CW/OPS/2/A.
25 IMA, CW/OPS/3/C.
26 IMA, CW/OPS/2/M.
27 IMA, CW/OPS/1/A.

Indeed, the sparse sources that survive from the republican side suggest that in some communities the warm reception usually reserved for National Troops (or so the local press would have the reader believe)[28] was also extended to the anti-Treaty side. On 5 October 1922, an unnamed soldier:

Returned from Tipperary on Tuesday evening, having travelled through most of the [third brigade] Area. Things are fine all through there and the civil population are most friendly. On Sunday I was at Mass in Rosegreen, and a column of 35 IRA men armed with rifles marched into the church for Mass. Returning from Mass the column was marching along the road quite openly and the people were all calling out hearty greetings to them. I slept in three different houses, miles apart, and found the same friendliness towards the boys everywhere.[29]

In memoirs first published in 1982, Liam Deasy claims that he and three IRA companions were well catered for as they passed through the county: from the 'Powells of Ballynaclough, a very friendly Protestant family', the soldiers received 'a typical Tipperary welcome'.[30] Geography was important, as ever, in the relative intensity of the republican struggle. The IRA was aware of its weaknesses and lack of support in certain areas, but knew how to use the landscape to their advantage. By late 1922, Deasy recalled, thanks to the imprisonment of many officers:

North Tipperary was considered dormant, with the exception of the district from Rear Cross in the west to Kilcommon north of Templederry, areas which included the north Tipperary mountains. Here with a very small force, we were more than holding our own in keeping the Free State forces at bay.

Following one failed expedition, Deasy and company retreated from the plains of Toomevara to the 'comparative safety' of the Tipperary hills.[31] A Free State Battalion operating around Nenagh reported that the 'civilian population in the mountainous districts are favourable to the Irregulars'.[32] O'Malley describes the 'sliding scale': 'weakly-held areas were often nearly eliminated, but again recruited and reorganised'.[33] Local knowledge was crucial to this republican leader. During the War of Independence, O'Malley had organized the IRA Second Southern Division (encompassing the 'greater part' of Tipperary, half of Limerick

28 Whilst residents of Bruree welcomed the 'striking progress' made by the Free State in their town, for example, Irregulars were defeated in a 'volley of machine-gun fire': *Limerick Leader*, 31 July 1922.

29 IMA, Captured Documents, Lot 4, A/0992/1.

30 L. Deasy, *Brother against brother* (Cork: Mercier Press, 1998), 92.

31 Deasy, *Brother against brother*, 91–2.

32 IMA, CW/OPS/3/C.

33 O'Malley, *Singing flame*, 162.

and a 'portion' of Waterford): 'I had cycled or tramped across it. . . . I understood the type of men there'. He was consequently annoyed with his civil-war appointment as Assistant Chief of Staff for the 'strange country' of Ulster and Leinster.[34]

The military strength of and support for the anti-Treaty IRA at any one time was also unavoidably linked to rise and fall of its leaders: the deaths of Tipperary's O/C Dinny Lacey (d. 18 February 1923) and IRA Chief of Staff Liam Lynch (d. 10 April 1923) had a particularly demoralizing effect. The capture of Breen, Donovan and Walsh in Co. Tipperary, in April 1923, was 'one of the biggest blows the Irregulars have suffered since the outbreak of hostilities, and should go a long way towards establishing peace in the area'.[35] The detention by the Free State of Breen, and other popular and prominent anti-Treaty men, 'finished any organised resistance to our troops in this area'; the 'civilian population' saw the 'downfall of the Irregulars' was near and were 'deserting the "cause" accordingly'.[36]

In Ireland, as often happens in civil war, simple, mercenary motives undoubtedly accounted for fraternization with one side or the other. 'Country people' in the vicinity of Newcastle West, for example, backed the republicans because, 'whilst chaos reigned', they could 'avoid payment of both their civil debt and their rates and taxes'. However, the 'town's people are supporters of the [Free State] Army for the same reason, that they will get their accounts paid when more lawful times arrive'.[37] The 'machinery of civilised life' tended to 'run with more or less smoothness' in areas where the government was in the ascendant, although, the *Church of Ireland Gazette* observed, 'the dislocation caused by Irregular occupation will take long to set right'.[38] A desire for respite, from the destruction and disruption dramatically depicted in the compensation evidence and local press, is perfectly understandable. Clonmel may have been 'spared the horrors of a stand-up fight in the streets', but the town was brought virtually to a standstill during the summer: 'the humiliations inflicted on the people and the deprivations which they had to endure was a sufficiently severe trial'. Industry, trade and commerce suffered under Irregular occupation.[39] By September 1922, the Free State had recaptured republican strongholds, but life did not

34 O'Malley, *Singing flame*, 139–40.
35 IMA, CW/OPS/3/C.
36 IMA, CW/OPS/3/C.
37 IMA, CW/OPS/3/C.
38 *Church of Ireland Gazette*, 4 August 1922
39 *Clonmel Chronicle*, 19 August 1922.

immediately return to normal: in late January 1923, Dungarvan, Co. Waterford, remained 'almost completely shut off from the outside world':

> No daily papers came here on Friday or Saturday.... Letters take a long while to come here and the general upset is felt very much by the inhabitants. But for the open port there would be intense suffering amongst the people for want of provisions.... We are thrown back almost to the middle ages and the upset to business is severely felt by the trading community.[40]

The Post Office reported to the Irish Government on the difficulty of getting messages through in July 1922: explosions on the railway line, 'impassable' roads and the cutting of telegraph wires isolated Limerick from everywhere but Dublin and Ennis.[41]

That is not to say that the republicans gave no thought to the unpopularity of their violent devastation: the Free State Army expected a 'cessation' in the 'War of Destruction' once the 'Irregular leaders wish to curry favour with the people'.[42] Many anti-Treaty soldiers were more realistic than Lynch, who 'clung to the illusion that he could transform the military situation once enough weapons were secured'.[43] Early in the conflict, Lacey had warned that republicans could become unpopular in Co. Tipperary if soldiers continued to 'scrounge on the countryside' and upset the local economy by, for example, burning Tipperary's famous creameries.[44] And this did happen: by May 1923, civilians had become 'fed up' with the 'constant drain on their resources'.[45] 'True we were still given food and shelter', said Deasy of the Civil War; but, whilst the 'hospitality... generosity and... bravery' of the people 'were the real backbone' of the War of Independence, by 1922–3 Deasy 'could not help feeling that for the most part we were being tolerated because of who we were or because of our success in earlier times'.[46]

The Irish Civil War was not as 'protracted' as the conflicts studied by Kalyvas. However, as happened in Greece and Spain, 'fatigue and suffering... undermine[d] preferences and sympathies'[47] in Irish communities – particularly in a violent county (Tipperary) already subjected to a two-year War of Independence.[48] The desire for the restoration of order

[40] *Munster Express*, 27 January 1923.
[41] NAI, S 567: 'Post Office reports'.
[42] IMA, CW/OPS/3/C.
[43] O'Halpin, *Defending Ireland*, 28.
[44] Hopkinson, *Green against green*, 151, 168.
[45] IMA, CW/OPS/2/M. See also Chapter 2, Section 1, on the 'commandeering' of private property by the republican (and sometimes Free State) armies.
[46] L. Deasy, *Brother against brother*, 96.
[47] Kalyvas, *Logic of violence*, 116.
[48] A county with a historical penchant for violence (see Chapter 1) and the largest share of the compensation claims (see Chapter 3, Section 1).

trumped pre-war social and political allegiances and ideologies; support was lent to the side that offered civilians protection. In the Free State, 'yearnings for peace and stability' even overrode qualms about draconian state methods: the 'Army Emergency Powers Resolution', introduced in the Dáil on 27 September 1922, allowed for indefinite detention without trial, control of firearms dealing by the National Army, and the establishment of military courts with the power to impose the death sentence on non-Army personnel.[49] There are some notorious recorded incidents of Free State cruelty: the Department of Justice files relating to the highly controversial 'Kerry mine explosions', at Ballyseedy Cross,[50] for example, have been released only recently.[51] However, the impression from the ground is that support lay mostly with the Free State, 'even at its most coercive'.[52]

2. Killing and Wounding

a) *Armed or Unarmed?*

The emergence, in the second-half of the nineteenth century, of new technologies and explosives (dynamite was patented by Alfred Nobel in 1867) had presented Irish revolutionary nationalists with new, spectacular methods of warfare.[53] The first famous explosion, at Clerkenwell prison in 1867, was accidental: an attempt to free a prisoner went tragically wrong. However, during the 'Skirmishing campaign', 1881–5, Fenian dynamiters systematically bombed a number of public targets in Britain, causing significant injuries, structural damage and, at Salford Barracks, the death of a young boy. From the mid-1880s, however, much of the earlier enthusiasm about the destructive capacity of the new explosives had been lost; the dynamiters' bombs turned out to be 'pinpricks, rather than serious subversion'.[54]

During the Civil War, bombs certainly were used less frequently than were simpler methods of warfare. Whilst smoke bombs 'were of great advantage in attacking buildings', republicans in Munster found 'incendiary bombs' designed to take human life more difficult to manufacture

49 C. Campbell, *Emergency law in Ireland, 1918–1925* (Oxford: Clarendon Press, 1994), 163–4.
50 Hopkinson, *Green against green*, 240–1.
51 NAI, Records of the Department of Justice, 2008/152/27.
52 Foster, *Modern Ireland*, 513.
53 N. Whelehan, *The Dynamiters: Irish nationalism and political violence in the wider world, 1867–1900* (Cambridge: Cambridge University Press, 2012), xiii, 21.
54 Whelehan, *The Dynamiters*, 302.

and use to any great effect.[55] A January 1923 reminder to all battalions in the Third Tipperary Brigade, from the Third Eastern Division of the anti-Treaty IRA, warned munitions officers and 'divisional chemists' to take care in handling and sourcing explosives: half the 'Mills Bombs' purchased 'from a member of the enemy Garrison', by the South Wexford Brigade, were found to be 'fitted with [an] instantaneous fuse'. This was a 'trick... intended to blow up any of our troops into whose hands these bombs may fall'.[56] This trade in unreliable munitions also highlights more controversial questions of allegiance: clearly not all links had been severed between the incumbent power and the insurgents. One republican recorded the 'considerable transfer of "stuff"' from undisciplined Free State ranks to 'our men' around Templemore, Co. Tipperary.[57] 'Stuff' may well have included these dangerous explosives and, whilst each side was mistrustful of the other, deals were done during the Civil War.

Whilst armament levels varied within and across the counties, the anti-Treaty IRA was much better equipped with rifles and revolvers than with bombs.[58] The impression from the military reports is that gunshot wounds were the more common cause of death and injury in the Civil War. 'Open conflict' and gun battles in the street lasted just a couple of months, but ambushes and sniping continued after towns like Clonmel had been secured.[59] In early October 1922, National Troops were surprised on the Clonmel-Cahir road 'for the third time in two months'.[60] A notice from the Third Tipperary Brigade Headquarters reprimanded one Commander-in-Chief because 'the "Activities"' of his (Eighth) Battalion were 'not up to the mark in the way of sniping'. He was reminded: 'the sniping of sentries, lorries and patrols demoralizes the enemy as well as inflicting casualties on them. You will see that these "Activities" are greatly increased for the future'.[61]

The press contrasted these 'mean tactics' with the military prowess and confidence with which the Free State defeated its enemies. On the Woodrooffe demesne, near Clonmel, National Troops took a 'gallant

55 IMA, Captured Documents, Lot 4, A/0992/1: 'smoke bombs' were thrown at Limerick city Civic Guards Barracks, John Street (26 March 1923) and placed in a barricade on the Foynes-Loughill Road (24 April 1923).

56 IMA, Captured Documents, Lot 110, A/1100.

57 IMA, Captured Documents, Lot 4, A/0992/1.

58 IMA, CW/OPS/1/A: Irregulars in Clonmel, for example, were 'well equipped' with 'Thompsons and Lewis guns', late into October 1922.

59 Campbell, *Emergency law in Ireland*, 155.

60 *Clonmel Chronicle*, 4 October 1922. See also numerous Free State Army reports on sniping: IMA, CW/OPS/1/A, CW/OPS/2/B.

61 IMA, Captured Documents, Lot 110, A/1100.

stand' against an Irregular ambush. The number of republican deaths was 'unknown', but, despite three dead and nine wounded National Troops, victory was claimed for the Free State, who 'put up a fight worthy of the traditions of Irish valour and routed the enemy, who withdrew to the mountains'.[62] Woodrooffe had been the site of a deadly War of Independence ambush and further deserved its 'unpleasant prominence in local history' after the burning of the big house on the estate in February 1923.[63] Just as the guerrilla tactics that had 'proved so successful against the British were now employed' against the Free State,[64] so the new Irish Government appropriated the discourse of the governor-oppressor in its response to this violence. Tags ('Diehard', 'Irregular') used in Free State Army reports, for example, denote the perceived illegitimacy of the republican cause and the immorality of their tactics. 'Those Free State people who had once glorified the ambush', remembered O'Malley, 'now spoke of it as cowardly form of murder'.[65] Deaths of Irregulars were not celebrated. No delight could be taken, for example, in the 'awful mutilation' of three young republicans, killed laying a mine outside the home of a former RM in Clonmel: 'a leg of one of the unfortunate victims was found hanging on to a tree close by'.[66] The ranks of the anti-Treaty IRA evidently included men of 'undoubted personal courage', such as 'well known' republican leader Patrick 'The Tank' Dalton, of Co. Tipperary.[67] Ultimately, however, it was for the Free State Army, and not republican rebels, that the moral high ground was reserved. Republicans were portrayed as bandits lacking in respect for civil and religious authority: attacks on Free State soldiers on their way to Mass were seen as particularly underhand and morally reprehensible.[68] The Catholic hierarchy condemned these attacks and the clashes in crowded streets that wounded 'peaceful citizens' as well as soldiers.[69] In a 'new form of frightfulness devised by the apostles of freedom' in their 'campaign against the people', republicans ambushed some Guards, stole their valuables and,

62 *Clonmel Chronicle*, 16, 19 August 1922. Woodrooffe is at the foot of the Comeragh Mountains; see Map 1.
63 See Chapter 3.
64 Campbell, *Emergency law in Ireland*, 160.
65 O'Malley, *Singing flame*, 152.
66 *Clonmel Chronicle*, 9 August 1922.
67 *Clonmel Chronicle*, 28 October 1922.
68 *Clonmel Chronicle*, 20 September 1922 and 14 February 1923.
69 Archdiocesan Archives, Monsignor M.J. Curran papers, Political papers, Box 2660: 'Pastoral letter of His Eminence Cardinal Logue, the archbishops and bishops of Ireland, to the priests and people of Ireland. To be read in all Churches and public oratories 22 October 1922'.

most despicably, threw their rosary beads and Sacred Heart badges on floor.[70]

Press attention focused on these local outrages and personal tragedies. At Woodhouse, in the deep ravine 'ideally suitable for the ambushers' purpose' between the villages of Millstreet and Ballinamult, Co. Waterford, three National Troops were shot at and killed. And so a fairly routine operation from Dungarvan – to round up an 'Irregular flying column' – ended suddenly for Vol Larry Phelan from Kilmacthomas (shot through the spine and killed instantly) and Vol Patrick Foley of Waterford city (succumbed in hospital to a serious head wound).[71] Twenty-three-year-old Phelan, it was reported, was a 'splendid type of man' and an 'immense congregation' gathered at his interment.[72] These public outcries of grief contrasted sharply, of course, with the lack of (at least demonstrable) local support at the funerals of British soldiers and policemen during the War of Independence. On 30 May 1920, in Co. Limerick, a guard of honour and coffin 'draped in the Union Jack' made its way to the Catholic churchyard in Killmallock as Constable Morton, who had been killed in an attack on the town barracks, was laid to rest. 'Few townspeople' attended the funeral but, as the coffin passed, 'small groups raised their hats'.[73] Certainly, the treatment of the victim after death can be as symbolic as the killing itself: mutilation of the body or the 'denial of a decent burial' has been observed across different cultures as a powerful show of strength on the part of the attacker.[74]

The loss of local lives in 'fratricidal strife' was marked with a particular bitterness:[75] eighteen-year-old Corporal John Kelly, for example, shot dead on the march into Clonmel in August 1922, had not died in glory on a faraway battlefield, nor joined the heroes of 1916, but had fallen victim to 'the policy of the Irregulars' – that is, their campaign of political violence against the new government. Yet he had, at least, been 'killed in action', and was armed and able to defend himself at the time of death. Indeed, whilst the horror of any death is not disputed, the manner of

70 NAI, Records of the Department of Justice, H 99/109: 'Attacks on Garda Síochána'.

71 *Waterford News*, 27 October 1922.

72 Many reports on Free State losses were followed a few days later with news of the soldiers' funerals. See for example: *Clonmel Chronicle*, 23 and 26 August 1922: at the funerals of Sergeant Finegan and Private Walter Cantwell, killed in ambush at Redmondstown, near Clonmel, 'every mark of sympathy and respect was shown, indicating the popular grief evoked by the sad occurrence'.

73 Abbott, *Police casualties in Ireland*, 82.

74 Blok, *Honour and violence*, 114.

75 *Clonmel Chronicle*, 12 August 1922.

Table 3. *Police casualties in the three Munster counties*

	Limerick	Tipperary	Waterford	TOTAL
1919	3	4		7
1920	14	22	3	39
1921	21	14	5	40
1922	1	3		4
TOTAL	39	43	8	90

Source: R. Abbott, *Police casualties in Ireland 1919–1922* (Cork: Mercier Press, 2000), 30, 33, 35, 39, 44, 51, 62–3, 68, 75, 77, 79, 87, 90, 92, 95, 96, 104, 110–11, 119, 121, 127, 148–9, 151, 156, 165–7, 184, 195, 199, 205, 211–12, 220–1, 225–6, 231, 239, 240–1, 249, 253–4, 261–3, 271, 278–9, 285.

Kelly's killing (and of Phelan and Foley, mentioned previously) was very different from the cases, explored in the rest of this section, where disbanded British policemen, off-duty soldiers and civilians were murdered at home or kidnapped and dumped after death.

Head-Constable Christopher Davis, RIC, is included in the casualty list – painstakingly compiled by Richard Abbott – of those 493 policemen who died in the discharge of their duty, 1919–22. Approximately 18 per cent of these deaths took place in Cos. Limerick, Tipperary and Waterford; see Table 3.[76]

Davis, a forty-two-year-old married man from Co. Galway, was killed in an affray in Tipperary town on 3 March 1922. As his 'Crossley tender' and another vehicle were leaving for Dublin, the party was ambushed in Michael's Street: Davis and another constable were shot and later died from their wounds. This high-profile case was brought to the attention of Parliament.[77] Davis's widow, Alice, and their five children, aged between six months and fourteen years, 'keenly [felt] the great loss they have suffered' and the family moved to England where, by the time Alice applied for compensation, in November 1926, they had joined the 'little colony' of ex-constables and their families in Letchworth garden city, Hertfordshire.[78] Davis was a Protestant and a 'most notable reference' from Rev. Horace Deane in Cahir, where Davis had been stationed 'for

[76] Jim Herlihy offers similar casualty figures for the three counties during 1919–22: 38 in Limerick, 43 in Tipperary, 7 in Waterford. See J. Herlihy, *The Royal Irish Constabulary: A short history and genealogical guide: With a select list of medal awards and casualties* (Dublin: Four Courts Press, 1997), 152.

[77] *House of Lords Debate*, 8 March 1922, vol. XLIX, cc372–83.

[78] *Clonmel Chronicle*, 16 December 1922; see Chapter 4.

some considerable time', probably helped to convince the IGC to make an award to Alice.[79]

However, what complicates this killing – and the shooting of other on-duty, but soon-to-be-ex-constables – is the disbandment of the RIC from 27 March 1922. The armed, centrally organized Irish policing system had always stood out from forces elsewhere in Britain and had struggled to escape its 'paramilitary image'.[80] Thanks to poor administration and intelligence gathering, and declining morale after World War I, the twentieth-century constabulary was even further out of touch with an increasingly nationalist public. From 1916, the RIC 'bore the brunt' of escalating republican intimidation and violence. After Sinn Féin's 1918 electoral victory, efforts to 'isolate and humiliate' the police became 'organised'. And, when dwindling officer numbers were boosted by the notorious 'Black and Tan' and Auxiliary forces, policemen became more than ever a legitimate target for IRA violence. Constables killed during 1919–22, then, were casualties of 'political violence', shot as symbols of British 'imperial power'.[81] Policemen were equipped and entitled to retaliate, and their murder scored a tactical point against the state. However, after disbandment, as members of the RIC began to disperse and return to civilian life, they began increasingly to come under personal attack and were no longer able to defend themselves.

The death of ex-RIC Sergeant Walshe, for example, took place in the context of disbandment and shows how the British policeman, once the enemy at the heart of the IRA campaign to undermine law and order in Ireland, had become in a matter of months a soft target, whose death was of little strategic value. Walshe was shot dead at the family house in Newport, Co. Tipperary, on 23 May 1922.[82] His killers – 'undisguised', in 'trench coats' and identifying themselves as 'IRA' – called him out of the room where he sat with his family and into the hallway, claiming they wanted Walshe at the barrack and 'would do nothing to him'. Yet, almost immediately, several shots were heard and Walshe 'fell back on the sofa with his hands crossed on his breast'. He never spoke again and his twelve-year-old daughter went for a priest. A native of Abbeydorney, Co. Kerry, there was no evidence of any personal or local vendettas against

[79] TNA, CO 762/53/6: Davis, Tipperary. The case was also heard in the Tipperary courts, under the Criminal Injuries Act, but the Free State was less generous than the IGC; see Chapter 2 on compensation policy and procedure.

[80] Abbott, *Police casualties in Ireland,* 14. See also: Regan and Augusteijn (ed.), *Memoirs of John M. Regan*, 9; Townshend, *Political violence in Ireland*, 72–3.

[81] Abbott, *Police casualties in Ireland,* 16.

[82] Abbott, *Police casualties in Ireland,* 293.

Walshe. Like the eighty-nine constables accounted for in Table 3, he was targeted largely because of the regime he represented. There was, however, a crucial difference: the disbanded policeman no longer had the protection of the old power when he was killed. Walshe was unarmed and defenceless at the time of death. It seems that Walshe had suspected that his old job would cause him trouble once the British departed: reports suggest that just prior to the attack the ex-constable was preparing to leave the county with his family (to return to Kerry, perhaps, because his service in Tipperary had ended).[83]

Walshe and his cohort were not nameless representatives of the British state killed in the line of duty; ex-policemen were sought out and targeted with deadly violence in their own homes. James Reilly, caught up in the violence surrounding the disbandment of the RIC from Tipperary town, was attacked for his property, as well as his past service. Reilly had served in the RIC for thirty-nine years and, on his retirement in 1920, had set up a restaurant and boarding house in Tipperary town, 'largely patronised by Crown Forces particularly the RIC'. His line of work 'brought him into great disfavour with the local civilian inhabitants', and he further attracted 'the unfavourable attention of the local IRA' by assisting wounded policemen in Tipperary in March 1922 'and helping with funeral arrangements'.[84] Under threat from the Irregulars, Reilly left for London three days after the receipt, on 18 May 1922, of his final threatening notice. One week later, his son was visited 'by IRA men' and 'told that if I returned I should be "plugged" [shot], as a prominent Irregular wanted my house and would have it at any price'. And, as a final insult, a boycott was enforced on the sale of his business.[85]

The ex-Serviceman was another former agent of the British state in Ireland who, by the Civil War, had been divested of the political and military credentials that had marked him out for attack during the War of Independence. Patrick Galligan was also killed in Newport, and in the same month as Walshe, although his death took quite a different form. In making her appeal for funds, Bridget Galligan naturally emphasized the financial impact of her husband's murder: Patrick, aged forty-seven, had been earning 35/- per week as a casual labourer and received an army pension of 15/- per week, which ceased on his death; his widow was left with 'no means of subsistence'. Bridget's situation was one 'of very exceptional hardship' and, in December 1926, the IGC granted

[83] *Limerick Leader*, 22 May 1922.

[84] Head-Constable Christopher Davis, discussed previously, was one of those killed on this occasion.

[85] TNA, CO 762/4/2: Reilly, Tipperary.

her £600. Bridget had until that time received no compensation for the attack, although the Free State's Compensation (Personal Injuries) Committee had ruled that, from 1 April 1923 until they reached the age of sixteen, an allowance of £1.5.0 per month be paid for each of her six children. The significance of this case, however, lies not in those left behind, but how the ex-Serviceman met his end. On 21 May 1922, Galligan's house in Newport, Co. Tipperary, was raided 'by a number of armed men' and Patrick pulled out of his bed and shot dead. Bridget explained:

> My husband an ex-British soldier who served in India, South Africa and also in France during the Great War was murdered by the Irregulars . . . in the presence of myself and my six young children . . . the eldest just over 13.[86]

That the family had to witness the death seems particularly cruel. Usually some distinction was maintained between what was in the eyes of the killers a justifiable, political target, such as an ex-solider or policeman, and his civilian relatives.[87] Friends of this ex-policeman were also at risk. Maurice O'Brien, a Loyalist cattle-dealer from Ashroe, Co. Limerick (just a few miles from Newport),[88] feared for his own safety after the shooting, and Edward Delany was frightened he would meet the same fate as 'two friends . . . Patrick Galligan and Sergeant J Walsh',[89] after he was fired on whilst collecting 'driven' cattle.

George Brophy's attackers also visited his home, but the killing was carried out elsewhere. The former Lieutenant in the British Army (demobilized with a pension after World War I) previously had been kidnapped and held for a month;[90] on the night of 1 May 1922 he was again 'forcibly taken from his home by republicans' and 'afterwards found to have been shot'. The body was not located and identified until November 1922, even though his wife, Mary, believed that George was killed prior to 8 May.[91] The source of Mary's suspicions about the timing of her husband's death is unclear; perhaps she had heard local rumours. Indeed, Mary seems to have known at least one of George's killers: of the party of seven armed men that called at her house in Upper Irishtown, Mary told the inquest she recognized one, O'Donoghue, who 'asked my husband why he did not leave the area when ordered'.[92] RIC men traditionally

86 TNA, CO 762/19/9: Galligan, Tipperary.

87 Walshe's killers, for example, murdered the ex-Sergeant out of sight of the family sitting-room; see earlier discussion.

88 See Chapter 2, Section 2a.

89 TNA, CO 762/83/12: Delany, Tipperary.

90 *Clonmel Chronicle*, 8 February, 1 March 1922.

91 TNA, CO 762/88/19: Brophy, Tipperary.

92 *Clonmel Chronicle*, 29 November 1922.

had been stationed outside their home communities, often in different counties, to prevent the development of local ties.[93] After independence, by contrast, disbanded constables and ex-Servicemen, such as Brophy, were murdered close to home and, as Mary's testimony suggests, perhaps even by perpetrators known to them. If Mary did not already feel isolated from her neighbours, as an ex-Serviceman's wife, this horrific ordeal cannot have left her in any doubt of the ill-feeling towards her family, which continued after George's death and left the widow in dire financial straits. Their small provision shop and egg-selling business in Clonmel, Co. Tipperary folded because of 'customer fear'. The local community was afraid, presumably, of patronizing a marked family like the Brophys. Certainly the circumstances of George's 'end frightened people away from the shop as in 1922 and 1923 the Irregulars saw to it that no-one had anything to do with their enemies'.[94]

'Kinship . . . is often enough to degrade a person's civilian status in the eyes of their enemy. . . . The fact that ordinary people are related to people in armed forces leads many to assume that they are inevitably helping [or] hiding . . . their people . . . and they must also share the same political views as their kin'.[95] Mary Brophy may have been seen, then, as an 'active sympathiser' in the eyes of George's killers. The Free State Army similarly kept a close eye on 'Mrs Edwards', who had stored arms in her home and become 'a notable personality amongst the "Die-Hards"', after the shooting of her son, Sean Edwards, in Kilkenny Prison in August 1921.[96] Yet, whilst these women experienced (very different kinds of) persecution, intimidation and isolation, they were not subject to violence against their person. Some deliberate shootings of women during 1919–21 were legitimized, Ryan contends, by the collusion of the females in question with the British authorities; 'women were defined through their relationship with the enemy; as spies or as girlfriends'.[97] Nevertheless, the gender distinction – apparent in the following account of a lethal War of Independence ambush – seemingly was maintained during the Civil War. On 14 May 1921, DI Henry Biggs and a military officer were travelling 'with three ladies . . . in a private motor car from Killorcully to Newport', Co. Tipperary, when they were surprised at Coolboreen by a party of twelve armed men. Miss Barrington was killed outright,[98] but, 'seeing there was a woman in the car an IRA man called out that the

[93] Regan and Augusteijn (ed.), *Memoirs of John M. Regan*, 12.
[94] TNA, CO 762/88/19: Brophy, Tipperary.
[95] Slim, *Killing civilians*, 95.
[96] IMA, CW/OPS/1/A
[97] Ryan, '"Drunken Tans"', *Feminist Review*, 83–4.
[98] The daughter of Sir Charles Barrington of Glenstal Castle, Murroe, Co Limerick.

attack was to stop' and, as one attacker left the scene, 'he told the other lady who had been slightly wounded that he was sorry that the women had been injured'. By contrast, when the 'leader of the group' found out that the wounded man by the side of the car was the DI, he and several others 'fired at him ten to twelve times with rifles'.[99]

Of course, we can never know for sure what exactly happened at Coolboreen, or indeed at the dozens of military encounters and unofficial episodes of murder and assault that took place during the Irish Revolution. Ambushing is a particularly controversial tactic. Although the fallout following their publication suggests otherwise, Hart's works on revolutionary Cork do not dwell excessively on the infamous encounter, between Auxiliary officers and IRA Volunteers, at Kilmichael on 28 November 1920. 'Military' episodes such as this, Hart explains, 'account for only a small proportion of revolutionary violence'.[100] Meda Ryan's biography of ambush leader Tom Barry, by contrast, sets out to defend the actions of this 'freedom fighter' and deals in detail with Kilmichael.[101] The public wrangling between Hart and the Aubane Historical Society over the 2004 anniversary of the ambush shows that interpretations of Kilmichael remain set along political lines.[102] This contentious and dangerous act of violence was not, however, meant to involve women. The account from Coolboreen, for one, portrays IRA men who shared a common understanding of the fair treatment of women in wartime and, as they committed a lethal act of violence, consciously acted in a socially appropriate way. Violence is often thought about in terms of its easily recognizable ends: killing or wounding an opponent. Yet, like other forms of social action and behaviour, the performance of violence is also important.[103] Murder has an unambiguous effect on the victim, but death – and the way in which the killing is carried out – can also communicate a message to the relatives, friends and local community of the deceased.

b) *Performance*

Chapter 4, on intimidation, reveals that threatening letters were posted on estates to warn off the landlord and grazier and – if the campaign

[99] Abbott, *Police casualties in Ireland*, 240.
[100] Hart, *IRA at war*, 82.
[101] Ryan, *Tom Barry*, 49–67. See also: P. Hart, P. O'Cuanachian, D.R. O'Connor Lysaght, B. Murphy, M. Ryan, J. Lane and B. Clifford, *Kilmichael: The false surrender in the War of Independence: Why the ballot was followed by the bullet* (Millstreet, Co. Cork: Aubane Historical Society, 1999).
[102] D. Fleming, '"War of words" over battle', *BBC News*, 26 November 2004 (http://news.bbc.co.uk/1/hi/world/europe/4043737.stm).
[103] Blok, *Honour and violence*, 108–13.

of intimidation was successful – claim the land for redistribution. The sinister notices used familiar vocabulary and historical pseudonyms; violence against the person also was accompanied by these stylized warnings. Thomas McGrath's bullet-ridden body was found on the road at Knockeevan, Clerihan, in March 1923. In the press, the death was portrayed as a cold-blooded killing: McGrath was taken, unarmed, and executed. The jury at his inquest 'deplored and strongly condemned crimes such as these against the country and the people'.[104] Yet, like RIC and British Army personnel before him, this Free State Army soldier was a valid target for republicans. According to the *Munster Express*, Sergeant McGrath did not work specifically in intelligence, but his killers seemed to believe he had passed on information about the republicans. As an informer, then, McGrath was 'tried' prior to his death (according to the parish priest called 'to minister to the unfortunate young man' in the house where McGrath was held). It was not known how the victim, who had been stationed in Waterford, was brought to the spot in Co. Tipperary where the body was found, nor what exactly happened in between. McGrath, married in Carrick, may well have been a native of Tipperary, and his corpse consequently left in familiar surroundings for added impact.[105] The motive for the killing, on the other hand, was more clearly spelled out: pinned to his coat 'was a paper which bore the words: "Convicted spy – Spies beware. By order, IRA"'. The bullet wounds in McGrath's head and body confirmed the soldier was 'wilfully murdered'; the note too was proof that the death was far from accidental.

The labelling of victims takes place first of all on an abstract level: one step in the 'basic sequence' of actions that enables a person to kill (or tolerate killing) is the 'de-humanising' of the enemy.[106] Victims are described as animals, for example, to make attackers forget their similarities with the enemy group.[107] This book records the range of identity labels ('grazier', 'Loyalist', 'Stater') used by local communities in wartime Munster to define self and other, friend and enemy, during the transition from British rule to Irish independence. Labels can also be used literally, to clarify and reinforce the deterrent message of violence:

Counterrevolutionary rebels in western France [during 1789–99] directed their violence against people accused of informing republican soldiers about their movements; they abandoned mutilated corpses near republican-held towns and

104 *Munster Express*, 10 March 1923.

105 Unfortunately, the Census cannot confirm this guess: there was no policeman named Thomas McGrath in Tipperary or Waterford in 1911 (although, of course, he may not have joined the force by that time). See Census of Ireland, 1911 (online database).

106 Slim, *Killings civilians*, 217–18.

107 Blok, *Honour and violence*, 109.

hung a tag around the informer's neck with his name and those of the victims who were avenged by his death.[108]

Notes tied to dead bodies in Munster during the Civil War similarly warned what lay ahead for alleged spies and traitors. Labelling the deceased with a threatening message had taken place during the War of Independence:[109] on 7 March 1921, James Maher, of Co. Tipperary, for example, met a gruesome end after giving information to the RIC. 'Taken away from his home by Sinn Feiners', to a bog eight miles from Thurles, James was 'riddled' with bullets and 'a label pinned to his coat marked "Spy Informer Traitor"'. His father's torment continued into the Civil War: as the parent of a 'spy', he was intimidated and could not keep his job at Thurles National Bank. Patrick Maher was dismissed in September 1922, his manager having received a letter, 'signed "IRA"', warning 'that unless he . . . wholly discontinued my services permanently as porter', then 'the Bank would be blown up immediately and that his life also would be a forfeit [and] that I would be shot anyway'.[110]

The Maher family posed no military threat to the republicans; 'spy' James and his backers, the British state, already had been removed. His father was a bank worker, not a soldier. The Civil War was not a straightforward continuation of the War of Independence, then, but was instead an opportunity to punish, for their past betrayal, remnants of British rule and relatives of its armed servants. The battle for people's loyalties, for information and support, continued when the Free State came into being. It cannot irrefutably be proved, of course, that the killers in the cases mentioned here belonged to the IRA and were not murderers with personal agendas borrowing provocative words and familiar tactics, such as the threatening notice, for show. James Cleary, a Tipperary labourer, 'had no enemies' and, according to his brother, 'took no part in politics'. The Free State military authorities confirmed that he had never given information. His employer, Walsh, and the local Vice-Commandant of the National Army testified to his 'excellent character'. Yet, on a December evening in 1922, Cleary was taken out of his employer's house and shot dead. Tied around the head of the corpse, discovered by his brother at New Inn, Co. Tipperary, was a label: 'Convicted spy. Spies and informers beware. One of many. IRA'.[111] Perhaps there had been a mix-up;

[108] Kalyvas, *Logic of violence*, 27.

[109] See English, *Ernie O'Malley*, 80, and Hart, *IRA at war*, 156.

[110] TNA, CO 762/55/14: Maher, Tipperary. Patrick made a separate appeal for compensation for the murder of his son, James, but the claim was dismissed as outside the IGC's Terms of Reference: TNA, CO 762/67/9.

[111] *Clonmel Chronicle*, 9 December 1922.

events leading up to the shooting are certainly confusing.[112] According to press reports, a young man entered the kitchen where Cleary sat with Mrs Walsh and, after enquiring of his name, retreated, it is presumed, to consult his comrades. The young man then returned, telling Cleary that he was 'wanted outside' and Mrs Walsh that 'I did not think there was any man of the name of Cleary in the district'. Cleary was never seen alive again. The motive for the killing (and, indeed, the identity of the victim) were thus far from obvious, even to the 'young man' sent to summon Cleary to his fate. The eight bullet wounds in Cleary's head and body, however, were more conclusive: the man was dead, the notice on his body was read and reported in the press, and a personal tragedy was assigned political meaning.[113]

Thomas Brennan was taken from his home near Lisvarrinane, Galbally, Co. Limerick, and shot through the head. The label attached to the body – 'Convicted Spy' – was meant for all to read; Brennan's body was discovered in a pool of blood, by passers-by on the road to Mass.[114] Brennan, a Catholic,[115] was a civilian and had not been convicted of a crime in any official sense. His supposed treachery may have been his position at the local big house: Brennan worked as a gardener on Robert Sanders' estate in the Glen of Aherlow (the mansion there, Ballinacourty, was burned down on 22 October 1922,[116] not long after Brennan's death). Yet, wherever Brennan's loyalties lay in life, it was his death, carried out like a military execution and made public by the dumping of the corpse with the threatening note attached, that warned the local community that 'Free Staters' (whether National Army soldier or big-house gardener) were punishable as spies and traitors of the republic.

The execution by the IRA of at least fifty people in Co. Cork during the War of Independence and Civil War, for various 'crimes against the Republic', is the subject of Gerard Murphy's recent and provocative study.[117] Murphy reveals that, in most cases, families received no information about the fate of the 'disappeared' or the location of the

112 It is also difficult to find out anything more about Cleary, without further personal details; the Census records a number of 'labourers' with this name in Co. Tipperary in 1911.

113 The manner of the killing (shots to the head) and the treatment of the corpse (attacks on the face, the pinning of a calling card) denote clearly a 'spy death'; see A. Dolan, 'Ending war in a "sportsmanlike manner": The milestone of Revolution, 1919–23', in T.E. Hachey (ed.), *Turning points in twentieth-century Irish history* (Dublin: Irish Academic Press, 2011), 21–38.

114 *Clonmel Chronicle*, 16 September 1922.

115 Census of Ireland, 1911 (online database).

116 See Chapter 3; a major labour dispute also took place on the demesne.

117 Murphy, *The year of disappearances*, xii.

body. The 'secret burials'[118] in Cork contrast with the public dumping of the executed traitor (sometimes with a notice attached) in the three Munster counties I studied. In terms of violence and the intensity of its revolutionary experience, Cork was – as Hart has shown – something of a special case;[119] civilian fatalities in the county and its capital were exceptionally high.[120] Murphy's foray into what remains a 'dark part' of Ireland's history is, nonetheless, highly valuable. His social profiles of the dead and disappeared in Cork make clear that, to be killed as a 'spy', one did not have to be actively engaged in espionage. So-called treachery covered a multitude of perceived sins. Hart explains: before the Truce, Protestant deaths could be justified as collateral damage in a war against British 'collaborators or informers'. Attacks on 'spies' during the Civil War, by contrast, had 'little to do' with the victim's actual behaviour.[121] Murphy concurs. IRA gunmen in the later period were fuelled by a 'cocktail of suspicion'; in the elimination of the spy-circles allegedly operating out of Cork's Protestant and Loyalist institutions (the YMCA and Boys' Brigade), civilians, including boys, were shot in groups and unceremoniously dumped.[122]

It may be difficult to see the military justification for the deaths uncovered by Murphy, but, in Cos. Limerick, Tipperary and Waterford, as in Cork, the killing of civilians and unarmed ex-officers was couched in powerful, official language. The 'trial' of republican prisoners and enemies before their 'execution', for example, lent legitimacy to the proceedings. A Protestant clergyman was allegedly 'arrested' and sentenced to death by 'court martial', for example, for helping local residents put out a fire at the police barracks in Portlaw. The sentence was not carried out and the clergyman escaped with his life, but he was made to face up to his crime and 'compelled to apologise'.[123] Civil wars 'by their very nature, break down the distinction between combatant and non-combatant', leading to the targeting of those unable to defend themselves. In interstate war, by contrast, the distinction between armed and unarmed, or soldier and civilian, is 'meant to be at its clearest'. Historically, it was assumed that warfare between European states was in some measure 'rule-bound and subject to codes of morality'.[124] However, World War

118 Murphy, *The year of disappearances*, 256.
119 See Chapter 2, Section 3b.
120 Murphy, *The year of disappearances*, 39.
121 Hart, *IRA at war*, 234, 243.
122 Murphy, *The year of disappearances*, 248–9.
123 *Waterford News*, 28 July 1922.
124 J. Horne and A. Kramer, *German atrocities, 1914: A history of denial* (New Haven: Yale University Press, 2001), 423.

I – and the horrific 'atrocities' committed between German soldiers and the Belgian population in the first months of the war – showed that the normal rules no longer applied. Irish Irregulars, too, defied expectations, acting not like guerrillas or bandits, but as a proper army. Republicans competed for authority with (in their eyes) the flawed and morally weak Free State. Liam Lynch met the 'savagery' of the Irish Government's 'Public Safety' policies, for example, with a campaign of execution: supporters of the coercive legislation were to be 'sentenced to death'.[125] Yet, whilst the Free State's summary execution of four prominent republicans on 8 December 1922, in revenge for the shooting of Sean Hales TD, was performed 'without any pretence of legality', Lynch ordered that republican violence against the other side be controlled and – like a state legal system – commensurate with the offence committed. Provisional Government troops or officials 'convicted' on a list of charges (including the maltreatment of republican prisoners) were to be executed on the production of 'definite evidence', which was to be properly 'recorded' and sent to General Headquarters.[126]

Attacks on civilians recorded in the compensation claims, and now in this chapter, show the Civil War was a bitter and sometimes cruel conflict. Perpetrators on both sides undoubtedly strayed from the military codes of conduct aspired to by Lynch (and in reality his centrally issued missives carried little sway in such a highly localized and disparately fought conflict). Other prominent Munster republicans nonetheless attached a great deal of importance to the way violence was carried out and at the very least paid lip service to the idea of a fair fight. As West Cork Brigade leader during the War of Independence, Barry, for example, allegedly ordered his men not to shoot off-duty soldiers, only revising his policy after the 'callous' treatment of his brigade by one British regiment.[127] Then, during the Civil War, after Barry's escape from prison and return to the fighting in Munster,[128] he again 'asked his men not to shoot an unarmed soldier: "We'll get them in a fight," he said'.[129] We cannot trust unquestioningly Barry's (or his biographer Ryan's) version of events. Ryan's research on Barry's career is valuable, but her 2003 biography had a clear agenda: to restore to Barry the legacy that was being eroded, in her eyes, by revisionists who challenged nationalist shibboleths and

[125] O'Halpin, *Defending Ireland*, 34–7.
[126] IMA, Captured Documents, Lot 110, A/1100.
[127] Ryan, *Tom Barry*, 185.
[128] Ryan, *Tom Barry*, 180–4.
[129] Ryan, *Tom Barry*, 186.

scrutinised heroes.[130] Yet, even if his ideas were not always turned into action, there is, in Ryan's work and Barry's own memoirs, evidence of a dedicated soldier with a strong belief that 'the only way to fight a war was in a warlike fashion'.[131] Whilst Barry joined the British Army simply 'to see what war was like, to get a gun, to see new countries',[132] he subsequently learned about military armament, organization and morale, using this training in Ireland to fight for 'an aim higher than . . . political freedom': 'for the dignity of man and all mankind'.[133]

'Commitment to soldiership' was also a key aspect of O'Malley's 'Revolutionary mentality'.[134] He took pride in his militarism and studied extensively 'explosives, firearms, strategy, and the techniques of warfare'. O'Malley wanted to fight the war properly; 'leadership and calmness' defined his contribution to the 1916–23 struggle.[135] Writing from Mountjoy Prison in January 1923, O'Malley anticipated an 'elaborate trial' by the Free State. He refused to engage, however, with the legal niceties of his case, confident instead in his morally superior position as a soldier of the historic Irish republic. Asked by a Free State captain if he required legal assistance:

> I informed him that I did not require legal assistance; that, as a soldier, I had fought and killed the enemies of our nation, and would do so again, so that a trial for the express purpose of passing sentence did not require a defence on my part.[136]

Neither did Dan Breen recognize the authority of the Free State apparatus: collapsed from 'exhaustion and hunger', at the Glen of Aherlow, Breen was captured and taken to Tipperary, 'where I was put through some form of trial'.[137] Breen also contrasts his alleged poor treatment at the hands of the new government, including the 'humiliation' of being marched through his native town,[138] with his own good conduct in war. Responding to claims from a Tipperary Labour candidate, supposedly intimidated by Breen during the 'Pact' election of 1922, Breen hoped

130 See Section 2a (in this chapter) on the fallout, between Ryan, Peter Hart and others, over the anniversary of the Kilmichael ambush.
131 Ryan, *Tom Barry*, 185.
132 Barry, *Guerilla days in Ireland*, 8.
133 Barry, *Guerilla days in Ireland*, 15
134 English, *Ernie O'Malley*, 73–4.
135 English, *Ernie O'Malley*, 74.
136 English and C.K.H. O'Malley (eds.), *Prisoners: The Civil War letters of Ernie O'Malley* (Swords, Co. Dublin: Poolbeg, 1991), 25, 28.
137 D. Breen, *My fight for Irish freedom* (Dublin: Talbot Press Ltd, 1924), 257–8.
138 Breen, *My fight for Irish freedom* (1924), 258.

'my countrymen know me well enough not to believe that I would ever put a gun up to an unarmed opponent'.[139]

Care must be taken with Breen's reminiscences. *My Fight for Irish Freedom* was 'a ghost-written memoir constructed hastily from Breen's dictation' and in 'blockbusters of revolutionary biography', such as this popular publication, the soldier naturally foregrounds the 'exemplary morality of the Volunteers' ahead of the actions of British forces.[140] The shooting of disbanded British policeman and kidnapping of unarmed Free State soldiers, explored in this section, also complicates his claims of proper behaviour. O'Malley and Breen did take lives and, like paramilitaries on the Continent in this period, were motivated to destroy their British and Free State enemies by the 'holiness of the cause' (in their case, the historic Irish republic, declared in 1916, but betrayed by the Treaty).[141] However, Irish resentment at the Treaty's failure to establish the longed-for republic did not lead to anything close to the 'ultra-violence' unleashed on the civilian populations of Germany, Austria and Hungary, by counter-revolutionary groups frustrated by the rise of socialism and territorial disintegration of the post-war years. World War I produced 'brutalised' veterans across Europe: in Ireland, ex-soldiers became IRA guerrillas, or practiced lethal violence and retribution within the ranks of the notoriously undisciplined Black and Tan and Auxiliary forces.[142] However, it was in Central Europe, not Britain or France, where violent subcultures emerged most obviously after 1918 and where men, hardened by 'four years of organised mass killing', found a new outlet in paramilitarism.[143] Activists no longer 'restrained' by military discipline mounted campaigns of a 'wildness and grimness' not seen during World War I: women and children were burnt alive in their homes, socialist workers were dragged into barracks and beaten senseless.[144]

The majority of the more than 16 million German, Austrian and Hungarian soldiers who had fought in, and survived, World War I, returned to civilian life in November 1918. However, when the German government called for volunteers to fight the Bolsheviks in the Baltic lands, the Poles

139 Breen, *My fight for Irish freedom* (1924), 254.

140 F. Flanagan, '"Your dream not mine": Nationalist disillusionment and the memory of revolution in the Irish Free State', Unpublished D.Phil. thesis (University of Oxford, 2009), 24, 30–1.

141 Gerwarth, 'The Central European counter-revolution', *P&P*, 195.

142 J. Lawrence, 'Forging a peaceable kingdom: War, violence, and fear of brutalization in post-First World War Britain', *Journal of Modern History* 75, no. 3 (September 2003), 557–589.

143 S. Berger, 'Germany', in Gerwarth (ed.), *Twisted paths*, 184–209 at 185.

144 Gerwarth, 'The Central European counter-revolution', *P&P*, 194–5.

along the eastern frontiers, and the internal Communist enemy, 'thousands were eager to enlist, to prolong the life of violence to which they had become accustomed'.[145] In Austria, the *Heimwehren* sprang up in opposition to 'red' Vienna and, in Germany, Great War veterans continued to 'defend the Fatherland' as members of the *Freikorps* (Free Corps).[146] Chapters in this book on arson and intimidation analyze the powerful urge, experienced across Ireland's civil-war communities, to drive from Munster and Ireland the local enemy (Protestants, landlords, graziers and 'Staters'). Republicans did not easily forget past offences. Service during the war, contact with British troops, and the unfair acquisition of land were met, as this chapter reveals, with murder and assault. However, Irish paramilitary groups (namely the anti-Treaty IRA) did not use the breakdown of law and order caused by the Civil War to perpetrate unfettered violence against civil society. Stark contrasts between the British Isles and mainland Europe are obvious in this regard: during Central Europe's White Terror, and the Russian Civil War of 1918–20, gruesome torture and death were 'so common people became inured to it'.[147] Casualty figures in Russia reached 3 million,[148] although total deaths in this country, from the war and the terror, as well as the famine and disease that followed, numbered around 10 million.[149] Post-War Continental Europe had become the site of some of the most barbaric acts of mass murder in recorded history and the killing did not stop: during 1933–45, 14 million civilians perished in the 'bloodlands' in the east.[150]

c) *Motivations*

'No pardon is given', boasted a student volunteer during the post-World War I suppression of a communist uprising in the Ruhr (Germany); 'we shoot even the wounded'.[151] When Co. Waterford magistrate Godfrey Greene was 'put on trial' by his captors, by contrast, his life allegedly was spared because: 'we never shoot wounded prisoners'.[152] Greene returned fire when, on 4 June 1922, a 'large party' shot at his home near Carrick-on-Suir (in Knock-na-Creha, Co. Waterford) where his father-in-law,

145 F.L. Carsten, *Revolution in Central Europe, 1918–1919* (London: Maurice Temple Smith Ltd, 1972), 18.
146 Carsten, *Revolution in Central Europe*, 18.
147 O. Figes, *A people's tragedy: The Russian Revolution 1891–1924* (Harmondsworth: Penguin, 1998), 774.
148 Gerwarth, *Twisted paths*, 2.
149 Figes, *A people's tragedy*, 773.
150 T. Snyder, *Bloodlands: Europe between Hitler and Stalin* (London: Bodley Head, 2010).
151 Gerwarth, 'The Central European counter-revolution', *P&P*, 192.
152 *Clonmel Chronicle*, 10 June 1922.

Matthias Walsh JP, also resided. The *Waterford News* reported the 'thrilling tale' of Greene's 'single-handed resistance with the aid of a double-barrelled shot-gun'.[153] By Kalyvas's definition, Greene was a civilian – that is, he was not a full-time soldier. Yet, whilst the violence at Knock-na-Creha cannot be characterized as a military encounter, Greene was at least able to defend himself, unlike the unarmed ex-constables and Free State soldiers taken from their homes and executed. Greene's trial and release as a 'wounded prisoner' also suggest a fairly organized and targeted attack on his person. Evidently he had committed some serious offence in the eyes of the 'armed men' who returned to the house on 8 October 1922, fired several shots and 'warned Greene to leave the district or take the consequences'. Greene suggested the violence was motivated by pre-existing anti-British sentiment: refusing to resign from his magistracy, he had become over the years the 'object of much hostility' and, for this longstanding demonstration of loyalty, he was subject to a vicious and 'prolonged attack'.[154]

Greene's injuries were serious indeed. A doctor testified to the severity of the wounds to his head, chest and arm. Greene suffered shock, loss of blood and for a year was 'incapacitated from doing business'. During this time, his lands lay derelict and stock went missing or was commandeered.[155] The effect of the attack on Greene's ability to make a living from his farm is telling; local press reports suggest that current land issues, rather than past service as a magistrate, explain the campaign of hostility against him. There had been, according to the *Clonmel Chronicle*, a number of similar incidents of 'intimidation of farmers' candidates'.[156] Greene was a member of County Waterford Farmers' Union and was due to stand in their interests at the June election. Greene may have been 'well known' throughout Cos. Waterford and Tipperary as an ex-JP, strong farmer and aspiring politician, but these credentials did not make him well liked; a number of resentments thus converged in the attacks against him.

Instances of violence against the person are rarely explained by a single motivating factor. We can identify Greene's economic and political interests, speculate how these clashed with a potential attacker's, and observe the violent tactics used in the expression of this conflict, but neither pre-existing ideological cleavages, nor irrational factors, explain completely the violence against him. Nevertheless, a key difference

[153] *Waterford News*, 6 October 1922.
[154] TNA, CO 762/71/16: Greene, Tipperary.
[155] TNA, CO 762/71/16: Greene, Tipperary.
[156] *Clonmel Chronicle*, 21 June 1922; see Chapter 3, Section 2a on the Farmers' Party.

between the Irish Civil War and the conflicts observed by seminal civil-war theorist Kalyvas, is the salience in the Irish case of the overarching national conflict (over political loyalty and British allegiance) in local episodes and experiences of violence. Kalyvas strives to distance his analysis from the widely held theory that on-the-ground dynamics in civil wars are an 'irrelevant manifestation of the macro level'.[157] Individual grievances and local rivalries do sometimes align and interact with broader political and military forces, but, Kalyvas argues, civil-war violence inevitably becomes centred on personal 'revenge'; violence in these conflicts has become 'an end in itself rather than a means to a political ends'.[158]

In Munster, by contrast, the 'end' of violence may not have been overtly political or military in every case, but the formation of conflicting national identities, and the desire to purge from the Free State those loyal to the old administration, recur in contemporary explanations of these ostensibly personal attacks. George Holland looked to recent history and older resentments of British rule to account for his assault. Holland's attackers 'accused me of supplying food and lodging . . . to Crown Forces. The allegation was true . . . I was always a staunch supporter of the British Government'. Indeed, 'prior to our troops, Police, Gentry . . . leaving the country', Holland catered for: 'Balls, Dances, Wedding Parties, Receptions, Evening & Tennis Parties, Garden Parties, Flower shows'.[159] The Catholic food-supplier and 'confectioner' from Clonmel, Co. Tipperary had previously served in the British Army and also owned a 'motorcycle and car business' (his stock was stolen and damaged during the Civil War). On 3 August 1922, Holland was badly beaten ('ruptured') on the road and left with a painful reminder of the encounter: he 'had to wear a truss' and could not work.[160] One reason the compensation claims are indeed so valuable as evidence is that they offer an insight into both the immediate experience of violence and the ways in which, through severe wounding or assault, an 'attack lives on and is embodied in the community long after the event'.[161] The horror that 'lived on' for Holland, and many others, was financial, as well as physical. SILRA supported Holland's claim to the IGC, corroborating the impact of his injuries on his 'earning power'.[162]

157 Kalyvas, *Logic of violence*, 390.
158 Kalyvas, *Logic of violence*, 58–61.
159 TNA, CO 762/196/5: Holland, Tipperary.
160 Truss: (MEDICINE) support for hernia.
161 Slim, *Killing civilians*, 59.
162 See Chapter 2 on British 'Loyalty' and organizations (such as SILRA) established to help injured Loyalists.

On the night of 16 December 1922, Henry Murphy of Ballinakill, Co. Waterford, was 'mercilessly beaten and maimed' by five men whilst on duty as a railway policeman at GSWRC premises. Murphy's was a new, and dangerous, job. The Free State's own police force, the Civic Guard, was formed in February 1922, but, as guerrilla war and criminality continued into autumn 1922, the Government directed the Guards towards civil duties such as railway security, leaving the conduct of the war to the military.[163] The serious and permanent damage caused by the attack, to Murphy's spine and left eye, rendered him 'totally disabled from work', and he asked the IGC to compensate his 'material financial loss'.[164] As the anti-Treaty army endeavoured to sabotage infrastructure and communications, the railways certainly were a dangerous place to be during the Civil War. Cornelius Hanafin, a GSWRC employee on the Kilorgan and Cahirciveen branch, Co. Kerry, for example, was allegedly treated to the republican policy, usually reserved for ex-constables and Free State soldiers, of abduction, trial and sentencing to death. His grave had been dug and he was being brought out for execution, 'by Irregulars', when National Troops intervened.[165] The local press and compensation claims catalogue other attacks on railway workers and their homes: Irregulars 'sniped' at railway repairmen in Co. Tipperary,[166] and Edward Scales's stationmaster's cottage in Foynes, Co. Limerick, was completely gutted by fire on 29 June 1922.[167] Recorded, too, were hundreds of incidences of damage to tracks and theft from derailed trains.[168]

In the eyes of the IGC, Murphy's was another such unfortunate case: he was 'in the way' of the raiders and 'got hurt'. The Committee rejected his claim that the injury was sustained on account of his allegiance to the UK, ruling that his attackers were merely 'out for loot' and had no political motivation. Press reports agree that this was a robbery gone wrong: Murphy found the men attempting to steal a box of groceries from a wagon and was set on. His own money was also stolen.[169] Murphy cited his RIC career as evidence to the contrary: as a policeman he secured the arrest of '158 men' during the 'Enniscorthy rising' and was devoted to 'suppressing and frustrating' the IRA during 1916–20.[170] It appears that Murphy simply was in the wrong place at the wrong time; the IGC was

163 C. Brady, *Guardians of the peace* (Dublin: Gill and Macmillan, 1974), 90.
164 TNA, CO 762/163/3: Murphy, Waterford.
165 *Clonmel Chronicle*, 11 April 1923.
166 *Clonmel Chronicle*, 11 October 1922.
167 See Chapter 2 on Edward Scales's fate.
168 See Chapter 3 on the damage to the railways caused by arson.
169 *Munster Express*, 3 February 1923.
170 TNA, CO 762/163/3: Murphy, Waterford.

not convinced by Murphy's attempts to account for the violence against him in terms of his past British service. However, during this intimate war conducted 'within homes and neighbourhoods, often between people who knew each other',[171] I believe it likely that Murphy's attackers did know about his police record and that he was victimized for his dubious loyalties. It emerged in court that the attackers were known to Murphy: he was able to identify two of the men as Simon Keane and Patrick O'Brien, and admitted he knew a third, Hennessey, after cross-examination.[172] The night watchman suffered horrendous injuries; there was more at stake than a consignment of food.

The wounding of off-duty National Army Captain J.J. Cummins and J. Maher looks like an opportunist raid for arms on the one hand, but it was also an example of 'malicious denunciation' in action in which the 'information used to make violence happen' comes from 'civilians, usually closely linked to the victims'.[173] The civilian-informant in this case was the girl who recognized the soldiers and gave the cue to shoot.[174] The *Waterford News* alleged that the pair had come to Maher's native village, Kilmacthomas, to get cigarettes for troops quartered in a local workhouse. In such familiar territory, neither saw the imminent danger: when Maher 'sauntered out into the street', a girl's voice was heard – 'There they are; shoot, shoot' – and a volley of gunfire rang out. Cummins, unarmed, was shot through the back and approached by attackers looking for arms and ammunition. Maher sustained a less serious flesh wound in the thigh. But this was more than a simple ambush: the attack on local men on their very own doorstep caused a 'painful sensation' in the area (Cummins, from Stradbally, around six miles south of the village, was also a local). The girl who cried 'shoot' may have identified the pair as Free State soldiers, but it also seems likely that she and other villagers knew the individuals. Both were familiar to the anti-Treaty IRA as past comrades: Cummins was Captain of the Stradbally Volunteers during the War of Independence and, two months before this encounter, had received a threatening notice ordering him to leave the district. Maher earlier had been 'taken prisoner . . . by Irregulars operating round Kilmacthomas'.[175] If the Kilmacthomas shooting was characterized by opportunism, then, it was about taking the chance to punish known enemies and former friends.

171 Hart, *IRA and its enemies*, 18.
172 *Munster Express*, 3 February 1923.
173 Kalyvas, *Logic of violence*, 176–9.
174 Kalyvas, *Logic of violence*, 79–80.
175 *Waterford News*, 1 September 1922.

Henry Murphy knew his attackers. Mary Brophy (see Section 2a) could identify at least one of the men who murdered her husband. Digby de Burgh, a Co. Limerick landowner intimidated persistently during the war (and whose mansion, Dromkeen, was burned) recalled that James McCarthy, the only labourer left in his service at the time of his attack, had been 'restless' on the day de Burgh was surrounded by 'armed men' and assaulted on his lands.[176] It seems that this member of de Burgh's own household knew in advance something of the violence planned for his employer. Local communities may well have shared information on the timing of attacks and identity of perpetrators that was not passed on to the authorities. Concerns were continually raised in Free State Army reports about how 'freely' or not intelligence was received from 'the people'.[177] Chapter 4 argues that the success of tactics such as boycotting depended on the complicity of the local community. And so those averse to undertaking homicidal violence themselves can become involved – indirectly – in harming their enemies during civil war. They do this through 'denunciation' (snitching) and 'collaboration' with the insurgent group.[178] Munster's conflict has in this sense something in common with civil war across the world; the Irish Civil War provided the 'many people who are not naturally bloodthirsty and abhor direct involvement in violence' with 'irresistible opportunities to harm everyday enemies'.[179] There were worries amongst Church of Ireland leaders that 'young men, and even young women' had become accustomed to killing: 'the doctrine of physical force has been preached for such a long time in Ireland that it has become almost an axiom of our national life'.[180] The Catholic hierarchy also feared that the 'moral sense of the people' had been 'badly shaken' by the war.[181] Free State officials particularly condemned female participation in the bloodshed: in response to his request for the release of Mary MacSwiney,[182] Archbishop Byrne was warned by the Government about the 'prominent and destructive part played by women in the present deplorable revolt'.[183] However, despite this reasonable measure of moral

[176] TNA, CO 762/37/10: De Burgh, Limerick.
[177] IMA, CW/OPS/3/C.
[178] Kalyvas, *Logic of violence*, 110.
[179] Kalyvas, *Logic of violence*, 389.
[180] *Church of Ireland Gazette*, 16 February 1923.
[181] Archdiocesan Archives, 'Pastoral letter [22 October 1922]'.
[182] Mary MacSwiney (1872–1942): Political activist famous for her Dáil speech against the Anglo-Irish Treaty. Supported her brother, Terence MacSwiney (Sinn Féin lord mayor of Cork, died on hunger strike in 1920), and was herself imprisoned during the Civil War.
[183] Archdiocesan Archives, Government papers, Box 467: Letter from the President's Office to Byrne, 18 November 1922.

panic, qualms remained about the taking of life. Irish civilians had not become inured to death and devastation.

Ordinary people are able to kill if the order comes from a 'legitimate authority'; they are understandably even more comfortable with 'indirect killing' (ethnic cleansing, for example, is not carried out by 'fanatics', but sanctioned by bureaucrats).[184] Hugo Slim cites the '80% rule': given certain conditions, 80 per cent of us will either collude or directly participate in acts of violence, whilst 10 per cent of people refuse or take on other duties in war and 10 per cent actively resist.[185] These 'conditions' hinge on 'our passions as human beings': emotions must be inflamed (or sufficiently cooled) for people to overcome inhibitions and be able to kill.[186] Once a person has entered this 'altered state', they may become accustomed to the previously unimaginable act of inflicting harm on others; a habit of killing can develop in individuals and societies.[187] Robert Gerwarth has shown how the 'culture of defeat' and competitive, masculine mentalities made killing 'an entirely plausible form of political communication' in Central Europe in 1918.[188] Men who fought with the IRA during the War of Independence felt sufficiently alienated from their community and from the state 'to cross the very high social and psychological barriers against violence' and murder local constables and British officials.[189] Yet, even those soldiers hardened by the guerrilla warfare of 1919–21 were not necessarily hungry for a further, gory fight. In *My Fight for Irish Freedom*, Breen recalls inflicting casualties on the British at numerous ambushes and raids on barracks. After a clash at Oola on 30 July 1920, for example, Breen's column 'retired without losing a man or receiving a wound', but the 'enemy had three dead and three wounded' following the 'fierce encounter' on the main road from Limerick to Waterford.[190] Tipperary's 'gallant son' is silent, by contrast, on civil-war violence.[191] He laments the loss of his 'old brothers in arms',[192] but reveals nothing of the conflicts in which they took part. Similarly, the *Fighting Story* pamphlets of county skirmishes and IRA heroism do

184 Mann, *Dark side of democracy*, 26–7.

185 Slim, *Killing civilians*, 214.

186 On human strategies for overcoming the powerful emotional barriers to interpersonal violence, see also: Collins, *Violence: a micro-sociological theory*.

187 Slim, *Killing civilians*, 215, 227, 244.

188 Gerwarth, 'The Central European counter-revolution', *P&P*, 179–181.

189 Augusteijn, *From public defiance to guerrilla warfare*, 87–123, 335–52.

190 Breen, *My fight for Irish freedom* (1924), 175–7.

191 Breen, *My fight for Irish freedom*, rev. ed. with an introduction by Joseph McGarrity (Tralee: Anvil Books, 1964), xi.

192 Breen, *My fight for Irish freedom* (1924), 255.

not cover the period after 1921.[193] There are no civil-war memoirs to match the boastful accounts of violence from the Continent.[194] It is the 'banality of violence' says Kalyvas, which gives civil wars 'a great deal of their appalling connotation'.[195] In Munster, by contrast, there is little evidence that serious violence against and amongst civilians, friends and neighbours had become commonplace. The cruelty of some individual cases of murder and maiming reverberated through the victim's family and wider community, but, unlike non-lethal attacks on persons, animals and property, this form of violence was not routine.

3. Sexual violence

Stereotypes of the 'fighting Irish' aside, Ireland was not a violent country by Continental standards.[196] There are no indicators in Munster of the mutilation and 'violation' observed in comparable conflicts elsewhere in Europe during this period: Tim Wilson shows that violence committed in Upper Silesia during 1918–22 took a more intense and brutal form than that occurring in another 'partition' region, Ulster.[197] Only a handful of compensation claims from the Civil War allege sexual assault, for example. Rape is never mentioned by name. Frank disclosure of such traumatic incidents perhaps is not to be expected in a conservative, rural society such as Munster in 1922–3. Nevertheless, cultural pressure to conceal the humiliation of sexual violence may well have been outweighed by the huge propaganda value in publicizing such allegations against one's enemy.[198] During the War of Independence, both the British forces and the IRA were keen to assert their own chivalry and 'depict the enemy as disorderly and unmanly'.[199] Though rare, serious physical attacks on women are still recorded: on 16 June 1922, four men assaulted Mrs Harriet Biggs at her home, Hazelpoint, near Dromineer, Co. Tipperary. This was a high profile case: Biggs and her husband were 'Protestant and connected with the landowning class' in the county.[200] The interest

[193] *Limerick's fighting story, 1916–21: Told by the men who made it* (Tralee: Kerryman, 1948).

[194] Gerwarth, 'The Central European counter-revolution', *P&P*, 196: *Freikorps* member Ernst von Salomon, for example, described the 'joyful' rituals of violence against property, individuals and 'undifferentiated crowds' during the 1919 Baltic campaign (it should be noted, however, that such accounts may be exaggerated; von Salomon later became a writer and wrote fictionalised accounts of his time as a soldier).

[195] Kalyvas, *Logic of violence*, 389.

[196] J. Bourke, *An intimate history of killing: Face-to-face killing in twentieth-century warfare* (London: Granta, 1999), 118–26.

[197] Wilson, *Frontiers of violence*, 66, 122–4.

[198] Wilson, *Frontiers of violence*, 77.

[199] Ryan, '"Drunken Tans"', *Feminist Review*, 84–6, 92.

[200] TNA, CO 762/4/8: Biggs, Tipperary.

of the press[201] and British Parliament is evidence that the case invoked shock and concern at the highest level. Lord Carson drew the attention of His Majesty's Government to the attack on this 'young married lady' and 'British subject' because 'of all the horrible outrages that we have had from Ireland since the British troops were withdrawn from that country, this to my mind is one of the worst'.[202] And, whilst Mr Biggs's reference, in his compensation claim, to 'assault' is ambiguous, the *Irish Times* report is much more suggestive. At the trial of the four young, local men charged with the crime,[203] the Prosecution called the case 'the most serious that had come under the notice of the Irish Government for the past twelve months and they were determined . . . to punish the offenders with the utmost rigour of the law'. A witness recalled: 'when she was liberated she was in a frightful state – almost unconscious. She told him that she had been molested by the men'. Mrs Biggs herself was 'not yet in a fit condition to attend and give evidence' in court.[204] Carson read out the victim's testimony to the Lords:

> [Whilst the house was ransacked] I was outraged by different men in turn, one after the other, and a guard was always kept in my room. Finally, I was taken out of my own room, to allow it to be searched for valuables, a light being required for that purpose, and no light being allowed there whilst I was in it. I was brought by a man in a green uniform into another bedroom, where I was once more outraged by this man. I believe I was outraged altogether on eight or nine different occasions.[205]

Rape is not mentioned explicitly, but the language used by William McKenna to describe the attack on his wife is indicative of sexual assault. The home of this steward on the Lloyd-Vaughan estate at Roscrea, Co. Tipperary, was raided in July 1922 and McKenna ordered to leave within twenty-four hours (the estate's big house, Golden Grove, had been attacked a number of times during May and June and the surrounding farm buildings were burned down on 28 July). The family only had moved to Roscrea, in March 1922, because of William's position as steward. Soon after, 'Republicans' found out that McKenna and his Ulster Volunteer son 'were Orangemen' and they began sending threatening letters.[206] The family eventually moved back to Belfast, via a stay in Scotland, 'to be amongst our own people'. But, following the July raids,

201 *Empire News*, 25 June 1922; *Freeman's Journal*, 9 August 1922.
202 *HL Deb*, 3 July 1922, vol. LI, cc196–202.
203 Michael Grace, Patrick and Edward Hogan (of Dromineer), James Grace (of Annabeg).
204 *Irish Times*, 9 August 1922.
205 *HL Deb*, 3 July 1922, vol. LI, cc196–202.
206 McKenna's IGC file contains a letter of support from a fellow Lodge member: 'I say with great confidence they indeed have been very loyal people'.

McKenna 'could not get away in time' and his attackers returned at around 10.30pm on 1 August 1922, taking cash, food, furniture, clothes and kidnapping his wife and son. The victims were tied to a tree and not discovered by McKenna until early the following morning. The incident left the seventy-five-year-old Mrs McKenna in 'shock' and her husband's account suggests something even more terrible: 'She will never recover from the outrage committed on her'. 'Outrage' has sexual connotations and the description of the ordeal, as one from which Mrs McKenna 'would never recover', does suggest rape. McKenna was in poor financial straits; the comfortable job he had hoped, aged seventy-two, to hold on to for another ten years was gone. He scraped together a living as a 'jobbing gardener'. But he did not mention loss of employment in his original compensation application and was encouraged by SILRA to resubmit the claim; what McKenna most wanted the IGC to consider was the 'torture which I and my wife went through'.[207]

Another sexual assault took place in Sopwell Hall, Cloughjordan – an attack particularly shocking for the callous separation of the two Protestant staff from the Catholic maid, who escaped the abuses of the armed raiders. The youngest son of the second Lord Ashtown, Sopwell's owner Cosby G. Trench was of noble Galway stock (Woodlawn, the family's huge, Italianate mansion in Kilconnell, Co. Galway,[208] was targeted, like many of its kind, during the Civil War).[209] On 14 August 1922, from the safety of his London home, Trench wrote to friend Henry O'Callaghan Prittie, the fourth Lord Dunalley, about the indecent assault of two servant girls employed at the mansion:

> Our troubles are small compared to yours [Dunalley's mansion, Kilboy House, near Nenagh, Co. Tipperary, had been burned down earlier that month], but I send you a true statement of what happened at Sopwell . . . I need hardly say that had the raid been confined to robbery, I should have thought little of it, as my neighbours have suffered in the same way – but what a prospect for me in one's old age! . . . We do not intend to return to Sopwell this winter.

Trench did 'not want back' the typed statement attached to the letter because 'the more these things are known in England the better'. In it he outlined events of 29 July 1922: five armed men demanded beds, looted the house and, separating the three women from the two men in the house, 'did their best to outrage them'. The two Protestant servant girls

207 TNA, CO 762/137/6: McKenna, Tipperary.

208 See Chapter 4 on threatening notices received by Lord Ashtown at Woodlawn.

209 Hon. Cosby Godolphin Trench (1844–1925): JP, DL, High Sheriff, Tipperary, 1886; formerly Capt 1st Royal Dragoons; contested North Tipperary (Liberal Unionist), 1892.

were 'bruised all over and nearly exhausted'. The attackers desisted only when promised money. Trench's statement continued:

> Of the party, two of the men can be identified and sworn to and the others are well known and they are all resident in the Parish. Father [space left blank] CC came out two days after, and saw the state of the house and the marks of the struggle and was greatly horrified. The whole thing had evidently been carefully planned some time beforehand. The Roman Catholic girl [reported to be Miss Flaherty, a kitchen maid] was not molested.[210]

Statements made in court by the housekeeper, Miss Alton, and housemaid, Miss Springer, corroborated this version of events. The women were able to identify two of the defendants, having met Hough and Mooney at a number of local dances; Flaherty was separated from the other two servants and escaped unharmed.[211] Press reports of the incident were highly charged and condemnatory: in the dead of night, innocent females 'in their night attire' had been subject to 'savage treatment' by a gang of men 'armed to the teeth'. The 'flying column' of five did not identify themselves as IRA; they ransacked Sopwell because 'they did not want the Republicans to get the arms'.[212] We must wonder whether these men belonged, in fact, to the Free State Army. The attack took place early in the war, which might explain their lack of uniforms. The culprits also were treated fairly leniently by the Free State legal system. And, whether soldiers or opportunistic raiders, these farmers' sons certainly were well equipped with rifles, revolvers and a 'naked bayonet'. Breaking into the cellar, they 'filled themselves with drink' before carrying out 'acts as vile as had ever been committed by the Huns in Belgium, with the difference that the crimes . . . were committed by native Irish upon their compatriots'.[213]

If reports were correct, the raiders had abused not only their national 'compatriots', but also local women with whom they had mixed socially. The attackers certainly knew the religious identities of the servants, and the conscious separation of the Protestants, Alton and Stringer, from Catholic Flaherty, reveals the cruel deliberateness of their actions. Neither the Egan brothers (male domestic staff left to keep Trench's 'ancient home' in his absence), nor the owner, were harmed in the attack. Violence was targeted at the most vulnerable. The exposure of female servants to attack was common during the War; many big-house owners had abandoned their homes before they were looted, damaged or burned,

210 NLI, MS 29,810(17).
211 *Irish Times*, 7 September and 7 October 1922.
212 *Irish Times*, 7 October 1922.
213 *Irish Times*, 7 October 1922.

leaving domestic staff in charge.[214] Trench, regarded as a generous and dynamic landlord, who had maintained 'good relations' with his tenants and employees,[215] certainly saw this as a heinous aberration, a one-off act of war, rather than a personal attack against him:

> I know it is confined to a small gang, I believe that are well known. The raid has been forcibly denounced by the priests and I have had a very nice letter from Bishop Fogarty. I think the raiders have rather overshot the mark this time; there is general condemnation. The Prov. Govt. have taken the matter up and I have some hopes (small, perhaps) that the culprits will be arrested and punished.[216]

Whilst it 'pained' the judge to sentence 'men of their class, under the circumstances which had been disclosed', severe penalties were handed out to the attackers by the Dublin court. Some absolution was nonetheless offered to the perpetrators by the judge's suggestion that the prevailing wartime conditions (the 'dreadful times' that had forced Trench from Sopwell in the first place) accounted for the men's crimes. Appeals for leniency were made for the young men who had, until then, 'borne a good character'. It was hoped that, 'when the country settled down', some 'mitigation of the penalties might be considered possible'. King, Downes and Mooney were sentenced to ten years' penal servitude. Hough, who, it was alleged, had remained outside the room where the attacks took place, received five years'.[217]

Social norms and expectations certainly are challenged during conflict. Civil war enables the invasion by males of the usually female-denominated domestic arena. House burning, for example, a viciously destructive yet common tactic, employed throughout 1919–23, affected directly those groups who would have otherwise avoided serious violence. Some men, Ryan points out, felt ashamed of turning women and children out and – in the words Louisa Bagwell of Marlfield, Co. Tipperary – making them 'stand and watch the darling old home burn'.[218] During the War of Independence, IRA raiders searching for arms, or a wanted male member of the household, showed 'courtesy' to female inhabitants.[219] O'Malley recalled that 'RIC reprisals' in the same period also left alone 'women and small children'. At a lodging house in Rineen, Co. Clare, which the police had set on fire, constables helped female visitors to

214 Graiguenoe Park, Charles Clarke's Tipperary mansion near Holycross, for example, was occupied by four servant girls on the night it was burned, 28 February 1923. See *The Nationalist and Munster Advertiser*, 3 March 1923.

215 *Irish Times*, Obituary, 10 December 1925.

216 NLI, MS 29,810.

217 *Irish Times*, 21 October 1922.

218 NLI, MS 32,617; see following discussion and Chapter 3.

219 Ryan, '"Drunken Tans"', *Feminist Review*, 84.

remove their luggage, but 'the men of the house' were not safe; 'it's men we want tonight', said the RIC, 'we're out for blood'.[220] A more polite warning often accompanied civil-war arson attacks, and servants, wives and children were given time to gather belongings and get out before the fire.[221] Some particularly 'courteous arsonists' visited Sir John Fox Dillon's big house, Lismullin, Co. Meath, in 1923. On opening the door to the raiders, the owner was told: "Sir John, we are very sorry, but we have orders to burn your house." The IRA 'helped him to remove some of his pictures and some plate and silver'. The family and male servants were kept in a locked room, but the armed men 'assisted the women in removing the property, much of which has been saved'.[222]

Other men may have experienced the 'thrill' of trespassing on female space and rifling through their possessions.[223] During 1919–21, in the context of a 'guerrilla war fought out in the countryside and isolated villages', women were 'easy targets for frustrated British soldiers and particularly vulnerable to attack', argues Ryan. She observes the 'danger and inequality' of the encounter of women (like the Sopwell servants discussed previously) dressed in nightclothes with uniformed, armed and often drunk men.[224] The family in flight from the burning house, without time to dress properly, is also a powerful motif in accounts of civil-war arson. 'We had no one but ourselves', wrote Louisa Bagwell to her mother-in-law, the day after the burning of Marlfield:

> [We had] only ten minutes to dress, with each of us a man in our rooms and they did not want us even to light a candle. The Republicans, we found, had stolen my bag and all the overcoats. Lilla was in bare legs, and we hadn't even a handkerchief; everything has gone – all my rings, pearls, watch.[225]

It is worth noting, though, that in a letter 'correcting some details' of a local press report on the fire at Marlfield, Louisa did stress that the arsonists 'offered no personal violence to us in any way' and 'appeared to acquiesce' in the family taking out their personal effects before the house was destroyed.[226]

220 English and O'Malley (eds.), *Prisoners*, 80.

221 Lilla Bagwell pulled down the Gainsborough from the drawing room after 'we insisted on their letting us take them out'; see following discussion and Chapter 3 on the burning of Marlfield.

222 Rathfeigh Historical Society, 'IRA's courteous arsonists', *A window on the past* 1 (Tara, Co. Meath: Rathfeigh Historical Society, 1987), 20.

223 Slim, *Killing civilians*, 238.

224 Ryan, '"Drunken Tans"', *Feminist Review*, 78, 82–3.

225 NLI, MS 32,617.

226 *Clonmel Chronicle*, 13 January 1923.

Contemporary observers of the Land War linked violence to male desire: late marriage at that time produced an 'abnormally large group of discontented single men, consigned to the status of "boys". The willingness of these young men, fuelled by 'social inadequacy' and 'sexual frustration', 'to go "out" with agrarian bands . . . may bear some relationship to the persistent cruelty of agrarian outrages' (such as animal maiming).[227] Attacks on the home during the revolutionary period arguably affected women more seriously than they did the men at whom the violence purportedly was aimed. Reports on raids and burnings used sexualized language to emphasize female vulnerability and suggest the deliberate desecration of the private sphere. However, violence against the female person was far less common. Ryan's supposedly 'convincing evidence' of widespread attacks and sexual violence on women and girls during 1919–21 is actually based on only a handful of examples. Sarah Benton found no evidence of mass sexual assaults carried out by British troops; rape was 'not a weapon of war'.[228] Female republican sympathizers received humiliating, gendered punishments (such as hair cutting),[229] but nothing to match the violent retribution and 'sexually charged torture' served on 'politicised women' by paramilitaries in Central Europe in the same period.[230]

Klaus Theweleit describes the extreme misogyny ingrained in *Freikorps* culture: in post-World War I Germany, violence against women was fantasized about and celebrated to a degree never recorded in the British Isles.[231] Indeed, besides a few shocking cases, there was no surge of allegations of abuse of women from Munster, following the Civil War. Some centres of conflict, such as the Balkans, see a repeated resorting to rape – a familiar weapon since the wars of 1912–13, the 'degradation and molestation' of women played a 'unique role' in the Serbian conquest and ethnic cleansing of Bosnia in 1992. Camps were constructed for the express purpose of sexual torture and rape served genocidal aims in places such as Prijedor.[232] Most post-World War I conflicts have seen a disproportionately greater number of non-combatants than soldiers injured or killed; women undoubtedly suffered in the Irish Civil War. But, whilst the modern context of 'systematic involvement' of the civilian population leads in some places to attacks on women as a 'conscious

227 Townshend, *Political violence in Ireland*, 113.
228 Ryan, '"Drunken Tans"', *Feminist Review*, 74.
229 Ryan, '"Drunken Tans"', *Feminist Review*, 83
230 Gerwarth, 'The Central European counter-revolution', *P&P*, 203–05.
231 K. Theweleit, *Male fantasies: Women, floods, bodies, history*, two vols. (Cambridge: Polity, 1987), vol. I.
232 Stiglmayer (ed.), *Mass rape*, x–xi, 54, 86, 206.

military strategy',[233] sexual assault has never been made a wartime tactic in Ireland.

4. Conclusion

The evidence available naturally shapes analysis: in terms of the compensation material, this book draws chiefly on claims submitted under the Damage to Property (Compensation) Act (1923). These un-catalogued files still exist, whilst the records of the Free State's Personal Injuries Committee, appointed in April 1923 to consider injury to the person and claims from the dependents of those who had died, do not survive.[234] There are hundreds more stories of burnt-out houses, stolen vehicles and damaged lands to draw on, than there are accounts of murder and maiming. The destruction of private belongings, public buildings and infrastructure was a powerful tactic; material damage to property during the war probably exceeded £30 million.[235] Acts of vandalism were not carried out on a whim, as O'Higgins' allusions to 'local turbulence' suggest.[236] The republicans' 'War of Destruction' was in fact highly planned and had a clear objective, 'to show the people that the Free State Government is unable to function'.[237] It was 'part of the tactics of the irregulars to do as much destruction as possible'.[238]

Detailed instructions left the Headquarters of the Third Tipperary Brigade, on 19 October 1922, for example, on making roads impassable: lay mines, dig trenches and create obstructions with trees and stones. Dozens of compensation claims filed against the Free State and British Governments relate to the specific damage caused by republicans building roadblocks.[239] The destruction was incessant: 'Lieutenant Engineers' were ordered to 'see that all telephone and telegraph lines in your area are cut, and if repaired they should be cut again as soon as possible'.[240] On 23 January 1923, 'Battalion C/Cs' in Tipperary were told 'to collect immediately all picks, crow-bars and sledges available in their areas and to dump same in a safe place'. These tools – along with 'one large wrench suitable for removing railways rails' – were to be used in the attack on the

233 Stiglmayer (ed.), *Mass rape*, 63.
234 See Chapter 2, Section 1.
235 O'Sullivan, *The Irish Free State and its Senate*, 115.
236 Townshend, *Political violence in Ireland*, 366.
237 IMA, CW/OPS/3/C.
238 *Church of Ireland Gazette*, 21 July 1922.
239 See for example: NAI, 392/362: O'Grady, Limerick; NAI, 392/20: James Teskey, Limerick: Teskey claimed 'the Irregulars were in the District and were continually knocking the trees and wall across the road'.
240 IMA, Captured Documents, Lot 125, A/1115.

network. The practical disruption caused by the wrecking of roads and rail was a tactical coup for republicans.

The anti-Treaty IRA in Munster certainly waged a costly war and succeeded, for a time at least, in undermining the authority of the new government. The insurgents did not, by contrast, regularly use lethal violence against the person, to coerce and control the populace. However, the fact that republicans waged a fiercer war on property than they did on people does not mean that all non-army fatalities can be accounted for as collateral damage. My exploration of the death and serious injury of the unarmed and those unable to offer physical resistance at the time of their attack raises important issues of civilian identity and draws out patterns in the performance of, and motivations for, violence in Munster in 1922–3.

'Civilians: Definition and Discussion' (Section 1) shows that the common assumption that, bar a few misguided and violent rebels, the vast majority of the Irish population supported the Treaty and new government's heavy-handed restoration order is not wrong, but is simplistic. Free State Army reports highlight the difficulties in telling friend from enemy. Local case studies complicate the notion of a passive, homogenous public subject to indiscriminate Irregular violence. Desire for respite from the disruption afflicting communities such as Clonmel, Co. Tipperary, and Dungarvan, Co. Waterford, is palpable in press reports and compensation claims. However, support for the republicans was not insignificant and varied according to geography, local leadership, personal ties and mercenary motives.

Open conflict and battles in the street lasted just a couple of months, but gunshot wounds remained the most common cause of death and injury whilst republican sniping, ambushes and a policy of kidnap, trial and execution, of unarmed civilians, as well as off-duty soldiers, continued into 1923; see Section 2a. Press attention focused on personal tragedies. The 'mean tactics' of the Irregulars, particularly the shooting of disbanded and defenceless ex-RIC and British Servicemen, were condemned as unfair and illegitimate. However, Section 2b, on killing and wounding, has suggested that, whilst some incidences of violence against the person took a more intimate form (attacks on female servants in the home; the savage beating of a railway policeman at his place of work), the performance of violence remained important. Rituals included the labelling of the corpse; notices pinned to the body assigned political meaning to an individual death, warning others not to follow in the deceased's traitorous footsteps. The battle for information and allegiance was bitterly fought. Murder punished those who betrayed the republican cause. High profile Munster republicans, including O'Malley and Breen, contrasted their idea of a fair fight, of carrying out killing like a proper army, with a Free State lacking in military and moral authority. In stark contrast to the gruesome violence perpetrated by paramilitaries in revolutionized Central Europe at this time, the anti-Treaty IRA did not use the breakdown in law of order to perpetuate unfettered violence against civilian society. 'Sexual violence' (Section 3) has concluded that rape never became a weapon of war in Ireland.

Fairly restrained by international standards, the Irish Civil War nonetheless was an intense and often cruel war: there is evidence that victims and perpetrators knew each other, and the community's complicity in violence was central to the success of the killing or forcible displacement of the target. Indeed, whilst the actual bloodshed was carried out by the two armed powers (the Free State and anti-Treaty armies) what the conflict in Munster has in common with the intense civil wars studied by Kalyvas was the opportunity it presented for 'indirect' violence against the person.[241]

241 Kalyvas, *Logic of violence*, 389, 413.

6 Conclusion

Violence is the *deliberate* infliction of injury on persons or property. Whether this injury is physical, psychological, life threatening or merely a source of harassment and inconvenience, violence is by definition behaviour with *intent*. It cannot be ignored or dismissed as a by-product of related, but distinct, terms such as war or conflict. The objective of this book, then, on violence in the Irish Civil War, is to seek meaning and purpose in the range of harmful and intimidating actions that occurred during, and in addition to, military encounters between the Free State and republican armies from 1922 to 1923. 'Everyday violence' is a necessarily broad category that includes actions categorized elsewhere in the historiography as 'political violence' and 'social violence'. In other words, this book looks both at anti-Free State subversion and destruction, carried out mainly by republicans, as well as violence traditionally dubbed 'agrarianism' (my investigation is not, however, limited to actions carried out in a rural setting; I examine collective, violent action directed towards local or legislative change, such as boycotts to undermine Protestants' commercial hold in the towns, as well as cattle driving to demoralize the grazier so as to redistribute his land).

The book deals thematically with three significant violent forms: arson, intimidation and harm (killing and wounding). Quantifying this violence, in any real, mathematical sense, is a difficult task. House burnings, for example, can be counted with some precision, and a survey of arson reveals that this highly destructive and serious category of violence was prevalent during the war: arson accounts for 18 per cent of compensation claims made for injuries sustained in County Limerick, 17 per cent in Tipperary and 12 per cent in Waterford; see Chapter 3. It is more difficult to pinpoint prolonged campaigns of intimidation; threatening words and actions combine over time to put pressure on an individual, but are not necessarily recorded as discrete incidents. It is fair to say, however, that the bulk of the primary evidence relates to intimidation (explored in Chapter 4, the longest chapter in the book). I analyzed more than 2,000 compensation claims relating to wartime injuries, and the majority concern non-lethal violence, particularly damage to personal property (excluding house burning) and financial loss associated with theft, boycott or the general disruption of trade and agriculture. Attacks on farm buildings and machinery, and the outright seizure of lands, certainly were common during the war; it is not surprising that the 'majority of claims presented to the [Irish Grants] Committee related to loss of farming profits'.[1] Daily work was interrupted by local violence, and compensation claims from the UK and Free State, and other contemporary sources, vividly depict the chaos reigning in many communities in 1922–3. Home Affairs Minister O'Higgins spoke derisively of 'local turbulence',[2] but, in Munster at least, the 'War of Destruction' succeeded in 'showing the people that the Free State Government is unable to function'.[3]

In the absence of a key set of records of killing and wounding,[4] it is also very difficult to accurately measure the harming of civilians during the war, and it is, further, impossible to enumerate those attacks about which victims did not come forward, even to the well-publicized and generally sympathetic compensation bodies. Yet, whilst the *frequency* of each violent form cannot always be charted exactly, its *function* is much clearer. No death, assault, fire, or other violent encounter ought to be dismissed as collateral damage of an intense and localized war. Violence was targeted deliberately at particular groups of victims – identified by their religion, political allegiance, economic status and gender – and served two clear objectives in the Civil War. The first key function of arson, intimidation and harm was to regulate community relations and purge from Munster unwanted persons. The perspectives of these victims are recorded in the primary sources on which this book is largely based; see Chapter 2. Indeed, whilst necessary caution is taken throughout with documents that are essentially insurance statements for the purpose of financial remuneration, the great advantage of the unexplored compensation material is that it captures otherwise unrecorded episodes and experiences of violence. The perspectives of perpetrators, by contrast, are not documented in comparable detail (although republican memoirs, from the likes of O'Malley, Barry and O'Donnell, do offer some insight into the mindset of armed actors during wartime). To avoid further an exclusively victim-centred account of the war, the book is structured around distinct violent forms (arson, intimidation and harm) and not specific religious

[1] TNA, CO 762/212: 'End of Committee Report'.
[2] Townshend, *Political violence in Ireland*, 366.
[3] IMA, CW/OPS/3/C.
[4] See Chapters 1 and 2 on archival problems: whilst the Free State's (albeit un-catalogued and difficult to quantify) Damage to Property compensation files survive, Personal Injury claims do not.

or political victim groups. Yet, whilst *Everyday Violence* does not set out to recount the 'plight of the Protestants' or 'decline of the big house', in Cos. Limerick, Tipperary and Waterford, the unavoidable trend that emerges is one of minority persecution.

Harriet Bagwell (Senator John Bagwell's mother) recalled Co. Tipperary in the early 1920s:

> Every man went in fear of his neighbour and the plight of Protestants living in lonely farms and cottages, of whom there were many in that country, was pitiable.[5]

Bagwell's words capture the tensions, between southern Irish Protestants and the Catholic majority, which, Heather Crawford argues, remain to this day:

> The sheer durability of this underlying current of something that is difficult to name but which could perhaps best be described as an alienating sensation of lack of safety, a 'strangeness'... is remarkable.[6]

Given, then, the deep-seated, almost subconscious, nature of inter-denominational resentments, it is vitally important to highlight the discrepancy between the 'soothing and evidently sincere' public statements in favour of minority rights (and indeed the religious freedoms guaranteed by the Free State constitution) and the lived reality for Protestants in the new country.[7] Ireland did not witness the state-sanctioned ethnic cleansing that haunted Central and Eastern Europe around this time. The Free State Government reserved the use of violence and repressive legislation for the anti-Treaty army wreaking havoc in the counties, and official records show an administration at pains to appear fair in its treatment of Protestants. However, analysis of local violence in Munster shows that the Free State's conciliatory rhetoric of early 1922 was not turned into action locally. Protestants were not murdered by the state or by angry Catholic mobs; more subtle, intimidatory tactics, including threatening letters, boycotts and cattle drives drove them out.

The relationship between migration and persecution on religious or political grounds is complex and controversial. The decline in the Protestant population of the twenty-six counties of the Free State was a trend already established before the war, and targeted violence is one of a number of social, economic and natural causal factors that contributed to the outflow; see Chapter 2. There are also important class and regional variations. Removing British-born Protestants from the equation, the

[5] NLI, MS 32,617.
[6] Crawford, *Outside the glow*, 3.
[7] Bowen, *Protestants in a Catholic state*, 24.

minority population decline (1911–26) was highest not in the Revolution's hot spots of Cork and Tipperary, but in the Connaught counties of Galway, Mayo and Roscommon,[8] suggesting that factors other than violence explain the Protestant exodus. Protestants at either end of the social scale (the Irish gentry in Bagwell's 'lonely' big houses and working-class Protestants employed in garrison towns and the industries based around the ascendancy's great estates) also fared worse during the Civil War than did the mercantile and professional classes in some of Munster's key urban centres; see Chapter 4.

Clearly not all Protestants experienced violence and expropriation during the war, but very few failed entirely to be affected by the threatening, sectarian atmosphere pervading many local communities in Limerick, Tipperary and Waterford. More intensive and personalized than earlier periods of conflict, it was indeed during the Civil War that Protestants found their loyalties violently challenged and their place in the country in jeopardy. No one, and nowhere, was completely safe. Boycotts of Protestant-owned shops and businesses successfully weakened the minority's commercial hold on areas where the non-Catholic population and influence traditionally were strong: the harassment and boycotting of Willie Roe, a Methodist grocer from Lismore, Co. Waterford, was shocking, but not atypical.[9] Threatening letters, many issued on behalf of the anti-Treaty IRA, made specific threats against the Protestant community. The compensation evidence suggests that the victim's denomination was important to the perpetrator. Attacks on Protestant institutions and religious personnel leave even less room for doubt about the attacker's sectarian agenda; see Chapters 3 and 5.

That is not to say that Catholics were exempt from targeted violence, as testified by hundreds of small farmers, and Loyalist ex-soldiers and constables, from Cos. Limerick, Tipperary and Waterford. Whilst pressure groups and support agencies such as SILRA and ICCA helped many Protestants, the 'Loyalist' they served was defined by his 'suffering' as much as his religion or politics. Ex-RIC and Servicemen and their families, even those with ostensibly tenuous business or social links with the British administration, were punished for their past allegiances (houses and crops were burned, hotels that had served troops were boycotted and so on). Identity politics certainly were complex – and shifting – during the Civil War. Catholic ex-constable James Coogan (Chapter 4) believed his 'right' to live in his 'own country' was under threat during the war, whilst prominent Protestant Unionists and big-house owners,

8 Bielenberg, 'Exodus', *P&P*, 205 (table 3).
9 See Chapter 4.

Keane and Bagwell (Chapter 3), failed to get full compensation from the British Government because, by accepting seats in the Seanad, they had demonstrated their allegiance to the Free State, not the British crown.

The heightened currency of a range of identity labels during the war ('Protestant', 'Loyalist', 'grazier', 'spy', 'Stater', 'traitor') suggests an urgency within the community to define self and other, friend and enemy, during the transition from British rule to Irish independence. Chapter 5, in particular, shows how brutally (and even literally, as seen in the tying of notes to corpses) these labels were stamped on victims, and how competing loyalties were contested in Civil War Munster. The death and serious injury of the unarmed, and those unable to offer physical resistance at the time of their attack, also raises important issues of civilian identity. The common assumption that, bar a few misguided rebels, the vast majority of the Irish population supported the Treaty and the sometimes heavy-handed restoration of order by the new government is simplistic. Support for the republicans took many forms. As important as any practical help or supplies offered by (or simply taken from) the people was their trust; civilians provided information about enemy forces when required and silent complicity in violent actions at other times. 'Malicious denunciation' (civilians informing on their personal and local enemies, by passing information to armed forces) is the chief motor for violence in internal conflict, according to seminal civil-war theorist, Kalyvas. In Munster, both sides struggled to control the flow of intelligence and the war provided some opportunities for 'indirect' violence for unarmed civilians; in some cases the information used to make violence happen came from civilians linked to the victim.

The second key function of violence during the Irish Civil War concerns not those who were chased away, but what was left behind. Land is a 'historical problem' in Ireland and a powerful motif in this book (Chapter 4, Section 5). The burning of the big house literally and symbolically reclaimed the Irish landscape from the Planter. Thanks to land purchase legislation, the assault on the landlord already was well underway by the Civil War; however, the fires that razed to the ground some of Munster's finest mansions represented the final step in the dismantling of the old order. The often unsympathetic handling of the claims of big-house owners, and contrasting displays of generosity, by both governments, in what were perceived as more worthy cases involving small farmers, also reveal broader shifts in state attitudes. The Free State Government in particular was mindful of its duty to the landless and rural poor; these priorities were informed, I argue, by the reality of violence on the ground in Cos. Limerick, Tipperary and Waterford. Haystack and outhouse burning (the most common category of arson attack in all three counties), land seizures, cattle driving and harassment turned the new government's attention to local grievances, and – where the Free State's Land Act (1923) did not go far enough in increasing peasant proprietorship – intimidation forced land redistribution outside the official channels. Violence targeted especially those who had recently acquired land or held large pastures; medium-sized farmers and graziers, in turn, jealously guarded their property. Animal maiming – of which there are some particularly cruel examples from this period – was used to settle personal vendettas over trespass and class rivalries within farming.

This book places the Irish Civil War in perspective. It charts the wide range of harmful actions that combined to frighten and isolate victims, over a period of weeks, months or years. But *Everyday Violence* is not a tale of prolific death and gruesomeness. The Civil War on occasion unleashed the brutal, intimate violence typical of internal conflict elsewhere in the world: the perpetrators of the savage beating of a railway policeman in Waterford, and indecent assault of two servant girls in Sopwell Hall, Co. Tipperary, were known to the victims in both cases. However, high-profile republicans, such as O'Malley and Breen, were obsessed with military procedure and conducting themselves as a proper army. Whilst it may be difficult to see the killings of off-duty Free State soldiers, and ex-British policemen and armed forces, in terms of a fair fight, the performance of violence nonetheless was vitally important to republicans; see Chapter 5. Usually the distinction between the victim and his civilian relatives was maintained. Neither the anti-Treaty IRA nor National Troops utilized the breakdown in law and order to carry out unfettered violence against women, children and the wounded, as did paramilitary groups in Central Europe after World War I. Rape never became a systematic tactic in Ireland. Neither was animal maiming matched by the mutilation of human bodies. Animals and private property bore the brunt of the severest actions.

The Irish Civil War certainly differs, in scale and intensity, from many of the conflicts analyzed by Kalyvas. The war in Ireland was far less protracted and bloodthirsty than the Greek conflicts (1943–9) at the heart of his *Logic of Violence*. What is also special about Ireland, compared with other conflict areas, is the *purpose* of civil-war violence. The Greek wars are Kalyvas's primary illustration of the process by which civil-war violence becomes 'an end in itself rather than a means to a political ends'. Local conflicts, he says, ultimately centre on personal 'revenge' and do not necessarily reflect the over-arching political or military dispute (the war over the Treaty, in Ireland's case).[10] I argue that individual grievances

[10] Kalyvas, *Logic of violence*, 58–61.

align and interact more closely with higher political, social and economic issues than Kalyvas concedes. I see a close connection between the micro and macro conflicts in Ireland: contested ideas of British and Irish identity – and a need to purge from the newly independent state those loyal to the old administration – recur as the most powerful explanation for violence in Ireland.

Arendt taught us to treat violence as a 'phenomenon in its own right' and, in trying to understand the Irish Civil War, there is indeed much value in separating violence from the military conflict in which it takes place.[11] This book engages with the strategies of the two armed forces, gauges official attitudes towards violence, and places death and destruction in Cos. Limerick, Tipperary and Waterford in an international context. However, what emerges is not a straightforward tale of rebellious republicans in conflict with a stable Free State. Violence was not the sole preserve of the Irregulars. Arson, intimidation, murder and assault surfaced in labour disputes, in conflicts over land, in sectarian and anti-Loyalist attacks, and violence was utilized across Munster to settle personal, local and historical scores. Indeed, the significance of my research – and where this book fits with the collection of local-historical scholarship now available on the topic – is in its characterization of the Irish Revolution as an intra-community, as much as an interstate, conflict. Overlaying and interacting with the familiar, political and military battle (ruling British state versus imagined Irish republic) was a social, cultural and religious war. Including this book, studies have now been made of the struggle for independence in Cos. Clare, Cork, Longford, Derry, Dublin, Mayo, Tipperary, Limerick, Waterford, Wexford, Sligo and Monaghan.[12] Together, these histories speak of 1916–23 as a process of establishing the kind of country independent Ireland would become, of deciding on the essence of Irishness. And, in some cases, violence was used to rid the new state of 'perceived outsiders, infiltrators, traitors, oppressors, and aggressors', in order 'to secure territory and unanimity [and] eliminate danger'.[13]

'Outsider' is not exactly synonymous with 'Protestant'. In the process of Irish identity formation, the 'confessional dimension' proved to be particularly inflexible;[14] but persons of dubious allegiance also included Catholic Loyalists and landowners, who were targeted in large numbers

11 Arendt, *On violence*, 35.

12 By Fitzpatrick, Hart, Coleman, Augusteijn, Farry and Dooley; see Bibliography. A new local history of Co. Waterford during this period is forthcoming with Four Courts Press: McCarthy, *Waterford and the Irish Revolution 1912–23*.

13 Hart, *IRA at war*, 258.

14 Crawford, *Outside the glow*, 3.

during the Civil War. We can never know for sure whether Protestants were targeted out of pure 'odium theologicum',[15] or because they were convenient symbols of the old regime. Few have yet claimed, with the conviction of Hart, that sectarianism was 'embedded in the vocabulary and the syntax of the Irish revolution'.[16] Yet neither have other local histories engaged, as I do, with violence and ethnic violence theory to fully understand the function of violence beyond its immediate military application (killing, infliction of hurt and destruction of property). In Limerick, Tipperary and Waterford, violence and intimidation were used to degrade a known enemy and homogenize the local community. Whilst the Protestant exodus from the twenty-six southern counties began before independence, violence and intimidation clearly accelerated the downward trend. Emigration was highest, argues Bielenberg, from counties where Irish-born Protestants comprised a very small minority (less than 3 per cent of the population) and this book shows how the lone, local Protestant (from Scales in his small stationmaster's cottage to Rose in his big house; see Chapter 2) became an easy target during the war. Yet this book also charts the experience of Protestants in the largely urban areas where the minority presence and culture remained strong; intimidation – particularly boycott – was used in Munster's towns and cities to destroy livelihoods and remove from their homes and businesses Protestants who, until the Civil War, had enjoyed relative prosperity and security.

No one was safe, in other words, because violence targeted Protestants and Loyalists of all classes. From Herbert Sullivan, the Protestant gentleman farmer forced out of Ireland for supplying milk to British soldiers during World War I, to Rachel Walker, the impoverished constable's widow who endured armed raids on her home and ostracism by the local community. From owners of picturesque mansions and cherished local landmarks (Rapla House, Graiguenoe Park and Gardenmorris) to small farmers ruined by the burning of their crops. From George Brophy, an ex-British Serviceman kidnapped and killed far from home, to Catholic 'big house' gardener and "Convicted Spy", Thomas Brennan, whose body was dumped publicly (with a threatening notice attached) for the local community to see. By bringing to light these largely unexplored episodes and experiences, *Everyday Violence in the Irish Civil War* both underlines the general importance of the non-combatant's perspective in war and captures the particular questions of loyalty and identity – facing armed actors and officials, as well as civilians – that beset the violent and chaotic establishment of independent Ireland through its Civil War.

15 McDowell, *Crisis and decline*, 129.
16 Hart, *IRA at war*, 240.

Glossary

TERMS

Anglo-Irish Treaty. Treaty that established the twenty-six southern Irish counties as the Irish Free State, a self-governing dominion within the Commonwealth: each TD (i.e. member of the lower house, Dáil Éireann) and Senator (member of the upper house, Seanad Éireann) was required to swear an oath of allegiance to the British crown on taking his seat in the Irish parliament (Oireachtas). Independence on these terms was anathema to republicans committed to the 1916 Proclamation (of the Irish Republic).

Cattle driving. Tactic made famous during the Ranch War (campaign of agrarian protest against large-scale stock rearing, focused on Cos. Meath, Westmeath, Galway, Roscommon and Clare, during 1904–08). On a drive, cattle and sheep were scattered far and wide (or illegally taken away) in order to cause trouble for, and harass, their owner (the **grazier**).

Congestion. In the 1880s and 1890s, this term referred to rural problems experienced in certain districts, namely the poor, boggy ground of the western seaboard; more generally, 'congests' or 'uneconomic holdings' are plots too small, or infertile, to afford adequate subsistence.

Grazier. Large farmers, small town businessmen and shopkeepers who had done well out of land reforms in Ireland; through nineteenth-century land purchase legislation (culminating in Wyndham's Act of 1903), 'graziers' acquired large ranches that were used for the grazing of cattle, rather than tillage.

Haggard. In Ireland and Isle of Man: a yard or enclosure beside the farmhouse where crops are stored.

Houghing. Cutting of hamstrings; first recorded in the 1690s as a quick and reliable method of disabling animals and humans.

Turbary. Right to cut turf, or peat, for fuel on a particular area of bog.

NOTE ON CURRENT VALUE OF OLD MONEY

In general, the compensation payments cited in this book are the amounts received at the time, in the old currency. In cases of particular interest and in order to give an idea of the generosity (or otherwise) of compensation bodies – and of the claimant's own boldness (or lack thereof) in seeking remuneration – I have used a factor of 44.5 to convert from pounds c. 1925 (when post-Civil War claims were submitted and awards made) to pounds in 2010, as is suggested for commodities, or lump sums, by the online tool: http://www.measuringworth.com/ppoweruk/. For example, a compensation payment of £100 is seen to be worth £4,450 today.

Bibliography

1. MANUSCRIPT AND ARCHIVAL SOURCES

Archdiocesan Archives, Drumcondra, Dublin

Archbishop Byrne papers

Government papers

Monsignor M.J. Curran papers

Irish Military Archives, Cathal Brugha Barracks, Rathmines, Dublin (IMA)

Captured Documents

Civil War Operation/Intelligence Reports by Command

Limerick City Library, Reference and Local Studies Department

Limerick City Trades Register 1769–1925, http://www.limerickcity.ie/webapps/tradesreg/Search.aspx (online database)

National Archives of Ireland, Dublin (NAI)

Records of the Department of Justice

Records of the Department of the Taoiseach

Records of the Ministry of Finance

Returns of the Census of Ireland (1911), http://www.census.nationalarchives.ie/ (online database)

Un-catalogued compensation files: Series 392 (Limerick), 401 (Tipperary), 402 (Waterford)

National Library of Ireland (NLI)

Correspondence re strike by labourers on the estate of Robert Sanders of Ballinacourty, Co. Tipperary [1920]

Dunalley Papers, of the Prittie family Lords Dunalley, 1665–1937

History of the Bagwell family by Harriet Bagwell

Public Record Office of Northern Ireland (PRONI)

Papers of the Irish Unionist Alliance

Papers of the Southern Irish Loyalist Relief Association

Propaganda material

Private papers of Col. F.H. Crawford concerning Unionism, the formation and security of the Government of Northern Ireland

Frederic Crawford's diary

The National Archives, Kew (TNA)

Domestic Records of the Public Record Office, Gifts, Deposits, Notes and Transcripts

PRO 30/67: First Earl Midleton papers
Records of the Colonial Office, Records of the Irish Office
CO 762: Irish Grants Committee: Files and Minutes
CO 903: Intelligence Notes
CO 906/38: The Weekly Summary

2. PRINTED PRIMARY SOURCES

BOOKS AND PAMPHLETS

Anonymous, *Intolerance in Ireland, facts not fiction, by an Irishman* (London, 1913).
Anonymous, *Limerick's fighting story, 1916–21: Told by the men who made it* (Tralee: Kerryman, 1948).
Barry, Tom, *Guerilla days in Ireland*, 6th ed. (Naas: Anvil Books, 1978).
Bowen, Elizabeth, *The last September* (London: Constable, 1929).
Breen, Dan, *My fight for Irish freedom* (Dublin: Talbot Press Ltd, 1924).
______, *My fight for Irish freedom*, rev. ed. (Tralee: Anvil Books, 1964).
Cork Incorporated Chamber of Commerce and Shipping, *Cork commercial handbook* (Cork: Cork Chamber of Commerce, 1919).
Irish Claims Compensation Association, *The campaign of fire; Facts for the public: A record of some mansions and houses destroyed, 1922–3* (Westminster, 1924).
Irish Free State Department of Industry and Commerce, *Saorstát Éireann: Census of population 1926*, 10 vols. (Dublin: Stationery Office, 1928), vol. III.
Lewis, George Cornewall, *On local disturbances in Ireland, and on the Irish Church question* (London: B. Fellowes, Ludgate Street, 1836).
O'Donnell, Peadar, *The gates flew open* (London: J. Cape, 1932).
O'Halloran, Alphonsus J., *The glamour of Limerick* (Dublin and Cork: Talbot Press Ltd, 1928).
O'Malley, Ernie, *The singing flame* (Dublin: Anvil Books, 1978).

NEWSPAPERS

British Library
Empire News
National Library of Ireland, Dublin
Clonmel Chronicle
Cork Examiner
Freeman's Journal
Limerick Echo
Limerick Leader
Munster Express
Nationalist and Munster Advertiser
Nenagh Guardian
Waterford News
Waterford Standard
Online Digital Archives
Irish Times
Manchester Guardian

Observer
The Times
Representative Church Body Library
Church of Ireland Gazette

PARLIAMENTARY RECORDS

Dáil Éireann Debates, Office of the Houses of the Oireachtas, Leinster House, Dublin, http://historical-debates.oireachtas.ie (online database)
Hansard (Houses of Parliament Debate), Hansard 1803–2005, Hansard Digitisation Project, Hansard Millbank Systems, http://hansard.millbanksystems.com (online database)
House of Commons Parliamentary Papers, ProQuest LLC, http://parlipapers.chadwyck.co.uk/home.do (online database)

3. PRINTED SECONDARY SOURCES

BOOKS AND ARTICLES

Abbott, Richard, *Police casualties in Ireland 1919–1922* (Cork, Mercier Press: 2000).
Archer, John E., *By a flash and a scare: Incendiarism, animal maiming, and poaching in East Anglia, 1815–1870* (Oxford: Clarendon Press, 1990).
Arendt, Hannah, *On violence* (London: Allen Lane, 1970).
Augusteijn, Joost, 'Irish Civil War', in S.J. Connolly (ed.), *The Oxford companion to Irish history*, Oxford Paperback Reference (Oxford: Oxford University Press, 2007), 277.
———(ed.), *The Irish Revolution, 1913–1923* (Basingstoke: Palgrave, 2002).
———, *From public defiance to guerrilla warfare: The experience of ordinary Volunteers in the Irish War of Independence, 1916–1921* (Dublin: Irish Academic Press, 1996).
Babington, Anthony, *Shell shock: A history of the changing attitude to war neurosis* (London: Leo Cooper, 1997).
Bardon, Jonathan, *A shorter illustrated history of Ulster* (Belfast: Blackstaff Press, 1996).
Barry, Sebastian, *The whereabouts of Eneas McNulty* (London: Pan Macmillan, 1998).
Bartlett, Thomas (ed.), *1798: A bicentenary perspective* (Dublin: Four Courts Press, 2003).
Beames, Michael, 'Rural conflict in pre-Famine Ireland: Peasant assassinations in Tipperary, 1837–1847', in C.H.E. Philpin (ed.), *Nationalism and popular protest in Ireland* (Cambridge: Cambridge University Press, 1987), 264–83.
Bence-Jones, Mark, *Burke's guide to country houses*, 3 vols. (London: Burke's Peerage, 1978), vol. I: *Ireland.*
Berger, Stefan, 'Germany', in Robert Gerwarth (ed.), *Twisted paths: Europe 1914–1945* (Oxford: Oxford University Press, 2007), 184–209.
Bew, Paul, *Ireland: The politics of enmity, 1789–2006* (Oxford: Oxford University Press, 2007).

______, *Conflict and conciliation, 1890–1910: Parnellites and radical agrarians* (Oxford: Clarendon Press, 1987).

Bielenberg, Andy, 'Exodus: The emigration of southern Irish Protestants during the Irish War of Independence and the Civil War', *Past and Present*, no. 218 (Feb. 2013), 199–233.

Blok, Anton, *Honour and violence* (Cambridge: Polity Press, 2001).

Bourke, Joanna, *An intimate history of killing: Face-to-face killing in twentieth-century warfare* (London: Granta, 1999).

Bowen, Elizabeth, *Bowen's Court; & Seven winters: Memories of a Dublin childhood; Introduced by Hermione Lee* (London: Vintage, 1999).

Bowen, Kurt D., *Protestants in a Catholic state: Ireland's privileged minority* (Dublin: McGill-Queen's University Press, 1983).

Boyce, D. George and Alan O'Day, *Parnell in perspective* (London: Routledge, 1991).

Brady, Conor, *Guardians of the peace* (Dublin: Gill and Macmillan, 1974).

Brennan, Niamh, 'A political minefield: Southern Loyalists, the Irish Grants Committee and the British Government, 1922–31', *Irish Historical Studies* 30, no. 119 (May 1997), 406–19.

Buckland, Patrick, *Irish Unionism, 1885–1922* (London: Historical Association, 1973).

Bull, Philip, *Land, politics and nationalism: A study of the Irish land question* (Dublin: Gill and Macmillan, 1996).

Busteed, Mervyn, Frank Neal, and Jonathan Tonge (eds.), *Irish Protestant identities* (Manchester: Manchester University Press, 2008).

Butler, David J., *South Tipperary, 1570–1841: Religion, land and rivalry* (Dublin: Four Courts Press, 2006).

Campbell, Colm, *Emergency law in Ireland, 1918–1925* (Oxford: Clarendon Press, 1994).

Campbell, Fergus, *Land and revolution: Nationalist politics in the West of Ireland, 1891–1921* (Oxford: Oxford University Press, 2005).

Carr, Raymond, *Modern Spain, 1875–1980* (Oxford: Oxford University Press, 1980).

Carsten, Francis L., *Revolution in Central Europe, 1918–1919* (London: Maurice Temple Smith Ltd, 1972).

Clarke, Peter F., *Hope and glory: Britain 1900–1990* (London: Penguin, 1997).

Clear, Caitriona, 'Cumman na mBan', in S.J. Connolly (ed.), *The Oxford companion to Irish history*, Oxford Paperback Reference (Oxford: Oxford University Press, 2011), 137–8.

Coffey, Leigh-Ann, *The planters of Luggacurran, County Laois: A Protestant community, 1879–1927* (Dublin: Four Courts Press, 2006).

Coleman, Marie, *County Longford and the Irish Revolution, 1910–1923* (Dublin: Irish Academic Press, 2006).

Collins, Randall, *Violence: A micro-sociological theory* (Princeton, NJ: Princeton University Press, 2008).

Connolly, Sean J., 'The Houghers: Agrarian protest in early eighteenth century Connacht', in C.H.E. Philpin (ed.), *Nationalism and popular protest in Ireland* (Cambridge: Cambridge University Press, 1987), 139–62.

Coogan, Oliver, *Politics and war in Meath, 1913–23* (Dublin: Folens, 1983).

Crawford, Heather K., *Outside the glow: Protestants and Irishness in independent Ireland* (Dublin: University College Dublin Press, 2010).

Cullen, Louis M., 'The overseas trade of Waterford as seen from a ledger of Courtenay and Ridgway', *The Journal of the Royal Society of Antiquaries of Ireland* 88, no. 2 (1958), 165–78.

Curran, Joseph M., *The birth of the Irish Free State* (Tuscaloosa: University of Alabama Press, 1980).

Curtis, L. Perry, 'Moral and physical force: The language of violence in Irish nationalism', *Journal of British Studies* 27, no. 2 (1988), 150–89.

Daly, Mary E., *The slow failure: Population decline and independent Ireland, 1922–1973* (Madison, Wis.: University of Wisconsin Press, 2006).

Darby, John, *Intimidation and the control of conflict in Northern Ireland* (Dublin: Gill and Macmillan, 1986).

Davis, Natalie Zemon, *Society and culture in early modern France: Eight essays* (Stanford, CA: Stanford University Press, 1975).

Deasy, Liam, *Brother against brother* (Cork: Mercier Press, 1998).

Delaney, Enda, *Demography, state and society: Irish migration to Britain, 1921–1971* (Liverpool: Liverpool University Press, 2000).

Deutsch-Brady, C., 'The cattle drive of Tulira', *Journal of the Galway Archaeological and Historical Society* 34 (1974–1975), 35–9.

Dolan, Anne, 'Ending war in a "sportsmanlike manner": The milestone of Revolution, 1919–23', in Thomas E. Hachey (ed.), *Turning points in twentieth-century Irish history* (Dublin: Irish Academic Press, 2011), 21–38.

Dooley, Terence A.M., *The murders at Wildgoose Lodge: Agrarian crime and punishment in pre-Famine Ireland* (Dublin: Four Courts Press, 2007).

———, *"The land for the people": The land question in independent Ireland* (Dublin: University College Dublin Press, 2004).

———, 'IRA veterans and land division in independent Ireland 1923–48', in Fearghal McGarry (ed.), *Republicanism in modern Ireland* (Dublin: University College Dublin Press, 2003), 86–107.

———, *The decline of the big house in Ireland: A study of Irish landed families, 1860–1960* (Dublin: Wolfhound Press, 2001).

———, *The plight of the Monaghan Protestants, 1912–1926*, Maynooth Studies in Irish Local History (Dublin: Irish Academic Press, 2000).

Dunbabin, J.P.D., *Rural discontent in nineteenth-century Britain* (London: Faber and Faber, 1974).

Elebert, Michael, 'Recollections of Rapla', *Cloughjordan Heritage* 1 (1985), 9–11.

English, Richard, *Ernie O'Malley: IRA intellectual* (Oxford: Clarendon Press, 1998).

English, Richard, and Cormac K.H. O'Malley (eds.), *Prisoners: The Civil War letters of Ernie O'Malley* (Swords, Co. Dublin: Poolbeg, 1991).

Fanning, Ronan, *The Irish Department of Finance, 1922–58* (Dublin: Institute of Public Administration, 1978).

Fanning, Tim, *The Fethard-on-Sea boycott* (Cork: Collins Press, 2010).

Farrell, James G., *Troubles* (London: Jonathan Cape, 1970).

Farrell, Michael, *Northern Ireland: The orange state*, 2nd ed. (London: Pluto Press, 1980).

Farrell, Sean, *Rituals and riots: Sectarian violence and political culture in Ulster, 1784–1886* (Lexington: University Press of Kentucky, 2000).

Farry, Michael, *The aftermath of revolution: Sligo, 1921–23* (Dublin: University College Dublin Press, 2000).

Figes, Orlando, *A people's tragedy: The Russian Revolution, 1891–1924* (Harmondsworth: Penguin, 1998).

Fischer, Conan, *Europe between democracy and dictatorship: 1900–1945* (Chichester: Wiley-Blackwell, 2011).

Fitzpatrick, David, 'The geography of Irish nationalism 1910–1921', *Past and Present*, no. 78 (Feb. 1978), 113–44.

______, *Politics and Irish life, 1913–1921: Provincial experience of war and revolution* (Dublin: Gill and Macmillan, 1977).

Follis, Bryan A., *A state under siege: The establishment of Northern Ireland, 1920–1925* (Oxford: Clarendon Press, 1995).

Foster, R.F., '"A strange and insistent protagonist": Colm Tóibín and Irish history', in Paul Delaney (ed.), *Reading Colm Tóibín* (Dublin: Liffey Press, 2008), 21–40.

______, 'Preface', in Nolan, William, and Thomas P. Power (eds.), *Waterford: History and society: Interdisciplinary essays on the history of an Irish county* (Dublin: Geography Publications, 1992).

______, *Modern Ireland 1600–1972* (London: Allen Lane, The Penguin Press, 1988).

Garvin, Tom, *1922: The birth of Irish democracy* (Dublin: Gill and Macmillan, 1996).

Gaughan, J. Anthony (ed.), *Memoirs of Senator James G. Douglas (1887–1954): Concerned citizen* (Dublin: University College Dublin Press, 1998).

Gerwarth, Robert, 'The Central European counter-revolution: Paramilitary violence in Germany, Austria and Hungary after the Great War', *Past and Present*, no. 200 (Aug. 2008), 175–209.

Greaves, C. Desmond, *Liam Mellows and the Irish Revolution*, 1st ed. reprinted with a new introduction by Gerry Adams (London: Lawrence and Wishart, 2004).

Grogan, Patrick, 'Letter from a war zone', *Decies* 67 (2011), 87–95.

Gullickson, Gay L., *Unruly women of Paris: Images of the commune* (Ithaca, NY: Cornell University Press, 1996).

Hallinan, Michael, *Tales from the Deise: An anthology on the history and heritage of Newcastle, the Nire Valley, and especially the parish of Newcastle and Four-Mile-Water* (Dublin: Kincora Press, 1996).

______, *Tipperary County: People and places: An anthology of the evolution of County Tipperary, some historic events and the history of the principal towns in the county* (Dublin: Kincora Press, 1993).

Harrison, Brian, 'Animals and the state in nineteenth century England', *English Historical Review* 88 (1973), 786–820.

Hart, Peter, *The IRA at war, 1916–1923* (Oxford: Oxford University Press, 2003).

———, *The IRA and its enemies: Violence and community in Cork, 1916–1923* (Oxford: Clarendon Press, 1998).

———, 'The geography of revolution in Ireland 1917–1923', *Past and Present*, no. 155 (May 1997), 142–76.

Hart, Peter, Padraig O'Cuanachian, D.R. O'Connor Lysaght, Brian Murphy, Meda Ryan, Jack Lane, and Brendan Clifford, *Kilmichael: The false surrender in the War of Independence: Why the ballot was followed by the bullet* (Millstreet, Co. Cork: Aubane Historical Society, 1999).

Hawkins, Richard, 'Liberals, land and coercion in the summer of 1880: The influence of the Carraroe ejectments', *Journal of the Galway Archaeological and Historical Society* 34 (1974–75), 40–57.

Hayes, William J., George Cunningham, and Moyne-Templetuohy History Group, *Moyne-Templetuohy a life of its own: The story of a Tipperary parish*, 3 vols. (Tipperary: Moyne-Templetuohy History Group, 2001), vol. III.

Hepburn, Anthony C., *Catholic Belfast and nationalist Ireland* (Oxford: Oxford University Press, 2008).

Herlihy, Jim, *The Royal Irish Constabulary: A short history and genealogical guide: With a select list of medal awards and casualties* (Dublin: Four Courts Press, 1997).

Hezlet, Arthur, *The 'B' Specials: A history of the Ulster Special Constabulary* (London: Tom Stacey Ltd, 1972).

Hobsbawm, Eric J. and George Rudé, *Captain Swing* (London: Lawrence and Wishart, 1969).

Hopkinson, Michael, 'The Civil War from the pro-Treaty perspective', *Irish Sword* 20, no. 82 (1997), 287–92.

Hopkinson, Michael, *The Irish War of Independence* (Dublin: Gill and Macmillan, 2002).

———, *Green against green: The Irish Civil War* (Dublin: Gill and Macmillan, 1988).

Hoppen, K. Theodore, *Ireland since 1800: Conflict and conformity* (London: Longman, 1989).

———, *Elections, politics, and society in Ireland 1832–1885* (Oxford: Clarendon Press, 1984).

Horne, John and Alan Kramer, *German atrocities, 1914: A history of denial* (New Haven, CT: Yale University Press, 2001).

Horowitz, Donald L., *The deadly ethnic riot* (London: University of California Press, 2001).

Inglis, Brian, *West Briton* (London: Faber and Faber, 1962).

Jackson, Alvin, 'The two Irelands', in Robert Gerwarth (ed.), *Twisted paths: Europe 1914–1945* (Oxford: Oxford University Press, 2007), 60–83.

Johnson, David S., 'The Belfast Boycott, 1920–1922', in J.M. Goldstrom (ed.), *Irish population, economy, and society: Essays in honour of the late K.H. Connell* (Oxford: Clarendon Press, 1981), 287–307.

Joll, James, *Europe since 1870: An international history*, 4th ed. (Harmondsworth: Penguin, 1990).

Jones, David J. V., *Rebecca's children: A study of rural society, crime, and protest* (Oxford: Clarendon Press, 1989).

Jones, David S., 'Land reform legislation and security of tenure in Ireland after independence', *Éire-Ireland* 32, no. 4 and 33, nos. 1 and 2 (1998), 116–43.

Jones, Edgar, 'Historical approaches to post-combat disorders', *Philosophical Transactions of the Royal Society: Biological Sciences* 361 (2006), 533–42.

Jordan, Donald, 'The Irish National League and the "unwritten law": Rural protest and nation-building in Ireland 1882–1890', *Past and Present*, no. 158 (Feb. 1998), 146–71.

Kalyvas, Stathis N., *The logic of violence in civil war* (Cambridge: Cambridge University Press, 2006).

Keaveney, William, *The land for the people: Robert Henry Johnstone and the United Irish League; A story of land agitation in the early twentieth century* (Dublin: Lios Rua, 2007).

Kennedy, Dennis, *The widening gulf: Northern attitudes to the independent Irish state, 1919–49* (Belfast: Blackstaff Press, 1988).

Keogh, Dermot, and Andrew McCartney, *Limerick boycott 1904: Anti-Semitism in Ireland* (Cork: Mercier Press, 2005).

Kiely, Maurice B., and William Nolan, 'Politics, land and rural conflict, c.1830–1845', in William Nolan and Thomas P. Power (eds.), *Waterford: History and society: Interdisciplinary essays on the history of an Irish county* (Dublin: Geography Publications, 1992), 459–94.

Kissane, Bill, *The politics of the Irish Civil War* (Oxford: Oxford University Press, 2005).

Lane, Pádraig G., 'Agricultural labourers and rural violence, 1850–1914', *Studia Hibernica*, no. 27 (1993), 77–87.

Lawlor, Pearse, *The Burnings 1920* (Cork: Mercier Press, 2009).

Lawrence, Jon, 'Forging a peaceable kingdom: War, violence, and fear of brutalization in post-First World War Britain', *Journal of Modern History* 75, no. 3 (Sept. 2003), 557–89.

Leeson, D.M., *The Black and Tans: British police and Auxiliaries in the Irish War of Independence, 1920–1921* (Oxford: Oxford University Press, 2011).

Lovett, Phil, 'Quakers in Limerick', *The Old Limerick Journal* 37 (Summer 2001), 3–9.

Lyne, Gerard J., 'Daniel O'Connell, intimidation and the Kerry elections of 1835', *Journal of the Kerry Archaeological and Historical Society* 4 (1971), 74–97.

Lyons, F.S.L., *Ireland since the Famine*, 2nd rev. ed. (London: Fontana, 1973).

Mac Suain, Seamus, *County Wexford's civil war* (Wexford: Séamus Mac Suain, 1995).

Magan, William, *Umma More: The story of an Irish family* (Salisbury, Wiltshire: Element Books, 1983).

Maguire, Martin, 'A socio-economic analysis of the Dublin Protestant working class, 1870–1926', *Irish Economic and Social History* 20 (1993), 35–61.

Maier, Charles S., *Recasting bourgeois Europe: Stabilization in France, Germany and Italy in the decade after World War I: With a new preface* (Princeton, NJ: Princeton University Press, 1988, c1975).

Malcolm, Elizabeth, 'Investigating the "machinery of murder": Irish detectives and agrarian outrages, 1847–70', *New Hibernia Review* 6, no. 3 (Autumn 2002), 73–91.

Mann, Michael, *The dark side of democracy: Explaining ethnic cleansing* (Cambridge: Cambridge University Press, 2005).

Marlow, Joyce, *Captain Boycott and the Irish* (London: Deutsch, 1973).

Marnane, Denis G., *Land and violence: A history of West Tipperary from 1660* (Tipperary: D.G. Marnane, 1985).

Martin, Peter, 'Unionism: The Irish nobility and Revolution, 1919–23', in J. Augusteijn (ed.), *The Irish Revolution, 1913–1923* (Basingstoke: Palgrave, 2002), 151–164.

McCarthy, Pat, 'Waterford hasn't done much either? Waterford in the War of Independence, 1919–1921: A comparative analysis', *Decies* 58 (2002), 89–106.

McDermott, Jim, *Northern Divisions: The old IRA and the Belfast pogroms* (Belfast: Beyond the Pale, 2001).

McDowell, R.B., *Crisis and decline: The fate of the southern Unionists* (Dublin: Lilliput Press, 1997).

McGarry, Fearghal, *Eoin O'Duffy: A self-made hero* (Oxford: Oxford University Press, 2005).

Milne, Kenneth, *Protestant aid 1836–1986: A history of the Association for the Relief of Distressed Protestants* (Dublin: Protestant Aid, 1989).

Mitchell, Arthur, *Revolutionary government in Ireland: Dáil Eireann, 1919–22* (Dublin: Gill and Macmillan, 1995).

Morgan, Austen, *Labour and Partition: The Belfast working class 1905–23* (London: Pluto, 1991).

Morris, Benny, *Birth of the Palestinian refugee problem revisited*, 2nd ed. (Cambridge: Cambridge University Press, 2004).

Murphy, Gerard, *The year of disappearances: Political killings in Cork, 1920–1921* (Dublin: Gill and Macmillan, 2010).

Muro-Ruiz, Diego, 'State of the art: the logic of violence', *Politics* 22, no. 2 (2002), 109–117.

Neeson, Eoin, *The Civil War in Ireland* (Dublin: Poolbeg, 1989).

O'Broin, Leon, *Revolutionary underground: The story of the Irish Republican Brotherhood, 1858–1924* (Dublin: Gill and Macmillan, 1976).

O'Connor, Emmet, *A labour history of Waterford* (Naas: Waterford Trades Council, 1989).

———, 'Agrarian unrest and the labour movement in County Waterford 1917–23', *Saothar: Journal of the Irish Labour History Society* 6 (1980), 40–58.

O'Connor Lysaght, D.R., 'County Tipperary: Class struggle and national struggle, 1916–1924', in William Nolan and Thomas McGrath (eds.), *Tipperary: History and society: Interdisciplinary essays on the history of an Irish county* (Dublin: Geography Publications, 1985), 394–410.

Ó Drisceoil, Donal, *Peadar O'Donnell* (Cork: Cork University Press, 2001).

O'Dwyer, Michael, 'Local happenings, 1922–3', *Oola: Past and Present* 9 (2000), 4–6.

Ó Gadhra, Nollaig, *Civil War in Connacht, 1922–3* (Cork: Mercier Press, 1999).

O'Halpin, Eunan, *Defending Ireland: The Irish state and its enemies since 1922* (Oxford: Oxford University Press, 1999).

O'Sullivan, Donal J., *The Irish Free State and its Senate: A study in contemporary politics* (London: Faber and Faber, 1940).

Parkinson, Alan F., *Belfast's unholy war: The Troubles of the 1920s* (Dublin: Four Courts Press, 2004).

Patterson, Henry, *The politics of illusion: A political history of the IRA* (London: Serif, 1997).

Powell, Martyn, 'Ireland's urban houghers: Moral economy and popular protest in the late eighteenth century', in Michael Brown and Sean Donlan (eds.), *Law and the Irish, 1689–1848: Power, privilege and practice* (Ashgate: Aldershot, 2011), 231–54.

Power, Patrick C., *History of South Tipperary* (Cork: Mercier Press, 1989).

Rathfeigh Historical Society, 'IRA's courteous arsonists', *A window on the past* 1 (Tara, Co. Meath: Rathfeigh Historical Society, 1987), 20.

Regan, John, *The Irish counter-revolution, 1921–1936: Treatyite politics and settlement in independent Ireland* (Dublin: Gill and Macmillan, 1999).

Regan, John M. and Joost Augusteijn (ed.), *The memoirs of John M. Regan: A Catholic officer in the RIC and RUC, 1909–1948* (Dublin: Four Courts Press, 2007).

Rumpf, Erhard and Anthony C. Hepburn, *Nationalism and socialism in twentieth century Ireland* (Liverpool: Liverpool University Press, 1977).

Ryan, Louise, '"Drunken Tans": Representations of sex and violence in the Anglo-Irish War, 1919–21', *Feminist Review*, no. 66 (Autumn 2000), 73–94.

Ryan, Meda, *The real chief: Liam Lynch* (Cork: Mercier Press, 2005, first published as *Liam Lynch, the real chief*, 1986).

———, *Tom Barry: IRA freedom fighter* (Cork: Mercier Press, 2003).

Ryan, P.J., 'Armed conflict in Limerick', in David Lee (ed.), *Remembering Limerick: Historical essays celebrating the 800th anniversary of Limerick's first Charter granted in 1197* (Limerick: Limerick Civic Trust, 1997), 274–6.

Slim, Hugo, *Killing civilians: Method, madness, and morality in war* (London: Hurst, 2007).

Smith, M.L.R., *Fighting for Ireland? The military strategy of the Irish republican movement* (London: Routledge, 1995).

Snyder, Timothy, *Bloodlands: Europe between Hitler and Stalin* (London: Bodley Head, 2010).

Stewart, A.T.Q., *The narrow ground: The roots of conflict in Ulster*, new ed. (London: Faber and Faber, 1989).

Stiglmayer, Alexandra, *Mass rape: The war against women in Bosnia-Herzegovina* (London: University of Nebraska Press, 1994).

Thackeray, David, 'Home and politics: Women and Conservative activism in early twentieth-century Britain', *Journal of British Studies* 49, no. 4 (Oct. 2010), 826–48.

Ther, Philipp and Ana Siljak (eds.), *Redrawing nations: Ethnic cleansing in East-Central Europe, 1944–1948* (Oxford: Rowman and Littlefield, 2001).

Theweleit, Klaus, *Male fantasies: Women, floods, bodies, history*, 2 vols. (Cambridge: Polity, 1987), vol. I.

Thompson, E.P., 'The crime of anonymity', in Douglas Hay (ed.), *Albion's fatal tree: Crime and society in eighteenth-century England* (London: Penguin Books, 1977), 255–308.

Thompson, E.P., 'The moral economy of the English crowd in the eighteenth century', *Past and Present*, no. 50 (Feb. 1971), 76–136.
Tilly, Charles, *The politics of collective violence* (Cambridge: Cambridge University Press, 2003).
Tilly, Charles, Louise Tilly, and Richard Tilly, *The rebellious century, 1830–1930* (London: Dent, 1975).
Tóibín, Colm, *The Penguin book of Irish fiction* (London: Viking, 1999).
———, *The heather blazing* (London: Picador, 1992).
Townshend, Charles, *Terrorism: A very short introduction* (Oxford: Oxford University Press, 2002).
———, *Political violence in Ireland: Government and resistance since 1848* (Oxford: Clarendon Press, 1983).
Vaughan, William E. and André J. Fitzpatrick (eds.), *Irish historical statistics: Population, 1821–1971* (Dublin: Royal Irish Academy, 1978).
Vaughan, William E., *Landlords and tenants in mid-Victorian England* (Oxford: Clarendon Press, 1994).
Wheatley, Michael, *Nationalism and the Irish Party: Provincial Ireland 1910–1916* (Oxford: Oxford University Press, 2005).
Whelehan, Niall, *The Dynamiters: Irish nationalism and political violence in the wider world, 1867–1900* (Cambridge: Cambridge University Press, 2012).
Wilson, Tim, *Frontiers of violence: Conflict and identity in Ulster and Upper Silesia, 1918–1922* (Oxford: Oxford University Press, 2010).
Younger, Calton, *Ireland's civil war* (London: Frederick Muller, 1970).

MUNSTER HISTORY JOURNAL

Cloughjordan Heritage
Decies
North Munster Antiquarian Journal
The Old Limerick Journal
Oola: Past and Present
Tipperary Historical Journal

4. UNPUBLISHED RESEARCH

Clark, Gemma, 'Fire, boycott, threat and harm: Social and political violence within the local community. A study of three Munster counties during the Irish Civil War, 1922–23' (D.Phil., University of Oxford, 2011).
———, 'The fiery campaign: New agendas and ancient enmities in the Irish Civil War. A study of arson in three Munster counties' (M.St., University of Oxford, 2007).
———, 'The Free State in flames: New politics or old prejudices? A study of arson during the Irish Civil War' (B.A., University of Oxford, 2005).
Flanagan, Frances, '"Your dream not mine": Nationalist disillusionment and the memory of revolution in the Irish Free State' (D.Phil., University of Oxford, 2009).

McCarthy, Pat, *Waterford and the Irish Revolution 1912–23* (unpublished manuscript; book forthcoming with Four Courts Press).

5. ONLINE SOURCES

'"Anti-English attack" hurts horse', *BBC News*, 7 Apr. 2008, The British Broadcasting Corporation (online news), http://news.bbc.co.uk/1/hi/wales/7333435.stm, accessed 8 Dec. 2010.

Fleming, Diarmaid, '"War of words" over battle', *BBC News*, 26 Nov. 2004, The British Broadcasting Corporation (online news), http://news.bbc.co.uk/1/hi/world/europe/4043737.stm, accessed 20 Dec. 2010.

'Online archived obituaries: Robin Torrie', *Munster Express*, 14 November 2007 (http://www.munster-express.ie/archived_obituaries/torrie-robin/), accessed 28 Feb. 2013.

'Pregnant horse slashed with knife', *BBC News*, 10 Mar. 2009, The British Broadcasting Corporation (online news), http://news.bbc.co.uk/1/hi/england/oxfordshire/7934216.stm, accessed 8 Dec. 2010.

Index